The Iraqi Predicament

Errata: Chapter 6, 'Russia and the Question of Iraq', was originally co-authored by Tareq Ismael and Andrej Kreutz for a special issue of *Arab Studies Quarterly*, entitled 'Iraq: Sanctions and the World', edited by Tareq Y. and Jacqueline S. Ismael, (Vol 23, Number 4, Fall 2001) and was updated by Andrej Kreutz for inclusion in this volume.

The Iraqi Predicament

People in the Quagmire of Power Politics

Tareq Y. Ismael
and
Jacqueline S. Ismael

Pluto Press

LONDON • STERLING, VIRGINIA

First published 2004 by
Pluto Press
345 Archway Road, London N6 5AA
and 22883 Quicksilver Drive, Sterling, VA 20166–2012, USA

www.plutobooks.com

British Library Cataloguing in Publication Data
A catalogue record for this book is available from the British Library

ISBN   0 7453 2150 X hardback
ISBN   0 7453 2149 6 paperback

Library of Congress Cataloging in Publication Data
Ismael, Tareq Y.
   The Iraqi predicament : people in the quagmire of power
politics / Tareq Y. Ismael and Jacqueline S. Ismael.
      p. cm.
Includes bibliographical references.
   ISBN 0–7453–2150–X (hardback) — ISBN 0–7453–2149–6 (pbk.)
   1. Middle East—Foreign relations—United States. 2. United
States—Foreign relations—Middle East. 3. Arab countries—Foreign
relations—Iraq. 4. Iraq—Foreign relations—Arab countries. 5. Iraq
War, 2003—Protest movements. I. Ismael, Jacqueline S. II. Title.

   DS63.2.U5I86 2004
   956.7044'3—dc22

                                                        2003025961

10   9   8   7   6   5   4   3   2   1

Designed and produced for Pluto Press by
Chase Publishing Services, Fortescue, Sidmouth, EX10 9QG, England
Typeset from disk by Stanford DTP Services, Northampton, England
Printed and bound in Canada by Transcontinental Printing

To Zayd,

who arrived in winter,
carrying the promise of spring and
the seeds for a new world.

Contents

Preface

The war on Iraq, initiated on 18 March 2003, and the occupation that followed, is a product of the degradation of international politics. This book provides a case study of that process through an examination of the international setting that has produced today's global environment, as reflected in the relationship between Iraq, the United States and a moribund United Nations since the 1990–91 Gulf War. As an exploration of a bounded system, a case study presents a microcosm of the larger world. By taking one problem, located at a particular point in space and time, the case study explores the problem to reveal the inter-relationship and inter-connectedness present. Iraq is a case study about the fate of people caught in the quagmire of international politics. It is this fate that reflects the degeneration of the international system built up from the ashes of two world wars in the twentieth century and embodied in the principles of international law and the United Nations charter.

'Misgovernment is of four kinds, often in combination', observed the prominent war historian, Barbara Tuchman.[1] State–society discordance in the Arab world is largely explained by the first three: tyranny or oppression; excessive ambition; incompetence or decadence. Arab state–international system discordance, on the other hand, appears to be largely a product of Tuchman's fourth kind – folly or perversity – which she explains as 'the pursuit of policy contrary to the self-interest of the constituency involved. Self interest is whatever conduces to the welfare or advantage of the body being governed; folly is a policy that in these terms is counter-productive.'[2] From this perspective the Iraq question in world politics has the aura of a 'march of folly' that there is every reason to believe will have repercussions for regional and international politics as profound and unpredictable as the repercussions of the First World War. As the lessons of history reflect, these repercussions reverberate on humanity as war and oppression, as well as the increasing resistance of people caught in the quagmire of world politics to the march of folly.

When the idea of this work first developed, our intention was to provide a more rational perspective on the Iraqi question: one that did not oversimplify or rely heavily upon dogmatic interpretations or orientalist approaches to this issue. Our methodology was to approach the issue from the angle of the effects of international power politics upon the population, caught between a dictator, a hegemony, and an ineffectual and bureaucratic international structure. While years of war and sanctions, followed by the Anglo-American invasion and occupation, have had an undeniably traumatic effect on the Iraqi social fabric, the identity and cohesion of Iraq remains intact and may be quite capable of overcoming this series of historic tragedies, if finally left to its own devices: hence the title of this book, *The Iraqi Predicament: People in the Quagmire of Power Politics*, which surely speaks for itself.

Directly or indirectly, this work is indebted to so many people, without whose efforts it could not have been possible. We would like to thank our research assistants, Mark Bizek, Warren Bridgewater, Mike Gladstone, Lisa MacIsaac, John Measor and Yousri Wagdi, who, through countless revisions, chased information, footnotes, etc. We would be remiss if we did not thank Professors Norton Mezvinsky and Christopher Vassilopulos for their helpful suggestions, input and constructive criticism. Also, Doreen Neville, for all of her amazing patience in dealing with our endless updating and reformatting, cannot be forgotten. We are especially indebted to Professors Raymond Baker and William Haddad for their patience, continuous input and editorial suggestions, which kept us grounded.

As authors of this book, we are solely responsible for its content and the ideas expressed. We also wish to acknowledge the support for this work provided by the Social Science and Humanities Research Council of Canada and the University of Calgary Research Grants Committee.

Calgary, Alberta, Canada
25 September 2003

1
Introduction: US Militarism and the Globalisation of Manifest Destiny

The hawkish National Security Advisor to President Carter, Zbigniew Brzezinski, explains the dynamics of the American global domination in his book *The Grand Chessboard*. He argues: 'Ever since the continents started interacting politically, some 500 years ago, Eurasia has been the centre of world power.'[1] Eurasia is the territory east of Germany, and includes Russia, the Middle East, China and parts of India. The newly formed EU enjoys sufficient economic and political resources to become a global hegemony, while Russia and China, which border oil-rich central Asia, constitute, by virtue of location, a threatening challenge to US dominance as well. In this strategic context, Brzezinski maintains that the US must be prepared to use military force against any state, or group of states, that challenges its superpower status.[2]

Brzezinski argues further that the interests of the United States in the former Soviet republics – and now independent states – of Central Asia, Turkmenistan, Uzbekistan, Tajikstan and Kyrgyzstan lie in oil and gas, in securing them from their immediate powerful neighbours: Russia, Turkey and Iran, and in blocking China's attempts at bridgeheads. He notes how the world's energy consumption keeps increasing; hence, those entities controlling oil and gas would be able to dominate the world economy. Brzezinski rationalises that the US wants nothing for itself, but rather, that it only wants to protect the identifiable 'good people' from the 'evil people'. In other words, America's primary interest is to ensure that the US has unhindered financial and economic access to resources. The thrust of Zbigniew's thesis leaves the reader with this subtle message: the establishment, consolidation and expansion of US military hegemony over Eurasia through Central Asia, and the Middle East (where oil is abundant) requires the unprecedented, open-ended militarisation of foreign policy, integrated with an unprecedented manufacture of domestic consensus behind this campaign of militarisation. With the publication of *The National Security Strategy*, it is clear that the Bush–Cheney power bloc has put this thesis into practice.[3]

What distinguishes Brzezinski's vision is not its novelty, but rather its assertive character of unapologetic rationalisation. Conditioned by the security afforded to them by two oceans, and a vast land of abundant economic resources, the American political culture gradually manifested a proclivity for controlling the 'other', while subverting the 'norm of co-operation' in favour of unilaterally imposed domination. Proclaimed in 1823, the Monroe Doctrine demarcated Latin America as the 'back yard of the US', under whose banner, thenceforth, a series of military interventions took place to consolidate America's pre-eminence over the American Hemisphere. With no credible justification, the US intervened militarily in Puerto Rico (1824), Mexico (1845 and 1847), Nicaragua (1857 and 1860) and in the province of Panama (1860). Alarmed, the governments of Chile, Bolivia, Ecuador, New Grenada (Colombia) and Peru met in Lima in 1847 to examine the increasing militarism and aggression of their American neighbour. The outbreak of war against Mexico in 1848 justified their concern: from Texas to California, the US annexed half of Mexico's territory. While the traditional European powers remained pre-eminent globally, the notion of 'manifest destiny' became clear during General Ulysses S. Grant's presidency (1869–77), highlighting American ambition to control the continent.

After the Spanish-American War in 1898, Spain gave up Cuba, the Philippines and Guam under American pressure, and was forced to accept an addendum to its constitution which gave the US the right to intervene 'for the preservation of Cuban independence' or to maintain a government protecting 'life, property and individual liberty'. Thus, Cuba lost its independence before ever having won it. Cuba was a US protectorate until 1934, ruled thereafter by governments without any real power. To ensure that the Latin American states might respect their 'international obligations and justice towards foreigners' and to 'bring about progress and democracy for backward people', marines landed in Mexico, Guatemala, Nicaragua, Colombia, and Ecuador. In 1912 President Taft stated: 'The whole hemisphere will be ours in fact, as by virtue of our superiority of race, it already is ours morally.'[4]

A consequence of the Spanish-American War was the development of the two-ocean naval supremacy cannon, which catapulted the US into the global arena and set the stage for their rise following the First and Second World Wars. Meanwhile, two successive wars had destroyed Germany's industrial base and it was no longer a European superpower, thus paving the way for an unchallenged US global role.

In 1941–42 the United States intended that France, together with soon-to-be defeated Italy, Germany and Japan, were to be part of a protectorate run by the Allied Military Government of the Occupied Territories (AMGOT). According to the agreement of November 1942 between Admiral Jean-François Darlan and US General Mark Clark, which secured France's commitment to the Allied cause, AMGOT would have abolished France's national sovereignty, including its right to issue currency. The US feared that despite the French defeat in 1940, France might reject the plan, especially if its presidency went to De Gaulle, who had vowed to restore French sovereignty. The US entertained serious concerns about the French obstructionist capacity, which France had manifested when it had opposed pro-German US policies after the First World War. With a De Gaullist regime, the US feared that France would not relinquish its empire, which was rich in raw materials and strategic bases, and on which the US had long set its eye by calling for an open-door policy for goods and investments in all colonial empires.

To negate the De Gaullist challenge, the US relied on the twin strategies of ignoring De Gaulle, and dealing with Pétain's regime through accommodation and toughness. US leaders realised that the Vichy regime in France, like the Latin American regimes, was more malleable than a government with broad popular support. After US forces landed in Morocco and Algeria on 8 November 1942, General Mark Clark courted Admiral Darlan, who was stationed in Algiers and served as Pétain's vice-premier and foreign minister from 1941 to 1942. General Clark had Darlan sign an agreement on 22 November 1942 placing North Africa at the disposal of the US and virtually rendering France a 'vassal' state, subject to unprecedented US rights over French colonies in Africa, including overseeing troop movements, ports, airfields, military defences and munitions, communications networks and the merchant navy. The agreement also provided for US requisitions of goods and services, tax exemptions, extraterritorial rights, and US-determined military zones. However, before the Vichy government could ratify the agreement, Darlan was assassinated by an anti-Vichyite with Gaullist connections on 24 December 1942. The US depicted De Gaulle as a right-wing dictator, but it had to abandon its plans to impose the dollar in liberated territories after the Allies, on 23 October 1944, officially recognised De Gaulle as head of the French government. The USSR had already recognised

De Gaulle as the head of France's government two and a half years earlier. On 10 December 1944 France signed a treaty of alliance and mutual security with Moscow, to offset US power. Nevertheless, France's position as a world superpower, already greatly diminished by the advance of German hegemony prior to the First World War, and further eviscerated by the destruction of its infrastructure in two world wars, evaporated. Excluded from the Yalta conference in 1945, France fell into the US sphere of influence in the post-Second World War order.[5]

After the Napoleonic Wars, global co-operation and conflict were organised around the empires of the 'Concert of Europe': Austria-Hungary, Russia/USSR, France, Great Britain and Prussia. One hundred and fifty years later, following the Second World War, the power of four of the five had been decimated: Germany lost its industrial base; France went into eclipse through defeat in war and the occupation that followed; Great Britain was bankrupted by the cost of war and its expansive empire; Austria-Hungary was dismantled following the First World War. Russia was the only European power to survive, and emerged from the Second World War under the leadership of Joseph Stalin as a global military and industrial power. However, while the traditional powers faded, the United States systematically matured and filled the gap with an expanded economy which supported massive military expenditures.

The world was left with two superpowers – the USSR and the US as nuclear powers, both competing for global supremacy. To contain Soviet influence, the US built a new structure of multilateral relationships (NATO, NORAD, CEATO). While American foreign policy during the Cold War was built on a global balance of power and deterrence, the US systematically invested billions of dollars in military technology from the late 1970s with the implicit goal of eclipsing the military capabilities of any existing or potential competitors. The resulting arms race bankrupted the Soviet Union, which collapsed in 1991, in effect bequeathing global supremacy to the United States.

Nevertheless, Russia remains an important power in the world, and a potential threat to America's global dominance, especially in the world's traditional and emerging oil centres, the Middle East and the Caspian Sea Basin. While the US enjoys enormous influence in the former Eastern bloc countries and has shepherded these states into NATO, Russia has not fully conceded its dynamic interests in the region. In the Middle East, although Russian influence has been minimal since the collapse of the Soviet Union, its strategic and economic interests in the region remain strong, if relatively dormant since the first President Bush declared a 'new world order' in the aftermath of his war on Iraq in 1991. In the Caspian Sea Basin, Russian influence continued to predominate after the collapse of the Soviet Union, but has met with increasing American competition because of the region's geopolitical significance for oil pipelines and resource wealth. Reasserting its presence in the region, in October 2003, Russia announced the establishment of a military base in Kyrgyzstan.

American military primacy and its unmatched technological prowess were starkly demonstrated to the world during the 1990–91 Iraq war. That war – conducted by a US-led coalition of 30 states against Iraq – represented the third world war of the twentieth century. Through the 1990s the US exercised modest multilateralism in its foreign policy, working through institutions where it exercised significant power, such as the North Atlantic Treaty Organisation (NATO), Asia-Pacific Economic Co-operation (APEC), the United Nations Security Council, the International Monetary Fund (IMF), the World Bank and the World Trade Organisation (WTO). The US government was typically content with what amounted to controlling access to these institutions and guiding their policies. With the ascension of George W. Bush to the US presidency in 2000, there was a more assertive militarist and corporatist agenda that shunned multilateralism and established astronomically high increases in defence spending. The events of September 11 provided a justification for this new orientation, and have been used since by the Bush administration to advance American hegemonic interests globally.

The American media, post-9/11, was filled with peremptory denunciations of unpatriotic 'conspiracy theorists'. In fact, it seems to be a quintessential article of faith that there are no conspiracies in American political life. However, about one year prior to the attacks on the World Trade Center, it became apparent that much of corporate America had been conspiring with accountants to 'cook their books' since the days of Reagan. Further, Stan Goff, a retired US Army veteran who taught military science and doctrine at West Point, asserts:

I have no idea why people aren't asking some very specific questions about the actions of Bush and company on the day of the attacks. Four planes get hijacked and deviate from their flight plan, all the while on FAA radar. I cannot fathom why the government's automatic standard order of procedure in the event of a hijacking was not followed. Once a plane has deviated from its flight-plan, fighter planes are sent up to find out why. That is law, and does not require presidential approval, which only needs to be given if there is a decision to shoot down a plane.[6]

It is becoming increasingly clear that September 11 will never be thoroughly investigated if George Bush has his way. On 29 January 2002, CNN reported that

> Bush personally asked Senate Majority Leader Tom Daschle to limit the Congressional investigation into the events of 11 September...The request was made at a private meeting with Congressional leaders...Sources said Bush initiated the conversation...He asked that only the House and Senate intelligence committees look into the potential breakdowns among federal agencies that could have allowed the terrorist attacks to occur, rather than a broader inquiry...Tuesday's discussion followed a rare call from Vice President Dick Cheney last Friday to make the same request.

What is certain, however, is that the 80-minute failure to put fighter planes in the air to protect American citizens and respond to the hijackings could not have been due to a breakdown throughout the entire Air Force command and control system along the East Coast of the United States. Moreover, mandatory standard operational procedures seem to have ceased with no explanation provided to a distressed American populace. In the post-9/11 period, the US Congress and the media became increasingly silent while the Bush administration put in place new and previously unimaginable structures to centralise its control and power – Homeland Security, a new department of state; TIPS, a civilian spy agency; the Patriot Act, enabling a dramatic curtailment of American civil rights.[7]

In addition, in the foreign policy sphere, on 14 September 2001 President Bush warned 'we will not hesitate to act alone, if necessary, to exercise our right of self-defense by acting pre-emptively against such terrorists'. In the immediate aftermath of 9/11, the international community, like the American policy, readily accepted the Bush administration's rationale for war on Afghanistan and joined in the US coalition for a 'war on terrorism'. A demonised Islam provided ideological logic for the war on terror both at home and abroad. Since the Iranian hostage crisis of 1979, Islamic revivalism had been demonised as a terrorist cult that encourages suicide attacks – contrary, it should be noted, to Islamic teachings. Osama bin Laden, portrayed as an Islamic fanatic rather than a reactionary political revolutionary, effectively cast the shadow of terrorism over the whole range of Islamic revivalist movements, and cast the shadow of a 'clash of civilisations' on Bush's declaration of war on terrorism. Internationally, the invasion of Afghanistan legitimated the principles of invasion and regime change as acceptable tools of international security and represented a milestone in the Bush administration's globalisation of manifest destiny.

While the capture of Osama bin Laden and regime change represented the overt motives for the invasion of Afghanistan, the covert economic agenda became manifest soon after. The American oil company Unocal (Union Oil of California) had proposed a pipeline from Turkmenistan to Afghanistan to Pakistan and the Indian Ocean port of Karachi but the project had been abandoned under the Taliban regime. Once the regime was toppled, the project was revived, thanks to the efforts of John J. Maresca, a former Unocal employee who was installed as US envoy to the new Afghan regime set up after in the wake of the invasion, and whose president, Hamid Karzai, was also a former employee of Unocal.

With Afghanistan effectively brought under US hegemony, Osama bin Laden was abruptly replaced with another personification of evil: Saddam Hussein. The marketing of Saddam Hussein as a serious threat to international security was more challenging than the Bush administration anticipated. There was nothing to connect Iraq with 9/11, and after 13 years of sanctions, the Saddam Hussein regime was effectively contained. Nevertheless, widespread fears left Americans receptive to Bush's claims about Saddam's possession of weapons of mass destruction (WMD), which the media, the Bush administration, and the British government, all repeatedly portrayed as an immediate threat to Western civilisation, and indeed, to its very survival. While the American public bought the Bush administration's bill of goods on the necessity of war on Iraq, the rest of the world was unconvinced.[8] In late 2002, opinion surveys revealed that across the globe, fear of the United States had reached unprecedented levels, along with distrust of the political leadership. An international Gallup Poll in December, barely noted in the US, found virtually no support for Washington's announced plans for a war in Iraq carried out 'unilaterally by America and its allies' (in effect, the Anglo-American coalition).[9]

After a major effort at international diplomacy and much wrangling in the Security Council in its effort to win international support for a war on Iraq, Washington bluntly informed the UN that it could be 'relevant' by endorsing Washington's plans, or it could be reduced to a debating society. Colin Powell informed the World Economic Forum, which strenuously opposed Washington's war plans that 'the US has the sovereign right to take military action, and when we feel strongly about something we will lead, even if no one is following'.[10] Bush and Blair underscored their contempt for international law and institutions at their Azores Summit on the eve of the invasion. They issued an ultimatum – not to Iraq, but to the Security Council – that they would invade Iraq with or without Security Council approval.[11] True to their word, in March 2003, the United States and Britain invaded Iraq.

While there was considerable international consternation at the unilateral action, effectively represented in Kofi Annan's criticism of US unilateralism in his 23 September 2003 address to the General Assembly, the international community ultimately accepted the fait accompli. On October 16, 2003, after five drafts, the Security Council unanimously approved UNSC Resolution 1511 which in effect made Iraq a US mandate (a territory to be administered by another nation under the old League of Nations). Thus, the Bush administration's policy of pre-emptive strike was tacitly accepted by the international community, essentially completing the foundation for the global-isation of manifest destiny as a principle justified in international relations. Indeed, Michael Meacher, British MP and Environment Minister from May 1997 to June 2003, observed that 'the "global war on terrorism" has the hallmarks of a political myth propagated to pave the way for a wholly different agenda – the US goal of world hegemony, built around securing by force command over the oil supplies'.[12]

On the global chessboard of power politics, the United States is the current champion, and can now rule the way the game itself is played. Syria and Iran have already been placed on notice that they can be checkmated. While many critics of the Bush administration have decried his policies as outside the American tradition, this chapter has attempted to outline the trajectory of US foreign policy since the early nineteenth century. Sometimes overt and at other times latent, the drive for manifest destiny has been an inherent policy principle driving that trajectory. The chess metaphor is an apt representation for power politics. But power politics isn't a game. Politics is about people, and power politics is about the quagmire that engulfs people's lives.

2
The Iraq Question
in Arab Politics

Over the past twelve years Arab civil society and governments have steadily raised their voices to decry the impact on the civilian population of the economic sanctions first imposed on Iraq in 1990 and sustained thereafter. As evidence of the devastating effect that the sanctions have had on the civilian population, Arab intellectuals, civil society organisations and some governments have increasingly denounced the sanctions regime, and pointed to the double standard reflected in the Security Council toward Iraq and Israel. In Arab regional politics, the Iraq question has become a central pivot of Arab politics in the twenty-first century, perhaps more volatile to the region and the world than the Palestine question was in the twentieth century.

While the Security Council has applied sanctions on Iraq with rigour, and with devastating effect on the Iraqi population (in violation of international law),[1] at the same time it has failed to enforce UN resolutions against Israel intended to protect the Palestinian population from the deleterious effects of Israeli occupation.[2] Over the decade of the 1990s the Arab world's consternation over the quagmire of international politics in which the Iraqi people were trapped increased as the toll of sanctions was repeatedly documented and laid before the international community by a number of international agencies.[3]

It is in this context that US President Bush's subsequent war on terrorism in response to the 11 September 2001 attacks on the United States aroused the spectre of a crusade against the Muslim world. It appeared to many as a fulfilment of Samuel Huntington's 'clash of civilisations' thesis, predicting an imminent conflict between Western and Muslim civilisations.[4] Indeed, in the wake of Bush's war on terrorism, Russia unleashed a military onslaught on Chechnya and Israel on Palestine (West Bank), in both cases with devastating consequences. Contrary to the protestations of the Bush administration, from 9/11 onward the war on terrorism appeared to be targeted selectively at the Muslim world, and Muslim populations were exempted from the protection of international law and human rights. For Arab regimes the Bush administration's increasing threat of war against Iraq throughout 2002 and 2003 had intensified the problem of volatility in regional politics. The Anglo-American invasion and subsequent occupation only served to further exacerbate these tensions.

Since the Gulf War of 1990–91 volatility is both a domestic and regional problem for Arab regimes. At the domestic level, there is in every state a wide rift between the political elite and the population. This rift has economic, political and social dimensions: it is represented economically in terms of substantial socio-economic inequalities; politically in terms of the wide disparities of power and privilege that separate the rulers from the ruled; and socially in terms of human rights abuse.[5] While these inequalities and disparities pre-date the Gulf War, they have coalesced into a volatile rift in regime legitimacy. At the grassroots level throughout the Arab world there is increasing dismay over the plight of the Iraqi and Palestinian people, which has crystallised into overt political action.

At the regional level, volatility has been manifested in the widening rift between the rich, oil-exporting states (Gulf Co-operation Council members) and the rest of the Arab states of the Mashriq and Maghrib in all three sectors – economic, political and social.[6] The rift is marked by the increasing polarisation of Arab states into two camps: states with a US military presence and those without such a presence.

The pressure exerted by grassroots Arab and international civil society organisations finally forced Arab states to alter their position on the sanctions in an effort to placate their increasingly alarmed, domestic constituencies. Balancing between the clear voice of outrage expressed by the Arab people, and the stridently expressed entrenched policies of the United States, Arab regimes gradually acknowledged the immensity of the tragedy unfolding in Iraq. In May 2000, Jordan's Prime Minister, 'Abd al-Ra'uf al-Rawabdeh, said, 'the sanctions imposed on Iraq have lead to a great human catastrophe of unpredictable destructive impact in the short and long terms. We call for a lifting of the embargo on Iraq.'[7] Similarly, in July 2000, Egypt's Foreign Minister, Amr Musa, now Secretary-General of the Arab League, called the sanctions 'unacceptable' and 'void of logic'.[8] The governments of Oman,[9] Morocco,[10] Jordan[11] and Egypt had all added their voices to calls for an end to sanctions in spite of strong ties to the United States. Even Syria,[12] Iran[13] and Kuwait,[14] longstanding adversaries of the Iraqi regime, had joined the call for an end to the humanitarian toll on the Iraqi people, if not an outright call for the lifting of the sanctions regime. Further, most of these nations would later, at one point or another, denounce the US-led war and occupation.

This chapter is divided into three parts. The first examines the opinions of Arab academics, intellectuals and professionals and is culled from several decades of study, travel and discourse within and about the Middle East. The second part examines the dynamics of change in the Arab world. The third part examines the positions of Arab regimes, NGOs and intra-state organisations towards sanctions, war and occupation.

ARAB POPULAR OPINION

There has been a strong tendency in the West to view Arabs as incidental or accidental participants in their own social, political and economic development. During repeated crises and wars over the past 50 years, Western media have given the distinct impression that Arab people coincidentally happened to 'be there'. Usually passive, sometimes reactive, their presence was nonetheless incidental; the focus has usually been either on the tyrannical leadership or on minority extremist views. The nature of this orientation to the Arab people – indeed, to the so-called 'other' – has already been critically examined by Edward Said and others following him. The role of the media in the Middle East has also come under critical review by scholars.[15] These subjects need not be re-examined here. Rather, we propose to examine the broad contours of Arab public opinion. Contrary to the general presentation of the Arab people in mainstream Western literature, both popular and academic, the assumption adopted here is that what Arabs think and feel is politically significant, even if that significance is not manifest in the short term.

In an examination of the opinions of Arab intellectuals and opinion makers, we initiated on the eve of the 1990–91 Gulf War an exploration of the nature of Arab society, the crisis facing the Arab people and their leadership, and prescriptions for change. This research was conducted in 1990–91, since when we have been following the trends identified informally as reflected in Arab news media (print and radio) and Arab forums (intellectual, religious, and informal). We make no claim to scientific rigour here. Our analysis is based on our interpretation of what we have had the opportunity to observe informally, including the discourse of Arab intellectuals and opinion makers in public forums.

Our report on the research conducted in 1990–91 identified several trends in opinion.[16] The first trend relates to the cause of the ontological/phenomenological crisis in the Arab world precipitated by Iraq's invasion of Kuwait in August 1990. Before the initiation of war on 17 January 1991 many in the Arab world placed primary responsibility for the crisis on Saddam Hussein, citing his invasion of Kuwait as the precipitating event. Ideological orientation (classified as Arab nationalist, Islamic revivalist, or Marxist, based on questions related to the nature of the state and the nature of society) did not directly affect the assignment of primary responsibility. However, there was an association between ideological orientation and the assignment of secondary responsibility. Arab nationalists and Marxists held imperialism responsible for escalating the crisis into a military confrontation with the West, while Islamic revivalists held Saudi Arabia and Egypt responsible for allowing the West to interfere. The vast majority in the Arab world felt that a resolution of the Gulf crisis should be based on an Arab solution, along with international economic sanctions.

After the war, opinion began to shift. By May 1991 many considered that the war was a result of an externally hatched conspiracy. Ideological orientation played a secondary role in terms of the nature of the conspiracy.[17] The outcomes of the war, particularly Saddam Hussein's political and military survival, were the primary evidence used to substantiate this claim, with the increasing intransigence of Israel over the Occupied Territories also commonly cited as evidence. The external conspiracy perspective deepened as the Gulf war faded into memory, with the argument generally taking the form that the objectives of the war were the destruction of Iraq as both an Arab military power in the Middle East, and as a civil society in the Arab world. Saddam Hussein's invasion of Kuwait was merely the pretext legitimating the military destruction. In connection with this, credibility was given to the argument that Saddam Hussein was enticed into the invasion, and his remaining in power only served to legitimate the annihilation of Iraqi civil society, as well as an effort to boost arms sales to the region. Such sales were viewed as part of a strategy for the destabilisation of Arab civil society through the promotion and entrenchment of militarised dictatorial regimes.

It is important to emphasise that this was not a radical or fringe opinion, but rather the dominant Arab perspective in the 1990s. This opinion was evident in mainstream Arab media and newspapers, all of which are more or less conservative, and not prone to challenge official positions. An example is an editorial that appeared in a leading UAE newspaper, *Khaleej* (Sharjah), on 14 October 1991:

The absolute quarantine imposed by the Security Council on Iraq changed the political situation completely. It is not reasonable or convincing to talk about penalties, quarantine or monitoring because of the continuation of Saddam Hussein in power. When everything related to technology and industrialisation in Iraq is being effectively locked up, all claims of fighting dictatorship are discredited, and the nature of all claims (of international law) that single out one specific Arab state in the Middle East are revealed.

Today they are...completely erasing Iraq's civil, industrial and technological future before erasing its military (capacity) through the steps of an international quarantine. That means a decision to freeze Iraq in the pre-industrial stage...That means the transformation of 18 million Iraqis into intermediate and long-range time bombs. This dangerous action will strongly shake any sense of security among all Arabs, particularly when Israel is able to monopolise nuclear, chemical and ballistic weapons in the region. The Security Council decision changed the political scene. The continuation of the spirit of revenge against an entire people and closing all windows of development and democracy in its face will sow new seeds of instability in the area.

A second trend was in the area of the effects of the crisis. Before the initiation of war on 17 January 1991 ideological orientation more or less accounted for perspectives on these effects. Arab nationalists stressed both the end of the normative order of Arab unity as a legitimating goal in Arab politics and the demise of the role of Arab nationalist regimes in regional politics, as well as the ascendancy of the conservative bloc led by Saudi Arabia, leading to a weakening of the common Arab front against Israel and of support for the first Palestinian *Intifada*. Marxists cited the penetration of the region by western powers, the destabilisation of the Arab world, and the militarisation of the region as primary effects. Islamic revivalists stressed the penetration of the region by foreign powers, the weakening of Islamic unity, and the loss of political legitimacy of regimes throughout the Arab world.

Following the Gulf War, a shift in opinion on effects was also indicated, and rapidly consolidated, with a clear enunciation that the militarisation of the region and the destabilisation of the Arab world were the primary effects. Ideology played a small part in the primary effects, but a greater one in the assignment of secondary effects. In other words, just as opinion on causes converged around a particular causal interpretation, so also did opinion on effects. Increasingly, there followed a deepening sense of hopelessness and resignation over the future of the Arab world under existing regional and international political arrangements. The sphere emphasised was associated with ideological orientation, while the feeling of doom and gloom cut across ideological orientations. Such sentiments can only have increased as war, oppression and poverty have increased under the existing political regimes, whose stability has been dependent on the support they receive from Western powers, primarily that of the United States; with both the political leadership of the Arab world and the West being held responsible on the 'Arab street'.

Before the Gulf War prescriptions for change generally reflected ideological orientation; after the war, however, this association weakened, and answers to questions of strategies for change reflected both an ideological disarray and a deepening distrust of all ideological orientations. This disenchantment with existing ideological prescriptions for change seemed to be coalescing around a new consensus of what is necessary to improve future prospects, including democratisation, demilitarisation and respect for human rights, as prescriptions for redressing national and regional abuses of power, along with increased Arab and Islamic unity.

By February 2003 and the looming threat of a United States invasion of Iraq, any optimism following the Oslo Agreement among Arab intellectuals and opinion makers about a better future for the Arab people in general and the Iraqi and Palestinian people in particular, was shattered by 9/11 (the terrorist attack on the World Trade Center on 11 September 2001) and the anti-Arab, anti-Muslim backlash in both American culture and US foreign policy. Opinion trends first observed in 1991 crystallised into two broad groupings – religious and secular. Each grouping has a wide range of variation within it, but at the core of each is a set of general principles about right and wrong, good and bad, and the means and ends of political action. Thus, in spite of the wide variation, the religious grouping is distinguishable from the secular grouping by the religious versus secular nature of the general principles of political action.

Within the religious grouping variation spans a political spectrum from the far right of fundamentalist extremists, across a broad-based, moderate centre of Islamist revivalists, to the left of Islamic reformists.

Here the designations of right, centre and left are used heuristically to refer to the orientation of political ends and actions. Generally, fundamentalist extremists appear rigid in adopting a literal interpretation of right and wrong, good and bad from the Quran and in their interpretation of the Hadith, and advocate the use of violence as a legitimate means of political action that is an end in itself (a means of personal salvation) in the struggle for a justice that is ultimate or transcendental. Islamist revivalists, in contrast, appear relatively pragmatic in their interpretation of good and bad, and right and wrong, mainly from the Quran and Hadith. There is disdain for the use of violence as a legitimate means of political action. The pragmatism of realpolitik imbues their approach to political action in the struggle for a more just society in the contemporary world. On the left of the spectrum, Islamic reformists advocate the application of reasoning (*ijtihad*) to interpret the Quran and the Hadith (and other sources such as *Qiyas* and *Ijma'*) in the determination of what is right and wrong in the Umma's (the Muslim community's) struggle for social justice. They are mainly concerned with planning and strategising political action as a means to achieve a just society in this world that is consistent with the spiritual and social well-being of the Umma.

Secularists, on the other hand, may be more disparate as a grouping. Within the group, variation appears to be dispersed around right and left pivots. Here the designations of right and left are again used heuristically, this time to refer to orientation to power in the definition of the problem (that is, causal explanations), and orientation to political action as a prescription. For secular rightists political power is at the heart of the problem. The enhancement of political power is good, and its diminution is bad. It follows that whatever political action enhances political power is right by definition. An a priori ethic of right and wrong, in other words, does not exist. Power is an end in itself and any means that enhances it is justifiable. Thus, there is considerable pragmatism in the use of violence in the pursuit of political power.

For secular leftists economic power is at the heart of the problem. An a priori ethic of good and bad, right and wrong pertains to the politics of economic power. Economic power as an end in itself is bad and wrong. As a means to an end, political action, including violence, in pursuit of economic power is right only if the end is morally justifiable (good). The only morally justifiable end is economics in the service of a socially just society. Like the religious left the secular left are concerned with planning and strategising political action as a means to achieve a just society.

While opinion appeared to us to have crystallised around two groupings by February 2003, opinion about cause and effect had consolidated. There was almost universal agreement among Arab intellectuals and opinion makers that the crisis precipitated by Saddam Hussein's invasion of Kuwait and the war that followed was caused by a covert US-Israeli conspiracy. With George W. Bush's assumption of the US presidency in 2000, the conspiracy became overt and manifest in the war on terrorism. For the secular grouping the war on terrorism represents an onslaught against the Arab world. For the Islamists it is an onslaught against the Muslim world. In spite of this secondary difference, however, there is agreement that the regimes in the Arab world are all implicated in the conspiracy, either actively or passively.

There was also almost universal agreement about effects. Both groupings agreed that, by 2003, the entire Gulf region was essentially under American military occupation, and the West Bank under Israeli military occupation. Furthermore, both groupings identified the war on terrorism as a means to suppress all resistance to occupation (real, potential or perceived), and pointed to efforts by both the US and Israel to consolidate their control. In terms of differences between the two groups on effects, the religious grouping tends to focus on the Islamic world and the secularists on the Middle East.

On prescriptions for political action in the face of this deepening crisis of what has been generally identified as neo-imperialism, the religious grouping presents a range of alternatives to the old problem of imperialism that are idealised and relatively unsullied by modern history. These vary from the extreme of the far right with its emphasis on violence as a worldly end in itself and a means to transcendental justice, to the Islamist revivalists who focus on pragmatic political action to acquire the power to change society, and to the Islamist reformers who seem to be attempting to bridge idealism and realism within reason by strategising for political action. In contrast, the secularists, whether right or left, present variations on twentieth-century themes of focusing on political or economic power. These themes have been more or less sullied by twentieth-century political practice and political outcomes in the Arab world.

ARAB REGIONAL POLITICS

The Arab political system that was founded in the aftermath of the two world wars evolved around the dynamics of three inter-related structural properties: the state system, inequality and dependency.[18]

1. *The state system*: the states established in the Middle East by political settlements among allied victors after the two world wars had, at best, very fragile legitimacy and authority. While the degree of instability from this varied from state to state, the overall regional factor was, nevertheless, considerable. This is because the state system in the region was an international fabrication, not a product of political process among the region's peoples. The popular appeal of Arab self-determination and nationalist doctrines and the instability of political regimes throughout the second half of the twentieth century reflect the underlying tension between the state system and the dynamics of political process in regional politics.

   In this fabricated state system political actors were empowered by the symbols of state sovereignty rather than by institution-alised political processes. In their efforts to institutionalise the state, politicians relied increasingly on coercion to enforce their authority internally, and depended on external powers to maintain authority regionally. The Arab-Israeli conflict, itself a manifesta-tion of the externally imposed nature of states in the region, intensified and accelerated this dynamic. The dependence of the region's states on coercion and external powers reflects their failure to institutionalise, that is, to take root in the region's political culture. The intensity of this varied across the assorted states; nevertheless, a central dynamic of political development in the framework of the state system has relied on empowerment of political actors who rely on coercion and foreign support to enhance state legitimacy and authority, and the marginalisation of political actors who represent other visions of political development in the region.

2. *Inequality*: the Arab states set up in the post-Ottoman era invested anti-Ottoman intellectual and economic elites with political authority, mediated by external powers. Closely related to this, the central dynamic of economic development in these states has relied on Western economic aid, in effect empowering elites oriented to the international market, while marginalising regionally oriented and non-market-oriented economic constituen-

cies. Thus, in the economic and political spheres, elites oriented toward Western economic and political institutions displaced the old-guard elite of the Ottoman era. In the social sphere modern education displaced traditional patterns of socialisation, marginalising the cultural foundations of both economics and politics. In effect, this bifurcated the social world between traditional patterns of stratification and modern patterns of power, privilege and influence.

The emergence of oil-rich states in the second half of the century intensified inequalities within and between states. There emerged huge concentrations of wealth in sparsely populated states, states that are essentially the private domain of tribally constituted ruling families protected by Western powers, and comparatively large concentrations of the economically disenfranchised through unemployment in states that are essentially mortgaged to Western financial institutions by unstable regimes protected by elaborate security/military establishments. Patterns of employment/ unemployment and labour migration reflected the increasing disarticulation between the region's political economy and the state system over the post-Second World War period.

3. *Dependency*: the political elites of the post-Ottoman Middle East achieved political power through overt and/or covert co-operation with Western powers in the dismantling of the Ottoman Empire. Economically dependent on Western aid to finance their regimes, and strategically dependent on Western technology to modernise them, these elites tied regional political development to the global economy of the industrial world. A central dynamic of this dependency was the transformation of regional politics into an arena for competition between global powers. US–USSR competition after the Second World War was manifested in the nationalist struggles of the 1950s and 1960s, and in the shift of Middle East regional political hegemony from the nationalist states of Egypt and the Fertile Crescent to the Gulf states in the 1970s and 1980s.

Arab political process

The impact of these structural dynamics on Arab political development has produced antagonism between Arab politics (the process of interest articulation and aggregation), and the political culture of Arab society (the process of value determination and articulation). There is a clear distinction here between popular political culture, represented as the political values, norms and interests manifested in a nation, and public political culture, represented as the political values, norms and interests of the state. By 1990 the Arab regional system reflected only public political culture, which effectively marginalised popular political culture through the oppressive means of state suppression. In other words, the Arab political system encompassed the political culture, as well as the political actors and processes, of the Arab state system. By the 1970s it was the only legitimate sphere of politics in the Arab world, but it actually represents a narrow spectrum of political activity resulting from the marginalisation and isolation of opposition groupings.

The antagonism between politics and popular political culture has several dimensions. First, as the contemporary Arab state system was essentially culturally alien to Arab society, Arab political actors have sought cultural legitimacy to institutionalise Arab politics. Thus, the discourse of Arab politics has revolved around the symbols of Arab culture – history, religion, language, customs and traditions. However, the state has increasingly relied on the instruments of social control to impose its authority on society. As a consequence, the praxis of Arab politics has revolved around the symbols of political power – control of state military and security establishments. Historically, the dynamic between political discourse and political praxis in Arab politics in effect imposed culturally mediated limitations on the behaviour of Arab states. By the early 1970s this dynamic ceased to function in the internal politics of most Arab states. This separated regime legitimacy from many of the sources of traditional authority, removed societal inputs into the administration of the state while increasing the state's reliance on the instruments of oppression and suppression to establish hegemonic control. This led to an abandonment of any pretence of popular sovereignty associated with the nation-state system in the European tradition. At the regional level, however, this dynamic functioned among states to limit their behaviour to the bounds of culturally legitimate patterns of interaction. In effect, this bifurcated Arab politics into internal spheres where struggles for power were unmitigated by cultural norms, and an external sphere bounded by cultural norms. While the normative foundation of inter-Arab relations, manifested in the Arab League (organised in 1945) and Arab summit conferences (initiated in 1964), exercised only symbolic control, the significant degree of conflict management and co-operation operant among Arab states throughout the post-Second World War era reflects the influence this exercised in inter-Arab affairs.

Second, due to the overwhelming state dominance of the modern instruments of cultural articulation, modern avenues for the expression of popular political culture in the internal political sphere were cut off. As a result, the development of popular political culture, confined to traditional religious channels and modes of articulation, became distorted. The effective result was that by the 1980s Islamic activism was the dominant manifestation of popular political culture throughout the Arab world.[19]

Impact of the Gulf War

The Arab political system proved sufficiently viable to sustain itself through more than four decades, autonomously adapting to turbulence in the system produced by international, regional and internal instabilities. The Arab-Israeli wars of 1948, 1956, 1967 and 1973; the 15-year Lebanese civil war from 1975 to 1990; Israel's invasion of Lebanon in 1982; the eight-year Iraq–Iran war of 1980–88; Israel's occupation of the West Bank, Gaza and the Golan Heights since 1967, and occupation of southern Lebanon from 1982 to 2000; and the two Palestinian *Intifadas*, initiated in 1987 and 2000, all reflect this turbulence in the system. However, this was absorbed by and large through realignments among states and among political actors via the channels and processes of the Arab political system.[20]

The major impact of the Gulf War was the destruction of the dynamic between political discourse and political praxis in regional politics, and the destruction of the Arab state system's ability to sustain itself. In other words, like the internal sphere, Arab politics in the regional sphere became a struggle for power unmitigated by normative considerations and dominated by the interests of the United States. This was the result of the direct collusion of key Arab political actors with external actors to precipitate massive external military interference in the Arab political system, to resolve an inter-Arab problem. The most fundamental cultural norm of Arab politics established prior to 1990 was broken, essentially discrediting other key political actors and shattering the legitimacy of the Arab political system among participants at all levels – internal, regional and inter-national. The effective result was that the agencies of conflict management and co-operation that evolved in the Arab political system were divested of their normative authority.[21] As a result, the

Arab state system after the Gulf War of 1991 lost its self-sustaining dynamic and required increasing levels of coercion to be sustained.

The interaction between political discourse and political praxis has been the most fundamental dynamic underlying Arab politics since the advent of Islam. Arab nationalism was only the twentieth century's symbolic manifestation of this dynamic, and the Arab political system was the form it took in the post-Second World War international environment, as a representation of the political values, norms and interests dominant within Arab society throughout most of the twentieth century.[22]

ARAB REGIONAL POLITICS AND THE IRAQ QUESTION

The imposition of economic sanctions against Iraq following its invasion and occupation of Kuwait in August 1990 was seen by Arab leaders as a coercive measure short of war to be used in concert with diplomatic efforts to avoid the instability attendant on, and the destructive consequences of, a larger conflagration in the Gulf region. The imposition of sanctions was generally supported as a measure to avert a wider conflict. Sanctions were considered a vehicle under United Nations auspices to support diplomacy, in the form of an 'Arab solution', to the crisis. The rejection of the diplomatic path and the overwhelming destruction of both civilian infrastructure and retreating Iraqi forces by the coalition during the Gulf War quickly raised doubts within the Arab world as to the driving force behind UN actions and US policy.[23]

Historically, Saddam Hussein had successfully aligned his regime with the cause of liberating the Palestinian people, a connection that conferred legitimacy and brought popular support from many in the Arab world. When faced with the intervention of Western military forces following the invasion of Kuwait, the Iraqi leadership attempted to associate its decampment from Kuwait with an Israeli withdrawal from lands it had also taken through force of arms. Rejection of this linkage by US and UN negotiators was facile, but tacit recognition of its significance emerged in plans for a post-war conference to resolve regional issues long before Iraqi Scud missiles were launched at Israel. A just peace between Palestinians and Israelis, or the prospect that such a peace was within the senior Bush administration's capability, was crucial to the US effort to isolate Iraq, build a coalition that included regional states and execute the Gulf War. Thus, the Gulf War, in effect, established linkage as a central issue. While the formulation of linkage proposed by the Iraqi regime was overtly rejected, the United States, its Arab allies and Israel reinterpreted linkage to allow the building of a broad coalition against Iraq.

On 30 October 1991 the United States and the Soviet Union co-convened an international peace conference in Madrid, Spain, to discuss a diplomatic end to the Arab-Israeli conflict. The conference initiated two parallel negotiating tracks: a bilateral track that involved specific talks between Israel and individual Arab states, and a multilateral track that involved many delegations discussing regional issues. It was attended by delegations from Israel, Syria, Lebanon, Egypt, a joint Jordanian-Palestinian delegation, the United States, the Soviet Union and the European Community, as well as observers from other nations and organisations. The Gulf Co-operation Council (GCC) states were represented by its Secretary-General as an observer, and GCC member states also participated in organising the negotiations on multilateral issues. Lastly, the United Nations sent an observer representing the Secretary-General. The process undertaken proved successful in bringing Israel and the Arab states into direct negotiations in an effort to settle regional disputes. In addition, it granted Israel a legitimacy and status it had not been able to achieve through force of arms or diplomacy in its (then) 43 years of statehood. Enormous expectations were raised for the peoples of the entire region, as all expected to benefit from the bounty of a resolution of the conflict between Israel and the Arab states. However, the diplomatic successes of the conference, including tentative steps toward normalisation between the states of the region, recognition of the need for co-operation and dialogue to examine regional issues such as water, and eventually, a 1994 Israeli-Jordanian peace accord, all paled in the face of the failed Palestinian-Israeli negotiations.

It was not only the resolution of a just peace between the Palestinians and Israel that eluded US leaders. With the survival of the Ba'athist regime in Iraq, and the abandonment of the popular uprising against Ba'athist rule by the same Western governments who had called for it, Arab states were left with no answers to domestic criticisms of their apparent desertion of the Iraqi people in their support of US policy. The devastation faced by ordinary Iraqis through the ensuing years of sanctions saw the population further decimated while the regime apparently only gained strength, both over its own population and within the region, as the sole visible opponent of American dominance. In the face of growing US ascendancy in the region and the perilous negotiations between the Palestinians and

Israelis through the Oslo process, Arab governments were left powerless to respond to the growing concerns of Arab intellectuals and the (so-called) 'Arab street' over the plights of the Iraqi and Palestinian people.

The increasing acknowledgement of the humanitarian cost to the Iraqi people meted out by UN sanctions aroused calls within Arab civil society organisations, international NGOs, UN member organisations and individual campaigners around the globe.[24] These calls for an alleviation of the suffering played no small role in the diplomacy surrounding the implementation of the oil-for-food programme in 1996. As the scope of the humanitarian crisis continued to widen in Iraq, Arab leaders increasingly felt compelled to speak out. Egyptian President Hosni Mubarak declared during a CNN interview on 20 November 1997 that 'easing the suffering of Iraqi people under UN economic sanctions comes at the forefront of Egypt's priorities'.[25] While still calling for full Iraqi compliance with UNSC resolutions, he went on to express concern over the stalled Middle East peace process, and the need for US support to apply pressure on Israel to move the negotiations forward. The inadequacies of the Oslo process, the bankrupt leadership of the corrupt and authoritarian Palestinian National Authority[26] and a rejectionist Israeli government under Likud leader Benjamin Netanyahu, were hurtling the peace process toward an abyss.[27] With its apparent demise and the outbreak of the Al-Aqsa *Intifada* in September 2000, the link between the plights of the Palestinian and Iraqi people assumed centre stage in popular Arab political culture.

The moral implications of the sanctions regime, as opposed to realpolitik identification of oil as a principal factor in the maintenance of sanctions,[28] relied upon the acceptance of the Security Council's stated goal of Iraq's compliance with the ceasefire agreement. The disarmament of Iraq's weapons of mass destruction (WMD) was an ambitious undertaking without parallel in international relations since the Treaty of Versailles at the end of the First World War. However, by 1998 the disarmament programme, beginning with UNSC Resolution 687, was inherently compromised in the Arab world through its not being applied to other states in the region in possession of WMD. This raised questions about the impartiality and real motives of UNSCOM personnel. Although considerable debate existed within the anti-proliferation community, following more than seven years of UNSCOM inspections, many argued that the process had effectively eliminated Iraq's chemical and biological weapons, and its existing capacity to reconstitute its weapons programme.[29] UNSCOM was increasingly devoting its disarmament activities towards the discovery and collection of documentation regarding personnel associated with the Iraqi programme, and the imposition of a monitoring system called for under its mandate. This process was pursued aggressively by the UNSCOM teams, and increasingly brought them into conflict with the Iraqi regime. Confrontations between the Iraqi government and UNSCOM escalated, as Iraq claimed sovereignty over the materials while UNSCOM argued that Iraq had had its sovereignty abrogated under the terms of the ceasefire agreement. Iraq was also sensitive to UNSCOM's use of information relating to government and Ba'ath Party activities unrelated to WMD. Such sensitivities were identified, and portrayed to the world media as Iraqi admission of a WMD programme. It was unacceptable to the UNSCOM inspectors and the US and UK governments that the Iraqi government would be allowed to possess any privacy for state or party machinations. In the face of increasing US and UK hostility towards the regime, the punitive bombing of Iraq, and the increasing reluctance of the Clinton administration to accept even UNSCOM accreditation as sufficient for the lifting of sanctions, the Iraqis argued that the potential for abuse was sufficient to bar UNSCOM inspectors of US and UK origin.

These inconsistencies, including the desire for an equal application of the disarmament goals to all states possessing WMD in the region, the general ambiguity of US requirements to lift the sanctions, and a desire to see a peaceable resolution of the UNSCOM crisis, confronted all Arabs and challenged the pro-Western policies of all Arab regimes. The UAE Foreign Minister, Rashid Abdullah Al-Noaimi, addressed these issues at the 53rd Session of the United Nations General Assembly on 23 September 1998.

The establishment of a zone free of all kinds of weapons of mass destruction in the Middle East and Arab Gulf regions is a requirement that complements the peace process and represents a major factor in the security and stability of those regions. Accordingly, it behooves the international community to demand that the Government of Israel accede to the Nuclear Non-Proliferation Treaty and subject its nuclear installations to the control and safeguards regime of the International Atomic Energy Agency.

The UNSCOM crisis of 1998 resulted in a major four-day bombing campaign by the United States and the United Kingdom following the evacuation of UNSCOM in December of that year. Suspicions that UNSCOM team members had been working for various foreign intelligence organisations, accusations repeated by the Iraqi regime throughout the crisis and resolutely denied by UNSCOM chief Richard Butler were confirmed when, on 7 January 1999, the US government admitted its intelligence agents had posed as weapons inspectors to spy on Iraq. This admission was further confirmed when, on 23 February 1999, the CIA admitted that it had been in Iraq posing as weapons inspectors for a number of years. The admissions saw UNSCOM disbanded, UNMOVIC founded, and undermined the credibility of anti-proliferation efforts and, more important, the integrity of the United Nations as an impartial arbiter. On 2 March 1999 US and UK air strikes on Iraq intensified causing considerable civilian damage. On 9 April 1999 Iraq rejected efforts to end the impasse in the Security Council, and vowed never to co-operate with weapons inspections unless sanctions were lifted.[30]

The quandary of UNSCOM, and subsequent admissions that inspectors were spying for Western intelligence organisations, undermined the entire disarmament initiative. Public support for sanctions vanished from the Arab Middle East and, increasingly, Arab leaders were called upon by their populations to find a way to end the suffering of the Iraqi people.[31] In January 1999 the Arab League met in Cairo and invited a full Iraqi delegation for the first time since 1990. The summit centred on ways to ease the sanctions, while maintaining pressure on Iraqi President Saddam Hussein to comply with UN resolutions on arms inspections. Syrian Foreign Minister Faruq al-Shari' called for an 'end to sanctions on Iraq' in the conference's opening address. Al-Shari' implored the delegates: 'Is it not our duty to stop this dangerous and recurring game in which the whims and espionage of international inspectors are used to let the Americans flex their muscles and hit Iraq materially, and the Arabs morally?'[32] Syria was joined by demands from Jordan, Yemen, Sudan and Palestine who all called for the embargo to end. Following deliberations, the summit condemned the December 1998 US and British air strikes on Iraq, and backed the lifting of the sanctions. However, to achieve unanimity between its membership the statement also called on Iraq to implement UN resolutions on weapons inspections, and refrain from making any 'provocative actions' toward its neighbours.

The Arab League's stand brought increased public statements by Arab governments demanding an end to the sanctions. Oman's Foreign Minister called for the lifting of sanctions at the UN General Assembly's

54th session.[33] UAE Foreign Minister Rashid Abdullah Al-Noaimi also addressed the General Assembly, and following a call for the Iraqi government to live up to its regional as well as its international obligations, voiced a strong appeal on behalf of the Iraqi people:

> The inhuman conditions visited upon the Iraqi people make it incumbent upon all of us to seek an early end to their suffering. We, therefore, call upon the Security Council, and in particular, its permanent members, to reach consensus on the drafts before it, leading to the implementation of its resolutions in full in order to lift the international economic embargo imposed on Iraq, and emphasising the importance of respect for the integrity and unity of its territory.[34]

As the sanctions approached their tenth anniversary, the international campaign to end the suffering of the Iraqi people, and the erstwhile efforts of several Arab governments saw the sanctions debate remain at the top of the international agenda. The release of UNICEF's *Child and Maternal Mortality Survey 1999: Preliminary Report* in July and August 1999, the first independent national child mortality survey since 1991, provided those wishing to see an end to the sanctions with the most accurate and secure information on the deleterious effects of the embargo.[35]

In February 2000, building on its calls for solidarity with the Iraqi people, Syria re-established diplomatic ties with Iraq for the first time in over two decades. With Arab and international humanitarian organisations objecting to the continued maintenance of sanctions, on 24 March 2000 the Security Council convened a special session to examine the humanitarian situation in Iraq. UN Secretary-General Kofi Annan said the humanitarian crisis in Iraq posed 'a serious moral dilemma for the United Nations'. Annan continued: 'The UN has always been on the side of the vulnerable and the weak, and has always sought to relieve suffering. Yet, we are accused of causing suffering to an entire population.' He went on to argue that the UN was in danger of losing the debate in the court of international public opinion regarding its responsibility for the humanitarian crisis, 'if we haven't already lost it'. In a pointed remark to those who would dismiss UNICEF's report, and the work of other independent examinations of the humanitarian crisis, Annan stated: 'We cannot in all conscience ignore such reports, and assume that they are wrong.'[36]

In April 2000 the United Arab Emirates followed Oman, Qatar and Bahrain in the renewal of diplomatic ties with Iraq by reopening its embassy in Baghdad. Iraq followed suit by opening its embassy in Abu Dhabi in July 2000. Abu Dhabi stated its intention to serve as a bridge to promote normalisation between Iraq and the remaining GCC states – Saudi Arabia and Kuwait – who had yet to re-engage with Iraq. Such attempts to engage with the entire region, and reacquire normalcy in its relations with an ever-growing number of Arab states, was part of a progressive Iraqi effort to build its relations with the region generally, and the GCC in particular. Arab leaders continued their assault on sanctions through the summer of 2000, with Jordanian Prime Minister 'Abd al-Ra'uf al-Rawabdeh delivering a speech to the Inter-Parliamentary Union on 4 May 2000, in which he stated, 'the sanctions imposed on Iraq have led to a great human catastrophe with an unpredictable, destructive impact in the short and long terms. We call for lifting the embargo on Iraq, and for the preservation of its sovereignty and territorial integrity, so that it can resume its role in the regional and international arena.'[37] On 28 July 2000 Egyptian Minister of Foreign Affairs 'Amr Moussa, speaking to a press conference in Cairo, stated that 'continued sanctions on Iraq, are unacceptable and void of all logic for Arabs'.[38] The Arab diplomatic manoeuvres received support from what was often seen as a regional antagonist when, on 1 August 2000, Iranian Foreign Minister Kamal Kharrazi stated that 'efforts should be made to bring the sanctions, as well as the sufferings and deprivations of the Iraqi people, to an end'.[39] The efforts soon expanded beyond the Middle East when, on 10 August 2000, Venezuelan President Hugo Chavez became the first elected head of state to visit Iraq since the end of the Gulf War, while on a tour of ten fellow OPEC member states. Chavez called for an end to Iraq's isolation.[40]

The reopening of Baghdad's Saddam International Airport on 17 August 2000, without authorisation from the UN sanctions committee, demonstrated an increasing audacity in Iraqi actions, just as the support for sanctions demonstrated deep fissures in the international community.[41] The momentum continued when, on 5 September 2000, an initiative proposed by the government of Qatar, ignored when it was first advanced the previous June, was adopted for study by a meeting of GCC Foreign Ministers. The proposals aimed at 'ending the suffering of the Iraqi people' by opening a 'channel for dialogue' with Iraq.[42] On 16 September 2000, after more than a decade of sanctions, Oman's Foreign Minister, Yousef bin

Alawi bin Abdullah, summarised the bankruptcy of the sanctions policy, and the frustration of Arab government's efforts to see the people of Iraq delivered from the destitution brought on by ten years of embargo. Bin Abdullah stated:

> Despite all the serious international and regional efforts to alleviate the suffering of the people of Iraq, the general situation in Iraq continues to deteriorate as a result of the economic embargo imposed for the last 10 years. Therefore, we cannot now but call for the establishment of a mechanism to end the siege and to lift the embargo, which doubtlessly has done great harm to the people of Iraq.
>
> Despite the fact that the regime of sanctions was intended as a political mechanism to guarantee that governments implement their commitments in accordance with UN resolutions, this mechanism has now become a weapon that has harmed the basic rights of people and society. This no doubt contradicts the letter and spirit of the International Declaration of Human Rights. We call on the Security Council to adopt new policies and effective mechanisms that will relieve the suffering imposed on states such as Iraq, Libya and the Sudan. The Security Council with its responsibilities defined by the Charter, should without doubt play a positive and unifying role, to maintain security and stability, under international circumstances, which aim to develop a new vision for economic globalisation.[43]

Sanctions unravel and Palestine ignites

The easing of Baghdad's diplomatic isolation and the rising demand for oil due to increased energy prices, coupled with the reopening of Saddam International airport, provided an opportunity for the government of Iraq, anti-sanctions advocates, and states who wanted to expand business opportunities within the rubric of the United Nations sanctions regime to express their rejection of the embargo. Flights from around the world began to challenge the embargo by arriving in Baghdad without UN authorisation, arguing that it did not apply to civilian flights carrying humanitarian aid. Humanitarian relief suppliers, as well as officials, medical experts, politicians, entertainers and athletes, protested against the ongoing suffering of Iraqi civilians by visiting Iraq and breaking the embargo. The Security Council and its Sanctions Committee (UNSC 661) quickly became divided over the legality of the flights. It found itself divided between those members of the Security Council who wanted to see an end to the sanctions regime (France, Russia and China) and those who advocated strict enforcement (the United States and the United Kingdom). The former argued that flights delivering humanitarian supplies to Iraq were not barred by Security Council resolutions and would therefore only have to notify the committee, while the latter felt that any visitors to Iraq needed to receive the committee's explicit approval.[44]

The flights began on 17 September 2000 with a Russian delegation aboard a charter plane carrying Russian oil executives and humanitarian workers, which did not request official approval from the sanctions committee in New York. Instead, landing in Baghdad on 17 and 23 September, the Russian spokesperson argued that, as humanitarian flights, they had no reason to require clearance from the committee. On 18 September 2003 the Russian Foreign Ministry made clear its position publicly:

> We continue to proceed from the premise that the relevant resolutions...do not contain any bans on regular passenger flights to Baghdad...As for charter flights to deliver humanitarian relief to Iraq, the Sanctions Committee must only be officially notified of such flights on the understanding that no formal permission from it...is required.[45]

A French flight from Paris which reached Baghdad on 22 September carried a delegation headed by France's former foreign minister, Claude Cheysson. The French government had given him the approval for a chartered Paris–Baghdad flight that carried 60 physicians, athletes and artists. The French Ambassador to the United Nations, Jean-David Levitte, addressed the issue after the flight had landed, stating: 'There will be other flights...[F]or many years now, we have considered that there is no flight embargo.' After the Russian and French flights, several Arab nations followed suit, and the resumption of regular passenger flights to Baghdad was discussed by many national airlines. The flights were creating positive feedback within the community of Arab states as well, and Egyptian Foreign Minister 'Amr Moussa, stated that 'Egypt is working on lifting the embargo on Iraq, and putting an end to those sanctions detrimental to the Iraqi people', when he addressed a press briefing in Cairo on 21 September 2000.[46] In Morocco the Speaker of the Moroccan Chamber of Advisors,

Mohamed Jalal Essaid, while meeting with a delegation from Kuwait, promised that Morocco would 'defend Kuwait's unity and security, and call for lifting the embargo imposed on the Iraqi people', renewing the call made by King Mohammed VI the previous April.[47]

The positive momentum achieved through the efforts of Iraqi and Arab diplomats, aided considerably by international anti-sanctions activists and humanitarian organisations, saw calls from throughout the Arab world for an escalation of the sanctions-busting acts by Arab actors. The editor of the London-based *Al-Quds Al-Arabi* wrote an editorial imploring the Arab world:

> Why doesn't Syria resume civil flights to Iraq? Why doesn't Jordan do the same? What about Egypt, Sudan, and Yemen?...What can the Arabs lose? What do they have left to lose?[48]

On 27 September 2000 the Iraqi government notified all of its trading partners through the office of Trade Minister Mohammad Mehdi Saleh that future contracts with the Iraqi government should be denominated in the euro rather than the US dollar.[49] Iraqi businessmen had curtailed their transactions of US dollars following the 36th session of the Iraqi cabinet, which had appointed a committee of economists to examine the possibility of replacing the dollar in trade deals with the euro or another alternative currency as a symbolic measure against US control in Iraq. The following day, 28 September 2000, Syria's Foreign Minister, Farouk al-Shari', again called for lifting the sanctions after talks in Damascus with Iraqi Deputy Prime Minister Tariq Aziz.[50] Similarly, on 30 September, Egyptian Foreign Minister 'Amr Moussa adopted a more hard-line approach to the lifting of sanctions. When speaking to the international media, Moussa noted that 'the sanctions regime was not reasonable in its marked insistence on embittering, [and] humiliating Iraq and its people'.[51]

On 28 September 2000 Israeli Likud Party leader Ariel Sharon made a deliberately provocative visit to Haram al-Sharif, the location of the Al-Aqsa Mosque, in effect igniting the fertile 'kindling' Oslo had produced over the previous year's failed negotiations. The Al-Aqsa *Intifada* erupted with massive Palestinian civil disturbances and the increasing use of violence by both Palestinian militants and Israeli security forces. The ensuing bloodshed escalated unabated from that date forward. The David and Goliath image of fighters with small arms and Palestinian children with stones clashing with Israeli tanks and soldiers returned the Palestinian-Israeli conflict to a paramount position in regional and international politics.

In spite of the redirection of the world's attention to the bloodshed in Palestine/Israel, humanitarian and passenger flights continued in an escalating challenge to UN sanctions. In October 2000 Jordan sent a plane carrying humanitarian aid to Baghdad, becoming the third such flight in a week and the first from an Arab state. Yemeni, Moroccan and United Arab Emirates aircraft followed the Jordanian lead, landing at Saddam International Airport in October 2000. Those were soon followed by aircraft from Iceland, India, Turkey and Syria. On 2 October 2000 Syrian President Bashar al-Assad, facing the first major crisis of his presidency with the outbreak of the Al-Aqsa *Intifada*, spoke in Cairo on his first state trip abroad and stated unequivocally: 'Syria seeks an end to Iraq sanctions.'[52] Many of the flights carried teams of surgeons and ophthalmologists as well as medicines and medical equipment. Tunisia sent its national football team to play a friendly match in Baghdad on 6 October 2000.[53] On 10 November 2000 a group of British peace activists flew into Baghdad, led by Labour MP George Galloway, who expressed solidarity with the Iraqi people and stated: 'We didn't notify the British government, or the United Nations...we came here as free citizens of the world to this country that we love.'[54]

Iraqi regional isolation continued to erode when Iraqi officials travelled to Egypt and attended their first Arab League summit meeting in a decade. The desire to face Israeli attacks on Palestinians as a unified coalition of states, to draw further attention to the plight of the Iraqi people, and the desire of some Arab governments to undermine efforts by the Iraqi regime to champion the Palestinian cause, saw Iraq reintegrated into the Arab League fold. The diplomatic furore caused by the humanitarian flights was replayed when, in November 2000, a Baghdad trade fair drew twelve foreign trade ministers and some 18,000 business people representing 45 countries. It was a further erosion of the isolation Iraq had experienced due to sanctions, although the fiscal limitations imposed by the oil-for-food programme kept the measure from aiding in the rebuilding of Iraqi infrastructure so desperately needed. With world opinion firmly tilted towards ending the embargo, and with violence escalating in the occupied territories, one of the first acts of incoming US President George W. Bush's administration was to initiate a substantial aerial bombardment of Iraq in February 2001. The bombings were claimed to be in response to increased Iraqi opposition to US and UK fighter aircraft enforcing the no-fly zones.[55] For the first time, targets were located north of the 33rd parallel, the northern terminus of the southern no-fly zone.[56] US and UK military leaders argued that the increasing frequency and sophistication of the Iraqi air defences posed a growing threat to allied aircraft and their crews. On 27 January 2001 another call for a 'reassessment of sanctions' by Egyptian Foreign Minister 'Amr Moussa recognised widespread popular opposition to sanctions throughout the Arab world.[57] Egypt successfully mobilised regional opposition to the US air strikes, including that of Iranian Foreign Minister Kamal Kharrazi, who, while consulting with Moussa in Egypt, stated, 'the time is ripe for a review of the economic sanctions against Iraq, and at the same time measures should be taken to check its proliferation of weapons of mass destruction'.[58]

In the face of the Israeli onslaught on the Palestinians and the US-led bombardment of Iraq, the Arab regimes could only voice concern and confer, revealing their collective impotency in world politics. The 13th Arab summit in Amman, Jordan, on 27–28 March 2001 demonstrated their collective inability to do anything more than express concern. Jordanian monarch King Abdullah II welcomed Arab leaders to Jordan to what he described as a new era in Arab co-operative efforts. Abdullah recognised that 'Arab citizens have become bitter and frustrated, with no confidence in themselves or in their future', and called on his fellow delegates to focus on economic, social and political co-operation in what he identified as a 'more homogeneous and closer...regional economic grouping', than existed elsewhere in the world. Moreover, the necessity of bringing about peacefully the liberation of Arab land from Israeli occupation and Palestinian self-determination was paramount, as was the lifting of sanctions on Iraq, whose 'inconceivable suffering has gone on for far too long. It is time to end this suffering, and to lift the embargo on Iraq.' Abdullah recognised the central role Iraq played within the region, stating that Iraq 'has always been at the forefront of the [Arab] nation in defending its causes and rights. It has never failed to respond to the calls of duty, sacrifice and brotherhood.'[59] Arab leaders focused on this call to see the sanctions lifted, and passed a resolution calling for 'lifting sanctions against Iraq and dealing with humanitarian issues according to national principles and international commitments'. In attendance was Kofi Annan, Secretary-General of the United Nations, Abdelouhed Belkaziz, Secretary-General of the Organisation of Islamic Conference (OIC), and Salim Ahmed Salim, Secretary-General of the Organisation of African Unity (OAU) all lending an international dimension to the Arab League's call. Syrian President Bashar al-Assad called for the 'urgent lifting of sanctions imposed on Iraq' and for 'a decisive and united Arab united stance against any bombardment of Iraq'. UAE Deputy Prime Minister Shaykh Sultan bin Zayed al-Nahyan stated: 'We look forward to more humane relations everywhere, and for the elimination of the spectre of fear from unjust sanctions.'[60]

In April 2001 Egyptian President Hosni Mubarak visited the United States, urging his US allies not to disengage from the peace process, and to revise the sanctions regime.[61] Also on a visit to the United States in April 2001, Jordan's King Abdullah reiterated that: 'We all understand that the problem in Iraq is relieving the sanctions on the people.'[62] He linked Iraqi disarmament with regional efforts, in stating the Iraqi position that 'there should be a reasonable approach to limitations on weapons of mass destruction. They [Iraq] seem to be willing to say that they're willing to do it if others in the region are willing to do it, too.'[63] Further, he reiterated his call for the United States to take a more active role to prevent an expansion of the violence in Palestine/Israel.[64] On 30 April 2001 King Mohammed VI of Morocco voiced his 'solidarity with Iraq', a shift in the Moroccan position which had previously voiced considerable support for Kuwait, while calling on Iraq to implement the resolutions in full.

With the US administration focusing on 'smart sanctions' in an effort to alleviate international pressure for the lifting of the embargo, Jordan's King Abdullah, on 25 June 2001, called on the Iraqi leadership to 'take the lead in rebuilding confidence', and declared that it was the 'responsibility of the Iraqi leadership to eliminate the suffering of the Iraqi people'. Reflecting the increasing disparity between Arab regimes and Arab public opinion, the Jordanian Parliament demonstrated solidarity with Iraq by rejecting the imposition of 'smart' sanctions (i.e. targeted at military-related imports).[65] When the Security Council convened in June 2001 to discuss the implementation of smart sanctions, Arab diplomats made opposition to a continued embargo clear. Even the staunchest allies of the US opposed it on this. Zeid Ra'ad Zeid Al-Hussein, representative of Jordan at the UN, stated:

Iraq continues to pay a hefty price as a consequence of the comprehensive sanctions imposed upon it that will have an impact on future generations of the Iraqi population in terms of their food, livelihood, health and prospects for economic growth and development. The result is an unprecedented case of civilian suffering...This type of collective punishment, the most severe in the history of the United Nations, did not achieve its declared purposes of consolidating peace and security. On the contrary, those sanctions created conditions that in the long run may endanger the future of the whole region...We believe that the only way out of the current crisis lies in the lifting of sanctions imposed against Iraq by the Council.[66]

Similarly, Saudi Arabia's ambassador called for:

an overhaul of this regime to put an end to the suffering of the Iraqi people by enabling Iraq to import all its basic humanitarian needs, medical supplies, foodstuffs and educational material, without requiring the prior consent of the Council...Sanctions should be restricted to the acquisition of arms, military equipment and dual-use materials as stipulated in relevant Security Council resolutions.[67]

This denunciation of the sanctions and rejection of US and UK efforts to reinvent the regime under the guise of 'smart sanctions' failed at the United Nations, and the Arab states continued with their efforts to reintegrate Iraq into the regional fold. Saudi Arabia, long opposed to normalisation efforts with Iraq prior to full Iraqi compliance, appeared to soften its position when, on 24 August 2001, Sultan ibn Abdul Aziz, Second Deputy Prime Minister and Minister of Defence and Aviation of Saudi Arabia, stated: 'Saudi Arabia has absolutely no interest in imposing sanctions against Baghdad or creating any political and military tension...We welcome Iraq's return into the Arab fold.'[68]

September 11 and 'ending states'

The Bush administration's war on terrorism adopted an aggressive and expansive policy connecting acts of terrorism with Islamic political militancy, weapons of mass destruction, and dissident regimes. Following the failure of the US-led military campaign in Afghanistan to capture Osama bin Laden or eradicate al-Qaida, the Bush administration expanded the rhetorical affiliation of the war on terror to encompass Iraq. Bush identified Iraq as part of an 'axis of evil' along with Iran and North Korea, and repeatedly advanced the call for the use of force in an effort to bring about regime change in Iraq. The Bush doctrine, as the policy formulation came to be identified, maintained that any nation or group that tolerates terrorists was now 'a potential target for American military action'. The US administration even enunciated the doctrine in a letter presented to the United Nations Security Council by Ambassador John Negroponte. It stated that the US 'may find that our self-defence requires further actions with respect to other organisations and other states'.[69]

However, US attempts to expand the war met considerable resistance in the international community, as well as in the Arab world. The escalation of violence in Palestine/Israel, including Israel's military reoccupation of Palestinian-controlled areas following Bush's declaration of a war on terrorism destroyed the ostensible basis for any Arab support for the expansion of hostilities on Iraq by US forces. In an effort to ease the tensions surrounding the conflict, Saudi Crown Prince Abdullah proposed a peace plan in February 2002.[70] The Abdullah plan proposed peace and normalisation of Arab-Israeli relations in return for a full Israeli withdrawal from the West Bank and Gaza, an arrangement that had been implicit in the Oslo process as it was understood by the Arabs. Such an understanding, however, was not shared by successive Israeli governments during the Oslo process, and negotiations had repeatedly stalled on issues surrounding Israeli settlements and Israeli security arrangements in the territories. Nevertheless, the plan had the virtue of returning negotiations to the principle of land for peace, while stressing that all of the land conquered in 1967 would need to be surrendered for a complete and lasting peace in the region. Thus, pro-American Arab states, led by Saudi Arabia, responded to US designs against Iraq by calling for negotiations on the Palestinian-Israeli conflict. By initially avoiding outright opposition to US plans in the war on terror, it was hoped that the US would rein in Israeli forces and provide for further negotiations. The maintenance of Arab acquiescence regarding Iraq was presented as being dependent on substantive progress in political negotiations between the Israelis and the Palestinians. The Arab states were willing to bargain full support for US military action against Iraq in return for a determined effort to bring Israel to the peace table. In response, the US administration sponsored a Security Council resolution on the Middle East that, for the first time, spoke of a Palestinian state. In addition, US Vice President Dick Cheney was forced to adjust US objectives during his March 2002 tour of Arab capitals, as he found that he could not focus on US designs for Iraq while ignoring the Palestinian-Israeli conflict.

While directing US attention towards the conflict in Palestine/Israel, Arab diplomats turned their attentions back to Iraq and achieved the long elusive rapprochement between Iraq and Kuwait at the 14th Arab summit in Beirut on 27–28 March 2002. Oman and Qatar brought Kuwaiti and Iraqi representatives together in Beirut and Iraq renounced its claim to Kuwait and pledged not to invade Kuwait again. Iraq also stated its 'respect for the independence, sovereignty and territorial integrity of Kuwait'. The breakthrough came after Iraq provided the Kuwaiti government with a written commitment not to invade Kuwait again, as well as a public declaration to the summit that 'Iraq guarantees the security of all the Arab countries, including Kuwait.' The Kuwaitis maintained that Iraq would need to fulfil its obligations as outlined under UNSC resolutions, return properties stolen during the 1990/91 occupation, and co-operate in finding some 600 missing individuals, but quietly abandoned their demand for a public apology from Iraq. The Arab League summit's final communiqué urged that the economic sanctions imposed on Iraq be lifted, and the 'sufferings of its people ended, in order to ensure stability and security in the region'. Crucially, the League communiqué rejected 'the threat of aggression against certain Arab countries' then emanating out of Western capitals, and stressed absolute rejection of a strike against Iraq, or a threat to the security and peace of any Arab country, considering such an action as 'a threat to the national security of all Arab countries'.[71] The agreement, while not removing Iraq's need to oblige by UNSC resolutions, nonetheless undermined the momentum for a US attack by presenting Iraq as a state at peace with its neighbours. Jordan, Turkey and Kuwait expressed reluctance and Saudi Arabia refused to provide bases for a US attack against Iraq.

In spite of the public posturing by Arab states, however, the build-up of US military forces in the Gulf continued unabated. By January 2003 over 100,000 US troops were concentrated in the Gulf states, and the Gulf itself had been transformed into a parking lot for US warships. This was done under the guise of pressuring Saddam Hussein's regime to disarm. International protests against the war mounted, and on 15 February 2003 6–10 million people the world over marched in protest of the war. On the Security Council, France, Russia and China – permanent members of the Council – opposed the thrust of US policy towards war before UN inspections were fully played out, and countered a joint US–UK–Spain (an elected member of the Security Council) resolution, designed to legitimate the immediate initiation of war, with a proposal to extend UNMOVIC inspections in an effort to disarm Iraq peacefully. During this period Syria was the only Arab state sitting on the Security Council as an elected member and supported the anti-war coalition, as did Germany, also an elected member. Other elected members of the Security Council – Angola, Cameroon, Chile, Pakistan, Mexico, Bulgaria and Guinea – were the subjects of intense political pressure to win their votes. In NATO, France and Germany co-operated with Belgium to forestall an US military build-up on the Turkish frontier with Iraq.

During this high-level international diplomacy, Arab states continued anti-war posturing at the regional level, focused primarily through the Arab League. However, the reality of their positions as US client states compromised any real opposition to US policy, as reflected in the continuing build-up of US military forces in the Arab world. By mid-February all the Arab states bordering Iraq, except Syria – Jordan, Saudi Arabia, Kuwait – had accepted US troops and made their military bases available to the US for launching an attack on Iraq, and the build-up of US troops was over 150,000. Popular opinion in the Arab world, like popular opinion throughout most of the world, was diametrically opposed to war. With 225,000 US troops in the region by the end of February,[72] in preparation of a US invasion of Iraq, anti-war demonstrations in the Arab world reflected the intensity of the Arab public's opposition to US policy. In Morocco, on 25 February, and Cairo and Khartoum, on 27 February, anti-war demonstrations drew over 100,000 protesters each.[73] Commenting on the Egyptian demonstration, BBC News reported that by allowing the protest 'it seems the government is hoping to show it is sensitive to the undoubted anger many Egyptians feel about the threat of war'.[74]

In early March 2003, Egypt hosted an Arab League summit. With 250,000 US troops stationed in the Gulf region by this time waiting to invade Iraq, and Israel pounding Palestinian refugees camps in Gaza almost daily, Arab leaders could only convey their collective will to inaction in the final communiqué which stressed that they would 'refrain from participating in any military action that aims at the security, safety and territorial integrity of Iraq'.[75] In spite of such platitudes, however, the summit exposed the sharp division in Arab politics provoked by the irony that all the US troops present in the area and preparing for an attack on Iraq were stationed at US military bases in Arab countries. A Monte Carlo radio programme on 6 March polled public opinion in the so-called 'Arab street' which, by and large, reflected public contempt for the leadership of the Arab world.

Also on 6 March 2003 an Islamic Summit Conference held in Doha reflected even more sharply the division among Arab states over the stationing of US troops. Having failed to gain Security Council approval for a resolution to support an attack on Iraq, on 18 March 2003 the United States initiated the attack with the compliance if not direct complicity of other Arab states. Street demonstrations broke out throughout the Arab world, as in the rest of the world, to protest against the United States' unilateral action and flagrant violation of the UN Charter. As UN agencies predicted, within days the war threw the population of Iraq into what the UN calls a complex humanitarian emergency – that is, a catastrophe precipitated, and complicated, by the quagmire of world politics.

Placed under the administration of the Anglo-American occupation forces, Iraq, at least temporarily, had been removed as an actor in Arab regional politics. However, it still remains one of the top concerns for the Arab people in general, alongside the Palestinian-Israeli conflict, revealing once again the disparity between public will and political praxis in the Arab world.

3
The US, September 11 and the Invasion of Iraq

Although quick to respond to current crises, US foreign policy is shaped by a more durable underlying pattern. The global distribution of world power today resembles a three-dimensional chess game. The top level of the chessboard is military power, increasingly dominated by the United States. On the middle level economic power is multi-polar and includes the US, Japan, the European Union and increasingly, China.[1] (Indicative of the changing politico-demographics is the projection that the GDP of the European Union in 2004 is expected to be $9.6 trillion for a population of 450 million people, as against $10.5 trillion and 280 million in the US.[2]) At the third level lie transnational relations independent of government influence which are more commonly referred to as 'civil society'. Power on this level is widely dispersed among diverse groups of non-state actors that include, at one extreme, international capital flows largely through the electronic transfer of funds that are frequently greater than the budgets of many states, non-profit and non-governmental organisations, and at the other (illegal) extreme, terrorists and computer hackers of the Internet and other supposedly secure computer systems.[3]

Today all three layers of these levers are very much in play. Most important is the history-altering ascension of the US to the status of sole global superpower. Following the Second World War the US replaced the European imperial powers on the world stage, and filled the power vacuum left by those powers' withdrawal from their colonies. The American strategy in the Middle East region during the decades of the Cold War was driven by its overall goal of strategic containment of Soviet power through a network of alliances designed to guarantee access to oil, while enabling Israel to establish itself as a dominant regional power. The conclusion of the Cold War at the end of the 1980s left the US as the only global military superpower. As such it does not tolerate the emergence of any Middle Eastern hegemony that may exercise its power independently of US dominance and challenge Israeli superiority.

From the early 1990s, the indisputable military superiority of the US has forged a mindset amongst the influential inner circles of American foreign policy strategists who have led the call for, and propagation of, US global hegemony. One of the most influential representatives of this unilateralist mindset is Paul Wolfowitz, the present Deputy Defense Secretary who, as early as 1991, argued in a draft Defence Planning Guidance (DPG) position paper that the United States should retain a pre-eminent role in selectively addressing those global issues which he, and like-minded individuals, perceived to threaten not only American interests but also those of its allies and friends, and which had the potential to seriously destabilise those international relations which he saw as linked to US global interests. Contrary to historically accepted international norms, which typically would require the justification of self-defence prior to an attack, he advocated the use of pre-emptive force against belligerent nations that were identified as possessing weapons of mass destruction.[4] As a result of the DPG, by 1995 the US National Security Strategy of dual containment regarding Iran and Iraq was firmly entrenched in US foreign policy. It proclaimed:

> The broad national security interests and objectives expressed in the President's National Security Strategy (NSS), and the Chairman's National Military Strategy (NMS) form the foundation of the United States Central Command's theatre strategy. The NSS directs implementation of a strategy of dual containment of the rogue states of Iraq and Iran as long as those states pose a threat to US interests, to other states in the region, and to their own citizens. Dual containment is designed to maintain the balance of power in the region…USCENTCOM's theatre strategy is interest-based and threat-focused. The purpose of US engagement, as espoused in the NSS, is to protect the United States' vital interest in the region – uninterrupted and secure US/Allied access to Gulf oil.[5]

The mainstream mass media, which is the main engine in the public sphere for the shaping of the collective thinking of the American public, acts as an auxiliary to the American government. It employs some primary narrative-themes, or 'narrathemes', that structure, direct and control discussion despite the appearance of diversity. First, there is the use of collective 'we', as a national identity marker, which any of the ruling elite employs without concern for ulterior motives. Second, there is the use of the unexamined conviction that opposition to the official American policies is 'anti-American', and that international opposition is based on jealousy of American democracy, greatness, wealth and freedom. When it comes to the Middle East or Latin America, the narratheme is that the US is a well-intentioned, honest broker, and a benign international force that utilises its power for good, and that there is no place for issues relating to power, financial gain, resource grabbing, or forced regime change. Abuses of American power are often reported from within this framework, thus implying that such abuses (the ones that are actually reported) are aberrations and hardly representative of an ongoing systemic problem directly related to the unequal share of global power held by US elites. It is as though the dictum 'power corrupts and absolute power corrupts absolutely' is suddenly forgotten. Third, there is a seemingly blind belief in the moral wisdom of the officials of the administration that is expressed again and again in the media without a shred of doubt and despite contrary evidence. The fact that Elliot Abrams and John Poindexter, two convicted felons of the Nixon era, have been appointed to high government positions in the Bush administration, with virtually no comment, reveals the blind acceptance of authority by much of the American public. Fourth, there is the ignoring of history, and a refusal to see linkages when these contradict endemic notions about the morally noble purposes of American foreign policy. For example, the fact that the US had previously armed and encouraged Saddam Hussein and Osama bin Laden is rarely presented in an objective contextual analysis.[6] The result of such media-cultivated 'realism' is the abhorrent range of idioms, e.g. 'soft power' and 'American vision' that the think tanks and government officials repeat over and over again without ever alluding to unflinching American support for the Israeli campaign against Palestinian civilians, or the terrible civilian casualties incurred by the UN sanctions regime in Iraq. Such topics are inadmissible during any discussion of US policy, no matter how factual they may be. Given such a media-generated political culture, the geo-economics of Iraqi oil was never seriously raised as a major reason for the invasion of Iraq in American mainstream media.

This chapter proposes that post-September 11 US policy in the Middle East reflects a mutually reinforced dialogue between two intertwined themes – media exploitation and unilateralism. Its purpose is, thus, to consider how this dialogue has played itself out in the unfolding of American policy in the Middle East since September 11. It will argue that the US-led invasion of Iraq was an instrument of global domination, and a strategic step towards the reshaping of the global 'environment', and that the timing of the invasion was critical to maintaining the 'dollar hegemony', and protecting American consumerism, which the world has been indirectly financing.

Throughout the twentieth century, Eurasia (which includes Europe and Russia), China and Japan have all been locations of military and economic power. The recently rising economic growth of China and Japan, in conjunction with that of the EU in the twenty-first century, poses an economic and political challenge to the supremacy of American global power. Indeed, although the might of the American military is unmatched, and will probably remain so in the foreseeable future, its economic strength and political dominion in as such diverse and potentially powerful places as Eurasia, China and Japan (not to mention the rest of the world) are necessarily limited, and even subject to attrition over time. Facing the complexity of such geo-strategic and economic interests, the unilateralist mindset in the Bush Administration relies solely on America's unchallenged military might to secure US global domination by physically controlling the global oil resources which are simultaneously the life-blood of potential European and Asian challenges to America's global ascendancy.

THE DEVELOPMENT OF AMERICAN POLICY TOWARDS THE MIDDLE EAST

American foreign policy in general, much like European policies in the Middle East, is one of power intervention to bolster otherwise vulnerable regimes, primarily against internal challenges, and to prevent potential regional hegemonies from exercising their respective capacities by conquering or coercively integrating states, such as the Gulf states, Jordan and Lebanon in the Middle East that were the creation of imperial powers. Although large-scale violence and war have been the usual path for the creation of the imperial states, these powers, and particularly the US, have prevented the emergence of a regional power in the Middle East by hindering state-building wars from being successfully fought. The vocabulary of peace, co-operation and alliances has been, in reality, a barrier that contemporary global powers have used to obstruct regional hegemonies from attaining major power status.[7]

Any attempt to challenge American strategic interests – with regard to Soviet containment, oil and the territorial security of Israel – by an Arab state has been countered by covert, or overt, American intervention. Historically in the Middle East the pendulum of power has swung between Egypt and Iraq, as both possess the potential to become a regional hegemony. For example, Nasser's attempt in the 1950s to engage in state-building activities, including war, ended in his failure and demise as a result of American and Soviet intervention. Iraq's later attempt in 1978–79 to fill the leadership vacuum which was created by Egypt's exclusion from regional politics ended in catastrophe in the Iran–Iraq War a year later. In the 1990s, once more largely due to outside interference with the invasion of Kuwait and the subsequent Gulf War, Iraq was forced to endure hardship and the destruction of its infrastructure culminating in a third war in 2003.

Over the course of the last five decades, the Israeli lobby has grown in power to the extent that it now amounts to a third major party with a political programme that rivals the agendas of both the Republicans and the Democrats. The enhanced stature of the Israeli lobby is grounded in its financial ability and influential stake in media monopolies as well as in its close link to policy-formulation centres. Until the demise of the Soviet Union, American foreign policy in the Middle East was a part of its global strategy that focused on containing an expansive USSR. During this period the importance of the region was secondary, whether in the public's perception or for elite policy analysts. This allowed for the gradual build-up and entrenchment of two powerful domestic lobbies: Israeli and the oil industry.

The Israeli factor makes it impossible to understand the evolution of American policy without close attention to the dynamics of domestic US politics. The formulation of American policy in the Middle East is influenced heavily by pro-Israeli input from US think tanks and the Israeli lobby. In February 1998, members of the Committee for Peace and Security in the Gulf published a letter to President Clinton in which they strongly advocated the unilateral use of force to topple Saddam's regime and replace it with a provisional government from the Iraqi National Congress (INC). The letter was signed by 41 persons, six of whom now occupy influential positions in the present Bush administration, including Donald Rumsfeld, Secretary of Defense; Richard Armitage, Deputy Secretary of State; Richard Perle, foreign policy advisor and Chairman of the Pentagon's Defense Policy Board; Elliot Abrams, National Security Council Advisor; Douglas Feith, Under Secretary of Defense and Policy Advisor at the Pentagon; and Paul Wolfowitz, Deputy Defense Secretary. Apart from Rumsfeld and Armitage, the rest are Israeli spokesmen, with close ties to right-wing Israeli organisations, such as the Zionist

Organization of America and the American Israel Public Affairs Committee.[8] These Washington insiders form the nucleus of American foreign policy formulation. A study conducted by sociologist Laurence Toenjes identified 14 organisations, each with significant roles in the formulation of US foreign policy, attempting to lend a quantifiable analysis of group membership by cross-tabulating individuals with membership in two or more of them. The results are telling: Richard Perle was associated with 10 of the 14, Jeanne Kirkpatrick (US Ambassador to UN under Reagan) with 7, James Woolsey (CIA Director under Reagan) with 6. Over half of the linkages identified represented only nine individuals.[9] Furthermore, Dr Toenjes found that of the 14 organisations there were five with a considerable consolidation of membership. These five groups represent the current Bush administration's ideological atlas very well: they include the Project for a New American Century (PNAC), the Committee for the Liberation of Iraq (CLI), the Center for Security Policy (CSP), the Defense Policy Board Advisory Committee (DPB), and the Jewish Institute for National Security Affairs (JINSA).[10]

Richard Perle and Douglas Feith authored a paper in 1996 to Israel's Likud Prime Minister, Benyamin Netanyahu, advising him to make 'a clean break from the peace process with the Palestinians'. The paper, entitled 'A Clean Break: A New Strategy for Security of the Realm', also called for the removal of Saddam Hussein and the imposition of a Hashemite kingdom, similar to the more Israeli-friendly monarchy of Jordan, in Iraq. In 1993 Douglas Feith asserted that the League of Nations mandate granted the Jews irrevocable settlement rights in the West Bank, and in 1997 he called on Israel to reoccupy the areas under Palestinian control, even though 'the price in blood would be high'.[11] The remainder of this group exerts influence as a result of their positions in influential think tanks, 'departments of pundits' and the mainstream media, who, one should recall, are all interconnected.[12] These 'think tanks' create a network of Middle East 'experts' who not only share the same outlook but also permeate US television and influential newspapers, publish books, and are always available to testify to congressional committees. This network consists of a number of research institutes that vary in importance and influence, but what is unique about them is not only the fact that they disseminate the same line of thought and outlook on the Arab Middle East, but also that their personnel often float between organisations, reinforcing each other. Moreover, these think tanks are funded by tax-deductible gifts from unidentifiable donors.[13]

Among the influential institutes in this network are the American Enterprise Institute (AEI), the Middle East Media Research Institute (MEMRI) (which specialises in distributing articles that degrade Arabs), the Washington Institute for Near East Policy, the Middle East Forum and the Hudson Institute. For example, Richard Perle is, at the same time, the chairman of the Pentagon Defense Policy Board, 'resident fellow' at the AEI and a member of the board of trustees of the Hudson Institute; he is also a close friend to David Wurmser, who is the head of the Middle East Studies section in the AEI. In addition, Meyrav, Wurmser's wife, is the co-founder, along with the former Israeli intelligence colonel, Yigal Carmon, of MEMRI, runs the Middle East Section at the Hudson Institute, and also belongs to the Middle East Forum. Michael Rubin, who belongs to the Middle East Forum, and worked for the Washington Institute for Near East Policy, specialises in Iran, Iraq and Afghanistan and assists both Perle and Wurmser at the AEI.

The staffing of top-rank positions in such institutes is predominantly pro-Israeli and very few know who funds such policy-shaping research. While promoting opinions from only one end of the political spectrum, this network enjoys an extraordinary level of exposure for their views in articles, books, journals, magazines and TV appearances. One study of think tanks in 2002 showed that those leaning to the conservative end of the spectrum received 47 per cent of media citations, compared to 41 per cent for centrist and 12 per cent for progressive voices.[14] In total, citations relating to domestic issues dropped while those discussing foreign policy increased – namely, the Council on Foreign Relations, Heritage Foundation, American Enterprise Institute (AEI), Hudson Institute and the Washington Institute for Near East Policy (WINEP) which alone saw a 23 per cent increase.[15] In 2001 the Washington Institute boasted it had placed 90 articles, written by its members, in mainstream media, of which Michael Rubin had written 50. While the Washington Institute has strong links with Israel, and employs two people from the Israeli armed forces, the Middle East Forum regularly issues the *Middle East Quarterly*, and the *Middle East Intelligence Bulletin*. These two publications have also located themselves in Washington, close to the seat of government and the media, and have actively campaigned to discredit university Middle East departments. Indeed Martin Kramer, of the Washington Institute, Middle East Forum and former director of the Moshe Dayan Centre in Israel, has written a book, *Ivory Towers on the Sand*, which is a vitriolic stricture of Middle East departments in American universities. The Washington Institute published the book, the editor of the *Weekly Standard* journal, William Kristol, who is also a member of the Middle East Forum, wrote a warm review, declaring: 'Kramer has performed a crucial service by exposing intellectual rot in a scholarly field of capital importance to national wellbeing.' The strategy of this network is to sew ideas in the media and the American administration, which others cultivate to develop foreign policy decisions.[16]

The department of pundits refers to the self-proclaimed Middle East experts, like Bernard Lewis at Princeton or Fouad Ajami at Johns Hopkins. The former is a British orientalist whose general disapproval of Islam and the Arabs has made him one of the foremost pro-Israel advocates. His work is based on the notion that Arabs, dominated by Islam, are not predisposed towards rational thought, but instead are driven by emotion. These racist connotations of Lewis' orientalist views, which portray Muslims as more beastly by nature than Christians or Jews (who are in Lewis' perception, rationalists), have been criticised heavily by a number of leading scholars. Edward Said, in his classic expose of this ideologically tainted perception of Arabs and Muslims, *Orientalism*, claims that

> Lewis's polemical, not scholarly, purpose is to show...that Islam is an anti-Semitic ideology, not merely a religion. He has little logical difficulty in trying to assert that Islam is a fearful mass phenomenon and at the same time 'not genuinely popular', but this problem does not detain him for long...he goes on to proclaim that Islam is an irrational herd or mass phenomenon, ruling Muslims by passions, instincts, and unreflecting hatreds...According to Lewis, Islam does not develop and neither do Muslims; they merely are, and they are to be watched, on account of that pure essence of theirs (according to Lewis), which happens to include a longstanding hatred of Christians and Jews.[17]

Lewis' approach to analysis is not common sense or an honest pursuit of facts, but generalisations and the reduction of complex human experience to very simple pronouncements which, strangely enough, have turned him into an authority in contemporary Middle Eastern socio-political issues amongst American policy-making circles. He has managed to attain 'expert' status despite the fact that he has never lived in, or even entered, an Arab country in decades. His book, *What Went Wrong*, which came out after the tragedy of 9/11, is reported to be required reading for the military despite its often prejudicial and factually incorrect statements about the Arabs and the Arab world over the last 500 years. His simplistic assertions about 'weak and primitive' Arabs, who will welcome whatever a powerful America might bring them, have found their way into the planning of policy and the thinking of the Pentagon.[18]

Fouad Ajami is a Shi'ite Lebanese who, in the 1970s, earned his name as a pro-Palestinian commentator. However, in the early 1980s he changed his sides to become a fervent anti-Arab ideologue, and a protégé of the Zionist lobby. Ajami has become the Arab expert, the native informant, deploying 'we' (Americans) as an imperial collective, which along with Israel, stands for 'justice and what is good'. Arabs are the villains and therefore deserve 'our' contempt if not hostility.[19] In addition, he advocated the American destruction of Iraq in the 1991 war, and seems to have succeeded in imbuing the American strategic mind with the notion that their benevolent armed forces can set things right in Iraq following the 2003 invasion. In August 2002, Vice President Dick Cheney quoted him as saying that the Iraqis would welcome 'us' as liberators in the streets of Basra.[20]

Included alongside Ajami amongst the ranks of the Zionist lobby are Martin Peretz and Mort Zuckerman. Martin Peretz is the former owner of the right-wing *New Republic* magazine. He is also a longstanding and articulate defender of Israel and its interests. Media mogul Mortimer B. Zuckerman, in a warmongering cry, declared that if George Bush Jr failed to act against Iraq, it would 'ruin American credibility in the Muslim world'.[21] Zuckerman is the chief of the Conference of Presidents of Major Jewish Organisations, an ultra-Zionist, and the owner of the *New York Daily News*, *US News & World Report* and the *Atlantic Monthly*. In his pro-war parlance, however, he has failed to disclose to his readers any of his Zionist affiliations. On 2 January 1993, after buying the *Atlantic Monthly*, Zuckerman issued a ban on articles that challenged Israel's right to Palestine.[22]

Another prominently featured 'Middle-East expert' is Daniel Pipes, the director of the Middle East Forum, who serves on the Special Task Force on Terrorism and Technology at the (US) Department of Defense. He sits on five editorial boards, has testified before many congres-sional committees, and worked on four presidential campaigns.[23] Judith Miller of the *New York Times* joins Pipes at the Middle East Forum, and has become notorious during the invasion of Iraq for never ceasing 'to reassert that weapons of mass destruction are about to be found'.[24] On 22 August 2003 Daniel Pipes was appointed a

Member of the Board of Directors of the US Institute of Peace whose mission is to seek peaceful resolution to international conflicts. Additionally, he is a founder of Campus Watch, an organisation that monitors university professors who are too critical of US or Israeli policy in the Middle East and has been featured frequently in the mass media. Because he has always been a pro-Israel and anti-Muslim ideologue, voting on Pipes' nomination in the Congress on 23 July 2003 involved many passionate appeals against him, which led to the temporary withholding of his nomination.

Like many other Middle East scholars, Pipes sees a way to end the Israeli-Palestinian conflict. However, unlike most of his peers, he sees no room for negotiation, no hope for compromise and no use for diplomacy. 'What war had achieved for Israel', he explained at a recent Zionist conference in Washington DC, 'diplomacy has undone.' His solution is simple: the Israeli military must force what Pipes describes as a 'change of heart' by the Palestinians in the West Bank and Gaza – a sapping of the Palestinian will to fight which can lead to a complete surrender. 'How is a change of heart achieved? It is achieved by an Israeli victory and a Palestinian defeat', Pipes continued. 'The Palestinians need to be defeated even more than Israel needs to defeat them.'[25]

The monopoly and manipulation of the media by pro-Israeli organisations is further augmented by the absence of an organised mass campaign on behalf of Palestinian and Arab human rights regarding the Israeli-Palestinian conflict which could balance the Israeli-controlled media and go straight to the American people who, though sometimes uninformed, are historically open to appeals for justice.[26]

Islam and Arab society, however, are rarely portrayed or examined in the mainstream English-speaking media, except when terrorism and violence in the Middle East is being examined. Media analysis of such violence, whether on American TV or in influential opinion-shaping papers, like the *New York Times*, the *Washington Post* and the *Wall Street Journal*, is frequently presented without any context. It is in this missing context that propaganda for Israel has 'a free rein', and anything more than the slightest criticism of Israel is 'a taboo in the mainstream media'.[27] De-contextualisation reinforces the 'inadmissibility of linkage' in the public discourse, which affords those who control the mainstream media the power to disseminate notions and perceptions as unopposed facts. Thus, Palestinian resistance to Israeli occupation is transformed into Arab violence, Arab acts of self-defence become acts of terrorism, and criticism of American support for the ruthless Israeli military destruction of civilian property is portrayed as anti-Americanism.

The impressive power of the Israeli lobby across the political spectrum comes from the fact that it is a nationwide donor machine that provides soft money, and funnels out-of-state funds to pro-Israeli political candidates. According to Stephen Steinlight, the retired director of the National Affairs of the American Jewish Committee (known as AJC), the wealth of the Israeli lobby is such that it can 'divide and conquer' and enter into selective coalitions that support the Israeli agenda.[28] The lobby for Israel is a network of individuals and organisations, the most prominent of which is the American Israel Public Affairs Committee (AIPAC), a group that is credited as 'a veritable training camp for Capitol Hill Staffers'.[29] The Israeli lobby is united by a consensus on US policy towards Israel that procures massive funding and unconditional protection of Israel.

Another organisation, the Jewish Institute for National Security (JINSA), spends the bulk of its budget on flying certain retired US generals and admirals to Israel to indoctrinate them in the Likud line so that when they return to the US they can write op-eds and appear on TV shows supporting the Likud position. Men from the right-wing JINSA and from the Centre for Security Policy (CSP) populate the Pentagon and the State Department committees, including that run by Richard Perle. The Israeli journalist Alex Fishman wrote in *Yediot Aharanot* on 6 September 2002, quoting Sharon saying that 'the group of Perle, Wolfowitz, Cheney, Rumsfeld, Doug Feith and Condoleezza Rice dominates Bush's thinking'. Furthermore, many of these prominent administration officials are members of JINSA and connected, in one way or another, to the AIPAC.[30] Richard Perle, the ex-chairman of the Pentagon Defense Policy Board, had previously been an election advisor to Netanyahu, who served as Prime Minister of Israel between 1996 and 1999 and currently as Ariel Sharon's Finance Minister. Perle is reported to have counselled Netanyahu to scrap all peace attempts, to annex the West Bank and Gaza and to try to get rid of as many Palestinians as possible.[31]

The Israeli lobby has succeeded in turning the Congress into a body endorsing most Israeli policies in the Middle East, particularly in relation to Palestine. Illustrative of this, the Senate decided to periodically send unsolicited resolutions to the President stressing and underlining American support for Israel. There was indeed such a resolution in May 2002 when the Israeli forces were wreaking havoc in Palestinian territories,[32] leading Edward Herman to refer to Congress as 'Israeli occupied territory.' In early 2002 Ariel Sharon, Prime Minister of Israel, initiated a massive Israeli military incursion into the West Bank, under the pretext of rooting out a terrorist infrastructure – essentially the same pretext the United States used to attack Afghanistan, crush the Taliban and spearhead the invasion of the country – and destroyed not only the civil infrastructure of the Palestine National Authority but also the socio-economic infrastructure of Palestinian society. This mass invasion and wanton destruction was planned well in advance in a report entitled, 'The destruction of the Palestinian Authority and disarmament of all [Palestinian] armed forces', and was set to begin following the next successful Palestinian suicide bombing of Israeli civilians. It was felt that, following such an attack, it would help buoy Israeli military morale and 'enable Israeli ambassadors and other officials to claim in talks with foreigners that the military action was a justified retaliation'.[33] A report in *Le Monde Diplomatique* echoed what journalists were generally reporting in the aftermath of the Israeli assault:

> During the week we spent in Ramallah, Gaza and Rafah, all we saw was destruction: villages, roads and homes, all demolished. Crops have been burned and public services bombarded. Missiles from helicopter gunships or F-16 fighter planes have destroyed newly completed civilian infrastructure...Does anyone believe that all these sites were terrorist hideouts?[34]

The interests of the American legislative and executive branches have become virtually identical to those of Israel and dissent is usually subjected to some form of discipline or 'flak'. As one example, two members of Congress, Earl Hilliard of Alabama and Cynthia McKinney of Georgia, who had been critical of Israeli policies in the occupied territories of Palestine, were both defeated by two obscure candidates who received campaign money channelled from New York.[35] Hence, for many observers much of American foreign policy in the Middle East is a function of the overwhelming power of the Zionist lobby in Congress and the US Administration.

The Israeli lobby, however, is not the only domestic factor that shapes US Middle East policy. The 'military industrial complex', against which Dwight D. Eisenhower warned, is equally critical. The close relationship between government decision makers and those who produce military wares is frighteningly close. In a 1961 speech, Eisenhower spoke of the potential threat posed by the interplay between the powerful American arms industry and the US government, arguing,

> In the councils of government, we must guard against the acquisition of unwarranted influence, whether sought or unsought, by the military-industrial complex. The potential for the disastrous rise of misplaced power exists and will persist.[36]

What Eisenhower may have recognised was that the potential for enormous profits amongst defence contractors would lead to a permanent lobby forming, with a revolving door of defence experts who would oscillate between service to the government and the military industry. For example, the profitability of arms manufacturers such as Lockheed-Martin are highly dependent upon the threat of armed conflict in the world and maintaining a clearly articulated threat to the security of states is in their 'best interest'. Ken Silverstein, in his book *Private Warriors*, compares the threat vacuum left by the Soviet Union's collapse to that of the post-Second World War world, in which arms manufacturers found themselves in an uncomfortably competitive environment.[37] At that time the arms industry, after extensive lobbying of the US government, found refuge in the renewed threat of the Soviet advance over Europe, despite the fact that the Soviet Union was still attempting to recover from massive wartime losses. The perceived threat of Soviet expansion – the so-called Red Scare – paved the way for Truman's unparalleled military budget increase of 30 per cent in 1948[38] and helped to solidify the complex interdependence between the US arms industry and policy-makers.

The defence contractors in the administration of George W. Bush include Richard N. Perle, who served as the chairman of the Defense Policy Board, a Defense Department advisory group. According to *The New Yorker*'s Seymour Hersh, the military-industrial complex is very prominent in the Defense Policy Board and other similar organisations:

> Advisory groups like the Defence Policy Board enable knowledgeable people outside government to bring their skills and expertise to bear, in confidence, on key policy issues. Because such experts are often tied to the defence industry, however, there are inevitable conflicts.[39]

Perle provides a prime example of how the revolving door between White House policy-makers and military profiteers operates. Not only has he served as the chairman of the Defense Policy Board (a position in which one is considered to be a 'special government employee', subject to federal ethical regulations, including one that prohibits the use of office for private gain),[40] but from 1981 to 1987 he also held the position of Assistant Secretary of Defense for International Security Policy, among other commitments to US government inter-agency groups. In addition to his governmental positions, Perle has been active in a non-governmental advisory capacity through his participation in a number of think tanks, including the prominent American Enterprise Institute (AEI), the Jewish Institute for National Security Affairs (JINSA) and the Project for a New American Century (PNAC). These relationships are further complicated by his position in the world of military profiteering. He is a managing partner in a venture-capital company called Trireme Partners L.P. whose main business 'is to invest in companies dealing in technology, goods, and services that are of value to homeland security and defence'.[41] Needless to say, a number of his business dealings have placed him in the spotlight. One venture in particular, in which the legality of his advisory role for Global Crossing aroused public suspicion, culminated in his resignation from the post of chairman of the Defense Policy Board.[42] The exposure of his dealings with Global Crossing emerged in the *New York Times* on 21 March 2003, right on the heels of *The New Yorker* article of 17 March 2003, in which Seymour Hersh lambasted Perle for his shady dealings with the wealthy Saudi-born businessman Adnan Khashoggi, a middle-man between Oliver North and mullahs in Iran in the Iran-Contra scandal, among other questionable dealings. Hersh charged that Perle had been involved in Trireme's negotiations with Khashoggi while at the same time advising the Defense Department on the invasion of Iraq, of which he was an ardent advocate. According to Hersh,

> As Khashoggi saw it, Trireme's business potential depended on a war in Iraq taking place. '...if there's no war,...why is there a need for security? If there is a war, of course, billions of dollars will have to be spent.' He commented, 'You Americans blind yourself with your high integrity and your democratic morality against peddling influence, but they *were* peddling influence.'[43]

Perle responded to Hersh's accusations by threatening a lawsuit for libel and referring to the award-winning journalist as a 'terrorist' on CNN.[44] However, threats of lawsuits are often used as methods of what Chomsky and Herman might call 'flak' to discipline journalists.[45] Twenty weeks later, on 5 August 2003, Perle had yet to file any legal motions against Hersh in either a US or a British court as he had asserted he would in the *New York Sun*.[46] Furthermore, the Hersh controversy fuelled even more inquiries into Perle's dealings, and journalists such as *The Nation*'s Ari Berman would bring up further charges against Perle's shadowy dealings in defence contracting and his position with the US government.[47]

The case of Richard Perle, while anecdotal, is actually symbolic of a greater phenomenon within the US governmental military-industrial complex. Silverstein suggests that the revolving door between US policy-makers and defence profiteers is not only representative of a problematic relationship between defence policy and profit, but also can be used to explain incentives for policy directions.[48] In this regard, the policy manoeuvres of the US administration needs to be viewed not only from an ideological framework, but also as rooted in concrete, market-based, economic concerns, only one of which is the relationship of policy-makers to the military-industrial complex.

UNDERSTANDING DOLLAR HEGEMONY

Although the ideology of the policy-makers within the US is crucial to understanding the nature of US actions, we must also be aware of other factors that influence and propel international relations, such as those institutional and systemic relationships that are motivated by the market to manoeuvre policy in favour of the most profitable situation. The projection of American dominant power rests on an array of economic conditions, many of which originate in the Middle East. Much of American economic prosperity can be attributed to the globally hegemonising American dollar, to which oil sales have been pegged since 1973, which has inexorably deepened the US involvement in the politics of the Middle East.[49] Since the Bretton Woods Conference at the end of the Second World War the current international trade and finance system has been based on the US dollar. The dollar assumes the role of fiat currency for global oil transactions (the petro-dollar) as well as the international reserve currency. The US prints hundreds of billions of these fiat petro-dollars, which are used by nation states to purchase oil/energy from oil-producing countries and then recycled from oil producers back into the US via Treasury Bills or other dollar-denominated assets such as US stocks, real estate, etc. Thus, in essence, global oil consumption provides a subsidy to the US economy. The dollar has been a global monetary instrument that the United States, and only the United States, can produce by fiat. As of 2002, the dollar was at a 16-year trade-weighted high, despite record US current-account deficits, and the status of the US as the leading debtor nation. The US's national debt at 12 August 2003 was $6.745 trillion against a gross domestic product (GDP) of $10 trillion.

The world's interlinked economies no longer trade to capture a comparative advantage; they compete in exports to capture much-needed dollars to service dollar-denominated foreign debts, and to accumulate dollar reserves to sustain the exchange value of their domestic currencies. To prevent speculative and manipulative attacks on their currencies, the world's central banks must acquire and hold dollar reserves in corresponding amounts to their currencies in circulation. The higher the market pressure to devalue a particular currency, the more dollar reserves its central bank must hold. This creates a built-in support for a strong dollar that in turn forces the world's central banks to acquire and hold more dollar reserves, making it even stronger. This phenomenon is known as dollar hegemony, which is created by the geo-politically constructed peculiarity that critical commodities, most notably oil, are denominated in dollars. Everyone accepts dollars because dollars can buy oil. The recycling of petro-dollars is the price the US has extracted from oil-producing countries for US tolerance of the oil-exporting cartel since the 1973 oil crisis.

According to Henry C.K. Liu,

> By definition, dollar reserves must be invested in US assets, thereby, creating a capital-accounts surplus for the US economy. The US capital-account surplus in turn finances the US trade deficit. Moreover, any asset, regardless of location, that is denominated in dollars is a US asset in essence. When oil is denominated in dollars through US state action, and the dollar is a fiat currency, the US essentially owns the world's oil for free because all countries must buy the dollar to purchase oil. And the more the US prints greenbacks, the higher the price of US assets will rise. Thus a strong-dollar policy gives the US a double win.[50]

With careful documentation, William Clark argues that a unique geo-political agreement with Saudi Arabia in 1973 has worked to the American advantage for the past 30 years. This arrangement has eliminated American currency risk for oil, raised the entire asset value of all dollar-denominated assets/properties and allowed the Federal Reserve to create a truly massive debt and credit expansion. These structural imbalances in the US economy are sustainable as long as certain conditions remain fairly stable.

First, nations continue to demand and purchase oil for their energy/survival needs. Second, the fiat reserve currency for global oil transactions remains only the US dollar. These underlying factors, along with the 'safe harbour' reputation of US investments afforded by the dollar's reserve currency status have propelled the US to its economic and military hegemony in the post-World War II period. However, the introduction of the euro currency in January 1999, has constituted a significant new factor that appears to be the primary threat to US economic hegemony.[51]

In 2000, the US dollar accounted for 68 per cent of global currency reserves, 80 per cent of all foreign exchange transactions and 50 per cent of all world exports. At the same time the US share of world exports was 12.3 per cent ($781.1 billion out of $6.2 trillion) and its imports, in global terms, 18.9 per cent ($1.257 trillion out of $6.65 trillion). Thus, the global dollar reserves are disproportionately higher than America's share in global trade (68 per cent not 31.2 per cent, which is the sum of American exports and imports), and the share of the dollar in world trade is much higher than America's share in global trade.[52] The phenomenon of the oil-pegged dollar, and the dollar as the only international reserve currency, has allowed the US to expand its credit system and incur a huge cumulated national debt (two-thirds of GDP in 2002) without a corresponding expansion in domestic economic capacity. By the end of the fiscal year 2002 foreign interests controlled 14.8 per cent ($1 trillion) of the total debt of $6.745 trillion. In addition, they owned 43 per cent of all Federal Government treasury bonds, 13 per cent of all stocks, and 24 per cent of corporate bonds, all denominated in the US dollar.[53]

This is an exceedingly vulnerable situation, or more accurately, 'the Achilles' heel' that is self-censored in the American mainstream media, though it is fundamental in the creation and maintenance of the American consumerist lifestyle that George Bush Sr asserted 'is not negotiable'. In other words, the world must continue to finance the American debt per capita of $21,428 and rising ($6.745 trillion/280 million people). The US administration manages the huge debt by printing more dollars (monetary expansion) not as a function of its GDP, but in proportion to the expected increase in international trade and the demand for oil and reserve currency that are dollar-dominated. Global acceptance of this phenomenon is based on the perception of 'America as a safe haven' and on a face-value trust in the strength of the dollar.[54] In January 1999 the European Union introduced its new currency, the euro, set initially at 80 cents to the US dollar. At the end of 2000, the euro was at 82 cents when Saddam pegged the Iraqi oil sales to the euro instead of the dollar with the apparent monetary loss of 18 per cent in oil sales revenue.

BACKGROUND TO THE PRESIDENCY OF GEORGE W. BUSH AND SEPTEMBER 11

The presidential election in November 2000 brought George Bush Jr to the White House, though not without public questions about the integrity of the election and the character of Mr Bush as the leader of the world's most powerful state. George Bush's poor grasp of, and scant interest in, global political intricacies is common knowledge, as is his understanding of the fundamentals of the management of the international relations matrix that President Clinton bequeathed to him. This lack of understanding may explain why the pro-Israeli cabal in the administration has been able to dominate Mr Bush's thinking. In June 2001 a Fox News poll announced that nearly 60 per cent of the American public 'had not gotten over how Bush took over the White House – they are angry'. Millions of Americans across the political spectrum were feeling unsure, upset and off-balance.[55] In July 2001 an investigation by the *New York Times* cast further doubts on the legitimacy of the incumbent of the White House, and on the inauguration day, 20 January 2001, though it was cloudy and rainy, about 20,000 protesters shouted, 'Hail to the thief.'[56] A public mood of this magnitude can change history if left uncontrolled.

Exactly one day after Bush became President, the National Security Team held a meeting, at which the first item on the agenda was 'regime change in Iraq by use of force'.[57] However, public perception of the presidency, and the current international norms and relations would not justify this. To force a regime change in Iraq by employing military power unilaterally would require full mobilisation of public support around the American president who would have to convince the American people of the worthiness of the cause. The issue would have to be of such significant proportion and magnitude that it would override the importance that the public attached to the credibility of the election. Furthermore, only urgent issues of mass survival would cement American multicultural diversity and, until September 11, there had been no such cause or issue to galvanise the public behind a foreign policy that was so clearly in contravention of international law. Moreover, the Bush administration signalled a major change in American policy towards Iraq in indicating the end of the dual-containment policies of his father, George Bush Sr, and Bill Clinton. The tragedy of September 11 gave the Bush administration the ability actively to pursue its aggressive agenda.

Iraq, however, was not the only change of direction in foreign policy that the administration sought. Oil considerations were high on the agenda, and while they certainly played a role in the decision to go to war in Iraq, energy policy permeated much more of the Administration's policy agenda than that. The corporate oil culture of the Bush cabinet motivated the administration to decide to resume negotiations with the Taliban on oil pipelines, offering subsidies to sweeten the deal. After four days in office, Vice President Dick Cheney set up an informal group, the Energy Policy Task Force, whose priority was to develop new partnerships in Central Asia. In March 2001 Laili Helms, the niece by marriage of former CIA director Richard Helms, organised a trip to Washington for Sayed Rahmatuallah Hashimi (representative of the spiritual leader of the Taliban, Mullah Mohammad Omar) to resume talks about the development of an oil pipeline through Afghanistan. By the end of July 2001 negotiations had broken down, and the US threatened to go to war with the Taliban if they did not accept the offer.[58]

THE AFTERMATH OF SEPTEMBER 11

The immediate effect of September 11 was the overwhelming power that the Patriot Act (legislated in October 2001) delivered to the executive, purportedly to enable it to fight terrorism. The Act, for instance, gives the government vast new surveillance powers, allows the virtual unlimited detention of immigrants without charges, permits 'roving wiretaps', and imposes gag rules to prevent persons served with warrants from revealing any information in the arrest. It also expands the power of the government to obtain secret search warrants from secret courts to obtain any personal information about individuals in the United States, ranging from library books checked out to personal medical and financial records.

In April 2002 Albert Gidari, an attorney representing Internet Service Providers (ISPs) and telephone companies, reported that the number of subpoenas that carriers receive was roughly doubling every month, reaching levels of hundreds of thousands of subpoenas for customer records. Immediately after 9/11 federal agents spread out across the country, rounding up immigrants from Arab and Muslim countries (the 'Ashcroft Raids'). People simply disappeared into government custody without charges or due process. Hearings by immigration courts were suddenly closed to the public, and lawyers were often unable to find out where their clients were being held. (Not a single one of these detainees has been charged with a crime relating to September 11.) Tens of thousands of immigrants were ordered to report and register with the government, and 13,000 who did faced deportation.

According to a report in *Le Monde Diplomatique*:

An executive order on 13 November created exceptional military tribunals. More than 1,200 people arrested after September 11 were still in custody in December, yet no one knows who they are or what crimes they are accused of.[59]

On 15 February 2003, in New York, police refused to allow anti-war protesters to march anywhere in the city, blocked off streets to prevent people from gathering, attacked people from horseback, and confined those who did make it to the mobilisation site of a planned protest into fenced-off 'protest pens'. April 2003 saw police repression of dissenting politics go further still in Oakland, when rubber bullets were shot at peaceful protesters. It was later revealed that the firing was the result of recommendations from a state police agency on counter-terrorism. Meanwhile, artists like Tim Robbins, Susan Sarandon, Danny Glover and scores of others came under fire for speaking out against either the impending war on Iraq or the attacks on civil liberties. Bill Maher lost his TV show, *Politically Incorrect*, and the Dixie Chicks' CDs were destroyed in rallies after singer Natalie Maines dared to criticise the President on stage at a concert. Phil Donahue, an outspoken opponent of the war, lost his talk show in the increasingly pro-war atmosphere of the media, despite the fact that he was the highest-rated MSNBC host. Major anti-war organisations and leaders were attacked as treasonous, with ties to everyone from al-Qaida to the Cuban government being insinuated. These events reminded observers of news clips from 1930s Germany.

Much of the storm came from the administration. Ari Fleischer, speaking of the Bill Maher incident, warned the American people to 'watch what they say'. Attorney-General Ashcroft, speaking to the Senate Judiciary Committee, blasted any criticism of the Patriot Act:

> To those who scare peace-loving people with phantoms of lost liberty, my message is this: Your tactics only aid terrorists, for they erode our national unity and diminish our resolve. They give ammunition to America's enemies and pause to America's friends.[60]

Furthermore, the Patriot Act attempts to muzzle the freedom of expression and to curtail the liberties inherent in the nature of non-governmental organisations. The war on NGOs is being fought on two clear fronts: one buys the silence and complicity of mainstream humanitarian and religious groups by offering lucrative reconstruction contracts; and the other marginalises and criminalises more independent-minded NGOs by claiming that their work is a threat to democracy. The US Agency for International Development (USAID) is in charge of handing out the carrots, while the American Enterprise Institute, the most powerful think tank in Washington DC, is wielding the sticks.

On 21 May 2003, in Washington, Andrew Natsios, the head of USAID, gave a speech blasting US NGOs for failing to play the role assigned to them. He warned 'the NGOs have to do a better job of linking their humanitarian assistance to US foreign policy and making it clear that they are "an arm of the US government"'.[61] Then, in early March 2003, self-indulgent in this power, President Bush Jr responded to press questions about the effect of the hundreds of thousands of anti-war protesters that frequently demonstrated against the prospect of invading Iraq, by saying 'I do not make my decisions based on the opinion of focus groups.' It appears he meant civilian groups opposed to his policies, as compared to think tanks in support of them. It has been noted that the Patriot Act has had a serious impact on American foreign policy as well, in that it undermines the argument of legitimacy put forward by the administration: that it is defending civil liberties around the globe.[62]

In the aftermath of September 11 the US administration declared that the event was an act of terrorism which the Taliban and Osama bin Laden had orchestrated, although there was no single Afghan in the American list of the perpetrators. The fact that terrorism is amorphous, and terrorists have 'no address', makes it convenient to single out groups, or even nations that propound anti-American policies as 'potential terrorists, or in connection with terrorism', and label them as enemies of the US. Osama bin Laden and his organisation al-Qaida in Afghanistan were marked for capture or death. The US army decimated the Taliban militia, and occupied Afghanistan in October 2001. However, Bin Laden eluded capture, and the one-eyed, illiterate, spiritual leader of the Taliban, Mullah Mohammad Omar, escaped from the mightiest army in the world after he was arrested. During the past 18 months the American army and intelligence have failed to locate either Bin Laden or Omar and most of his lieutenants, and as long as Bin Laden is assumed to be alive, the presence of the American army is self-exculpatory, despite the increasing state of lawlessness and the resurgent drug smuggling that the Taliban had successfully ended in 2001.

From the American foreign policy perspective, September 11 is the tool of domination that the unilateralist, militarised cabal employs to execute its new grand strategy worldwide. The media, as an instrument of engineering consensus among the population, which is interlinked with the right-wing, pro-Israeli think tanks, disseminates a power discourse that pinpoints Islam and Arabs as the causes of terrorism while reinforcing the Israeli justification for its military operations against the Palestinians.

THE PRISM OF MEDIA POWER DISCOURSE

In the aftermath of September 11 strident patriotism has been the dominant tone and tenor of public discourse in the United States. Unrecorded or unregistered dissenters and anti-corporate globalisation protesters cower before braying jingoists and a militarised administration armed with the Patriot Act, while environmental concerns and a rational American foreign policy have been abandoned. On 20 September 2001 US President George W. Bush addressed a joint session of the US Congress and told the world 'you are either with us, or you are with the terrorists!'[63] In effect, this dogmatic discourse has served to disallow, or at least reduce and marginalise, any questioning of US policy in the Middle East. Furthermore, US policy-makers have essentially narrowed the definition of terrorism to an ethno-cultural term of reference.

Terrorism, in other words, means Muslim terrorism and may well refer to virtually any act of violence, protest, or resistance in the Muslim world. The connection between international acts of terrorism and 'dirty Arabs' has a long history in the United States. The danger of the post-9/11 world is that opposition to the militarised American government is now seen as support for terrorism – unpatriotic and treasonous.

The subtext of public discourse on the Middle East in the United States is based on a set of myths and metaphors that the American information media have orchestrated, circulated and reinforced in order to exploit the discharged energy of public paranoia and vindictiveness which emerged after September 11. These myths and metaphors direct the energy towards an easily identifiable foe: Muslims in general, and the Arabs, in particular, and is now made to include those who oppose the American administration. One definition of a myth is that it is a partial truth generalised to explain the whole. As a partial truth, there is always plenty of ad hoc and selective evidence to support it, so that it is particularly resilient to contrary positions. From this perspective, a metaphor creates an analogy that makes up caricatures of links between a people and policy-makers, institutions and processes, cultures and ideologies.

Public vetting of American policy options is filtered through the lenses provided by pro-Israeli lobbies posing as think tanks and other so-called 'experts'. Following September 11 the lens has provided an immensely homogenised Islamic Arab 'world', devoid of the humane, enlightened and magnanimous societal achievements of Western – more specifically American – civilisation. The discursive power of this phenomenon allows for racist notions to flourish and for the tremendous abuse of violent force to be used against the 'other'. Bernard Lewis, for example, has advocated a 'get tough' policy with the 'Arab world'.[64]

The oversimplification of Arabs by many American academics, journalists and policy-makers continues beyond the classic orientalist approach. To many, Arabs are seen as a monolithic community that can only be understood through the scholarly analysis of the Quran, the various schools of legal interpretation that have resulted from its teachings, and Bedouin tribal society. Such reductionism was identified by the French scholar Maxime Rodinson as 'theologocentrism', the referencing of Islamic theology to elucidate any action taken by Arabs.[65] That people living in the Middle East are politically informed, some even motivated to political action ranging from non-violent public demonstrations to the indiscriminate violence of terrorism, *and influenced by socio-economic forces other than Islam and ninth-century Arab tribalism*, is ignored. Such intellectual disconnection has led to clear associations in public discourse within the English-speaking world that equates Islam with 'terrorism', Palestinians with 'suicide bombers' or 'gunmen', and the profession of the Islamic faith with 'fundamentalism'.[66]

While religion generally, and Islam in particular, holds a central position within Middle Eastern culture and political discourse, it would be fallacious to identify any Arab state or political movement as being representative of Islam and its teachings. Ironically, the discourse promoting a monolithic 'Islam' in conflict with a monolithic 'West' exists in the Middle East in the teachings of many Islamic activists. Osama bin Laden's statements have repeatedly referred to the Christian 'crusaders' who occupy the land of the holy places in Arabia, and to the nefarious actions of the 'West' to deprive the Palestinian and Iraqi peoples of their freedom. This identification of the policies of the governments of the United States, United Kingdom, France, and so on reflects a theologism successfully transformed into the reactionary political vision of many Islamic political actors who oppose the corrupt and ineffectual Arab regimes, in a call for a return to a more pious existence. That this has spawned violent action is a tactical decision rather than evidence of any proclivity for violence inherent within Islam. Put simply, the motivations of Islamic activists are political and economic in nature and not predominantly theological.

Arab leaders make numerous references to their piety and religiosity in an effort to legitimise their rule, and increasingly, to co-opt the language used against them by their political opponents who are infused with religious beliefs and teachings, and are identified in the English-speaking media as 'fundamentalist'. This singularity of identification has been reinforced as Islamic 'experts' are given pride of place in mainstream media investigations of events as varied as the Gulf War in 1991, the earlier World Trade Center bombings in 1993, and the suicide bombings in Palestine and Israel. The religious legitimacy self-conferred on Arab regimes by their leaders is echoed by American calls for a cleansing of Islam from the 'violent' interpretation imputed to all opposition movements in countries as diverse as Algeria, Iraq, Lebanon and Afghanistan.

However, American political leaders, intellectuals, and the English-speaking media do not similarly stress the religious orientation or numerous references to the Christian faith by American, British, Canadian or Australian political leaders. Such language and imagery is not seen as having any bearing on the political decisions emanating from Washington, London, Ottawa or Canberra. Likewise, political violence perpetrated by pro-life activists who bomb abortion clinics or assassinate medical professionals is not taken by governments and media as being representative of the Christian faith. Groups as diverse as the Branch Davidians, the Unification Church, the People's Temple or any other aberrant Christian theological group are dismissed and not given legitimacy. Christian phraseology and references common in American political discourse are not seen as relevant, while religious references made by Arab political leaders are continually pointed out.

Indeed, examples of the influence of the Christian faith on the political discourse of the English-speaking states are profuse. The United States' national motto, 'In God We Trust', is prominent in both houses of its legislature, inscribed above the speaker's podium on the House floor, and above the entrance to the United States Senate. As the events of September 11 were unfolding, Senator Joseph Lieberman of Connecticut, who had been Al Gore's Democratic Party nominee for vice president in 2000, called for prayer as members of Congress were evacuated from the Capitol building in Washington. The following day, congressional leaders and several hundred staff members sang 'God Bless America' on the Capitol steps. A congressional 'day of prayer and reconciliation' – the first since the Lincoln presidency during the American Civil War – was held on 4 December 2001. Significantly, the resolution affirming this day was passed even before the tragic events of September 11 (H. Res. 548 on 24 July 2000). It called on Americans to 'humbly seek the blessings of Providence for forgiveness, reconciliation, unity, and charity for all people of the United States', and was heralded as evidence of the increasing influence of the religious right in American politics. The two-hour meeting included nearly one-quarter of the members of the House and Senate repeating the Lord's Prayer on their knees. This combination of patriotism and religion is not new in the United States, in spite of its profession of adherence to the principle of the separation of church and state. When examining the constitutionality of prayer in government, the US Supreme Court in a 1983 decision found that legislative prayer is 'deeply imbedded in [the] history and tradition of this country' (*Marsh v. Chambers*).[67]

American theologocentrism has emerged from a long history of similar views in Western Europe that have contextualised Islam as a 'threat' to its civilisation. 'Evil' motivations grounded in the teachings of the Quran are seen to imbue the motivations, not only of individuals, but also of the collective actions of the Arab Middle East.

With the terrorist attacks on New York and Washington, the public display of personal religious faith became both more widespread and more conspicuous. It is rarely, if ever, acknowledged in the mass media that this seems to operate in a similar fashion to the phenomenon that caused Islamic households in Lebanon to become more expressive of their commitments to the faith during the Israeli occupation, and Palestinians and Jews to become religiously and culturally defiant under their respective collective persecutions. This has important ramifications as further examination might reveal commonalities amongst people across cultural boundaries, and further challenge the 'Clash of Civilisations' theory. Additionally, the phenomenon seems to indicate that theocratic traditions are still prevalent in the modern state, both in the West and in the 'Islamic world'.

The connection between orientalism and Samuel P. Huntington's 'Clash of Civilisations' exists in the foreign-policy formulation of the Bush administration, by articulating a clear vision of the opponent based in theocratic dimensions, while at the same time representing the American view in the language of the Bible. While President Bush describes himself as a born-again Methodist, his head speechwriter was an evangelical Christian. Borrowing a phrase from a popular Protestant hymn about the blood of Jesus, President Bush stated: 'Yet, there's power, wonder-working power, in the goodness and idealism and faith of the American people.'[68] In an interview for the PBS show, *Religion and Ethics News Weekly*, Princeton University religion professor Elaine Pagels discussed the importance of political discourse in times of conflict over religious imagery.

> If we are going to talk about conflict among nations, our government traditionally establishes political discourse and discussion of those options. Now, even if that discussion were to result in the conclusion that Mr. Bush fervently desires, which is a resolution of war, it would be a political negotiation. The way he's setting it up attempts to just bypass that negotiation, it seems to me. What that does is distort the reality of the situation and make anyone who even engages him in discourse seem like somebody who is on the side of evil.[69]

What is clear from these two dynamics is that President Bush accepts that a 'Clash of Civilisations' is likely and is openly purporting to be fighting it in his 'war on terrorism', by labelling and defining his opponents with the same religious overtones he uses to describe himself. The difference being that one is on the side of good, and the other evil.

Well before September 11 the themes of Muslim and Arab terrorism were entrenched in the American media. In fact, since the 1967 Arab-Israeli war political violence in the Arab world and politically motivated violence by Arabs anywhere in the world have been highlighted more in the public media than violence occuring in any other part of the world. The media have been happy to play a passive role in portraying this situation in this fashion. For example, where the media strove to provide the political context for violence in areas like Northern Ireland, the political context of Middle Eastern violence was seldom reported. On the contrary, the *Lawrence of Arabia* perception of the Arab world as a violent place, and the Arab people as undisciplined and uncivilised tribal people was assumed to explain the context. Indeed, when the Oklahoma City bombing of 1996 occurred, the initial response in the American media was that it had been perpetrated by 'Arab terrorists'.[70] In this context, the almost immediate ascriptions in the American media of September 11 to Arab terrorists raised no eyebrows. On the morning of the attacks CBS News reported from the Pentagon that the Democratic Front for the Liberation of Palestine (DFLP) had claimed responsibility. When NBC reported that a spokesman for the DFLP denied responsibility, Tom Brokaw, its head anchor, noted that there are always 'claims and counter-claims' in 'situations like these'. Indeed, American news anchors and producers forged within the immediate coverage an image of war rather than focusing on the tragedy. The ABC news anchor, Peter Jennings, invoked the image of Pearl Harbor, and CBS labelled its coverage 'Attack on America'. Over video of the second tower's collapse, NBC's Tom Brokaw intoned: 'The profile of the United States has changed, and terrorists have declared war on the United States.' He then went on to say that Osama bin Laden may have been predicting the attack three weeks prior when he warned there would be a future terrorist event in the United States.[71]

This rush to provide viewers with a culpable party, including the (then) unconfirmed and repeated involvement of men of Middle Eastern descent in the attack, provided a convenient target when calls for revenge emerged almost immediately thereafter in an emotionally charged atmosphere. On the day of the attacks former Secretary of State Lawrence Eagleburger stated: 'There is only one way to begin to deal with people like this, and that is you have to kill some of them even if they are not immediately directly involved in this thing.'[72] The immediate condemnations of the attacks by Arab leaders and prominent Islamic clerics were ignored by the press, and 'terrorism experts' on every American network focused on the 'threat' of Islamic fundamentalism emanating from the Arab world. Though threats or responsibility by any Palestinian group remained unsubstantiated, the media made explicit connections between Arab grievances against Israel and terrorism.

Nevertheless, despite the fact that the attacks were condemned by many Islamic clerics and leaders, the *New York Times* columnist Thomas Friedman questioned:

> Surely Islam, a grand religion that never perpetrated the sort of Holocaust against the Jews in its midst that Europe did, is being distorted when it is treated as a guidebook for suicide bombing. How is it that not a single Muslim leader will say that?[73]

In reaction to the terrible events of September 11, while addressing the nation, President Bush proclaimed, 'We will make no distinction between the terrorists who committed these acts and those who harbour them.'[74] Rich Lowry exclaimed in the *Washington Post*: 'States that have been supporting, if not Osama Bin Laden, people like him, need to feel pain. If we flatten part of Damascus or Tehran or whatever it takes, that is part of the solution.'[75] As Bush proclaimed:

> Our military action is also designed to clear the way for sustained, comprehensive and relentless operations to drive them out and bring them to justice.
>
> Every nation has a choice to make. In this conflict, there is no neutral ground. If any government sponsors the outlaws and killers of innocents, they have become outlaws and murderers, themselves. And they will take that lonely path at their own peril.[76]

The media played an important role in highlighting Islam as a major focus on its coverage of September 11 and the 'war on terror'. Major television programmes – such as *60 Minutes* and Ted Koppel's *Nightline* – aired items featuring Islam, dialogues with Muslims, etc. PBS' *Frontline* broadcast 'Muslims: A Clear Picture of Islam', and specials on the 'Nature of Islam' and Arab society dominated media coverage. On its 30 September 2001 broadcast, *60 Minutes* produced an exposé on Islam. Host Ed Bradley asked:

> When the suspects in the September 11 bombings were identified as Muslims, people who follow the teachings of Islam, President Bush went to great lengths to point out that the overwhelming majority of the world's more than one billion Muslims are decent, law-abiding citizens. How then is it that a religion that promises peace, harmony, and justice to those who follow the will of Allah can have in their midst thousands committed to terrorism in the name of Allah?

On its 17 December 2001 broadcast, CBS news correspondent Andy Rooney, after reading the Quran in English, stated that all Americans should read it because: 'the [Quran] dominates the lives of 1.6 billion Muslims in the world, many of whom are unfriendly to us' and that 'there's no such thing as separation of church and state in most Muslim countries'.[77]

In this context[78] the initial reaction to September 11 and Bush's inflammatory rhetoric of 'crusade' and 'a monumental struggle of good versus evil'[79] suggested an American 'holy war'. This had two direct consequences in the US: widespread acts of violence against individuals and institutions like mosques and Islamic schools which terrorised people who were, or were mistaken for, Muslims, and a broadly based public outcry by Islamic scholars, intellectuals and Muslim community groups against the vilification of Islam. The White House reacted quickly to distance itself from these acts. The overt racism against individuals was condemned, and President Bush made a concerted public demonstration of respect for Islam, consulting Islamic scholars and clerics, hosting a Ramadan dinner at the White House on 19 November 2001 and on 17 September visiting the Washington DC Islamic Center.

Visibly ethnic Muslim American spokesmen for the 'American establishment', such as Fouad Ajami (see above) and Fareed Zakaria (*Newsweek*'s foreign affairs editor), were featured in the media, especially on television broadcasts. The public text of this campaign was the theme of 'saving Islam from the terrorists' but the subtext played on the theme that the Arabs are the bad boys of Islam.[80] This notion was prominently featured in Fareed Zakaria's feature story on 'Why Do They Hate Us?' in the 15 October 2001 issue of *Newsweek* magazine:

> Only when you get to the Middle East do you see in lurid colours all the dysfunctions that people conjure up when they think of Islam today. In Iran, Egypt, Syria, Iraq, Jordan, the occupied territories and the Persian Gulf, the resurgence of Islamic fundamentalism is virulent, and a raw anti-Americanism seems to be everywhere. This is the land of suicide bombers, flag-burners and fiery mullahs.

PRELUDE TO INVASION

On the governmental level, even prior to September 11, The Pentagon was bringing relentless pressure to bear on the CIA to produce intelligence reports more supportive of war with Iraq. According to former CIA officials, key officials in the Department of Defense were also producing their own unverified intelligence reports to justify war. Much of the questionable information came from Iraqi exiles, long regarded with suspicion by CIA professionals. In an ad hoc intelligence operation parallel to the CIA, the office of Under Secretary of Defense for Policy, Douglas J. Feith, collected information from Iraqi exiles, and scoured other raw intelligence for useful titbits to make the case for a pre-emptive war. 'This information sometimes went directly to the President', says Vincent Cannistraro, a former senior CIA official and counter-terrorism expert. The unit began as a two-person group, but later expanded to five people, and was set up to provide Rumsfeld, Deputy Secretary of Defense Wolfowitz and Feith with data they could use to disparage, undermine and contradict the CIA's own analyses. The unit's main focus was on Iraq, especially Iraq's alleged links to al-Qaida and its purported intent to use its alleged nuclear, chemical and biological weapons. Within the foreign policy, defence and intelligence circles a great many of the senior staff were opposed to an Iraqi invasion. However, because the less than two dozen neo-conservatives leading the war party in the administration had the support of Vice President Dick Cheney and Secretary of Defense Donald Rumsfeld, these war advocates were able to marginalise the opposition. Richard Perle, James Woolsey and the Pentagon's policy-makers made increasing use of the Iraq National Congress (INC) as their primary source of information on Iraq's weapons programmes, its relationship to terrorism and its internal political dynamics, making no distinction between intelligence and propaganda and freely using alleged informants and defectors who even fabricated information that went straight into presidential and vice-presidential speeches.[81]

In the context of international politics America's 'war on terrorism', with its doctrine of pre-emptive strike initiated a bandwagon effect among other states that had restive minority or border problems to use this doctrine to justify their efforts to settle their own political scores. Accordingly, India and Pakistan vis-à-vis Kashmir, Turkey vis-à-vis the Kurds, Russia vis-à-vis Chechnya, Spain vis-à-vis the Basques, and Israel vis-à-vis the Palestinians, welcomed the doctrine as allowing them a free hand to do wha they liked, and virtually everywhere throughout the so-called 'free world', states increased barriers to refugees and asylum seekers as well as to travellers from the post-colonial world. On 29 May 2002 *Euronews* reported that, since September 11, over 4500 persons arriving at European airports from the global south had been turned away as illegal immigrants following stepped-up border control measures in Europe.

Initially the United States 'watched with detached interest as Sharon dismantled the basic foundations of the Oslo process...In a December 2002 meeting between Sharon and Bush in Washington, Bush asked only that Arafat not be killed.'[82] While the Bush administration's call for the establishment of a Palestinian state on 2 October 2001 (and again on 4 April 2002) and its sponsorship of Security Council Resolution 1397 (12 March 2002) were initially celebrated as signs of a more balanced American policy on the Arab-Israeli conflict, in fact they rang hollow when set against events on the ground. The Israeli carnage of the West Bank intensified in March and April and President Bush dispatched Secretary of State Colin Powell to the region (8–17 April 2002) in an attempt to mollify world opinion in general and Arab opinion in particular. According to Geoffrey Aronson, director of the Foundation for Middle East Peace, Powell's itinerary made it obvious that the aim was to limit the conflict solely to Israel–Palestine. During planned visits to Morocco, Egypt and Spain, Powell joined in a statement with the United Nations, the European Union and Russian leaders which was more assertive against Israeli actions than anything coming out of the White House. Washington and the US press corps ignored it, and Israel continued its offensive.[83] Additionally, Bush and his spokespeople, while 'advocating' for a Palestinian state, have not emphasised sovereignty. This is, of course, in alignment with the Israeli line of considering more autonomy for the Palestinians in bantustan-style isolated enclaves (given that Israeli conditions are met), but not agreeing at any point to the full territorial sovereignty of a contiguous Palestinian state.

Colin Powell's junket to the Middle East essentially reflected an American policy of determined inaction on the Israeli-Palestinian front and was, in essence, an effort at damage control. It was Vice President Dick Cheney's earlier mission in March 2002 – which took him to Britain, Jordan, Egypt, Yemen, Oman, Qatar, Saudi Arabia, Kuwait, Bahrain, the United Arab Emirates, Israel and Turkey – where the Bush administration's determined course of action on the Middle East was revealed. At these meetings Cheney attempted to drum up support amongst Arab regimes in Morocco, Jordan, Egypt, Yemen, Qatar, Bahrain, Saudi Arabia and Oman (as well as Israel, Turkey, Spain and the United Kingdom) for a military build-up in preparation for a ground war in Iraq. CIA officials were reported to have surveyed three key airfields in northern Iraq, much to the embarrassment of Iraqi Kurdish leaders Massoud Barzani (Kurdistan Democratic Party) and Jalal al-Talabani (Patriotic Union of Kurdistan), who both told a high-level delegation from the US State Department visiting in 2001 that the Kurds would not act against Saddam Hussein unless they were certain that the US was determined to overthrow him, and had a plan to do so.[84] In early March 2002 the Bush administration called on Britain to supply a 25,000-man force[85] and US troops began arriving in Kurdish-held areas in the north of Iraq, in support of Kurdish Democratic Party militias.[86] A battalion of 24 Longbow Apache attack helicopters arrived in Kuwait, and more than 5000 US fighting vehicles, mothballed since the end of the Gulf War, were overhauled for use in the event of a ground war. More important, the US Central Command moved its service headquarters to the Gulf and US Special Forces set up a base in Oman. Unconfirmed reports in the US press and from Iraqi opposition groups announced that there had been a US military build-up in Kuwait to between 25,000 and 35,000 additional personnel.

At about the same time on the financial front, the euro was gaining against the US dollar. By the end of 2001 the euro had gained 25 per cent and was still climbing. This led some economists to predict parity with the dollar in the very near future. This meant that Saddam had made a tremendous financial gain by his early switch to the euro to which he had pegged the $10 billion on hold for the oil-for-food programme. However, the ramifications of the Iraqi switch were more alarming from the American perspective. In 2001 Iran converted more of its reserve currency to the euro and considered the economics of selling oil using the euro rather than the dollar.

In April 2002 Javad Yarjani, head of the Petroleum Market Analysis Department in OPEC, announced in Madrid:

> In the short-term, OPEC member countries, with possibly a few exceptions, are expected to continue to accept payment in dollars. Nevertheless, I believe that OPEC will not discount entirely the possibility of adopting the euro pricing and payments in the future. The Organisation, like many other financial houses at present, is also assessing how the euro will settle into its life as a new currency. Alternatively, there are other OPEC member countries that conduct most of their trade with Europe, which would be more likely to favour pricing in euros. It is quite possible that as the bilateral trade increases between the Middle East and the European Union, it could be feasible to price oil in euros, considering Europe is the main economic partner of that region. This would foster further ties between these trading blocs by increasing commercial exchange, and by helping attract much-needed European investment to the Middle East. Essentially, increased trade in euros, associated with a rise in the value of the currency, would also encourage people to view it as a safe bet in terms of savings, or as a store of value. For the euro to emerge as a serious competitor to the US dollar, it would need to replace or parallel the dollar as the currency of choice for hard currency reserves.[87]

By 2004 ten more nations will join the European Union, thus raising European oil consumption to 33 per cent above that of the US. At that stage the EU will be buying more than half of the OPEC production, and will increasingly press the OPEC to trade oil in the euro in order to mitigate currency risks.[88]

Given the fact that Middle East trade is structured around bilateral commercial agreements with the countries of the EU, whose currency has been appreciating against the dollar, the OPEC shift creates the possibility of a dislocation of the American economy, and results in serious financial problems. The effect of an OPEC switch to the euro would be that oil-consuming nations would have to flush dollars out of their (central bank) reserve funds and replace these with euros. The dollar would fall anywhere from 20–40 per cent in value and the consequences would be those one could expect from any currency collapse and massive inflation. Thus, there would likely be a foreign funds flood out of the US stock markets and dollar-denominated assets, there would almost certainly be a run on the banks much like the 1930s, the current account deficit would become unserviceable, the budget deficit would go into default, and there would be a world economic crisis.[89] In short, the economic dimension of global power threatened to overwhelm the military-strategic domain where American hegemony was most secured. The Bush administration was determined to act against this possibility, and to act using its military advantage.

The appreciation of the euro and Saddam's switch had created ripple effects so detrimental to the US that only regime change in Iraq would promise a solution. From the American perspective this was intended to send an immediate message to the OPEC countries, especially Saudi Arabia, of the dire consequences that would be in store if it made a similar move to the euro. At the same time, regime change was seen to initiate the new American 'grand strategy' in the region and around the world.

Saudi government refusals to allow air raids on Afghanistan to be launched from Saudi airfields, as well as unequivocal Saudi opposition to a military campaign to oust the Iraqi regime caused the United States to begin to transfer its forces to more pliable states. Saudi Arabia's Crown Prince Abdullah had been adamant in his opposition to a US attack on Iraq.[90] In the second week of March 2002 several sources reported that the US Air Force had begun preparations to move its Gulf headquarters from Saudi Arabia's Prince Sultan air force base which was reported to maintain a US garrison of some 4500 personnel as well as an unidentified number of aircraft that patrolled the southern no-fly zone over Iraq, to Qatar's al-Udeid air base, which has the longest runways in the Gulf.[91] It follows that the final plan would be to make Iraq the new headquarters for the US military machine in the Middle East. It is in a more strategic location, controlling the heart of the Middle East at the convergence of the Tigris and Euphrates rivers, and between Jordan, Syria, Turkey and Iran. Furthermore, by removing the US military from Saudi Arabia, al-Qaida would be denied one of its rallying cries: infidels on holy Muslim territory!

Although the move was initially explained as a temporary redistribution of American resources to pursue the Afghan war, the leaked request for bids to move sophisticated equipment suggested a more permanent relocation that would allow the US to conduct an air campaign against Iraq despite Saudi refusals to collaborate. Also, it went some way to alleviating the threat to the stability of the Saudi royal family posed by Sunni Islamic militants, for whom the US military presence has been, and continues to be, controversial. Qatar was seen as a more stable and willing host. Its Emir, Sheikh Hamad bin Khalifa al-Thani, has received strong US backing since overthrowing his father in 1995, and he has been a strong advocate of increased Arab ties with Israel. While the deployment proceeded without incident, and was largely unnoticed in the Western media, Cheney met unexpected resistance on his visits with Arab leaders.

After hearing objections in every country he visited on his Middle East tour (aside from Britain and Israel), on his return to the US, Cheney sought to minimise the difficulties in rallying support for the inevitable confrontation with Iraq.[92] He acknowledged the need for an American role in mediating the increasing Israeli-Palestinian violence. Cheney extended an invitation to Crown Prince Abdullah, the de facto ruler of the most important US ally in the Gulf, to visit the US to advance the Saudi peace initiative which was based on recognition of the State of Israel by all Arab states in exchange for the return of occupied land and permanent peace.[93] Abdullah declined the invitation in June 2002 to visit the White House in an exceptional display of solidarity with the Palestinian cause over the Bush administration's continued refusal to become involved in brokering an agreement. In spite of US efforts and public pronouncements to the contrary, the Palestinian and Iraqi issues were increasingly conjoined. Israel's violent repression of the *Intifada* in March and April 2002, and the Bush administration's determined pursuit of support for its policy of a military response to overthrow the Iraqi regime, saw an increasing international public discussion of the double standard in American policy towards the Middle East. In mid-March Bush even declared that 'all options are on the table – including nuclear weapons – to confront states that threaten to use weapons of mass destruction'.[94] However, the international solidarity afforded to the US as a result of September 11 had by then dissipated and, in the face of the Israeli assault on the West Bank, the darker contours of the so-called 'war on terrorism' were becoming apparent and problematic as protests against a war in Iraq spread across North America and Europe. Nevertheless, on 4 April 2002 Bush reiterated his message that 'everyone must choose; you're either with the civilised world, or you're with the terrorists'.[95]

American policy in the Middle East was increasingly criticised by America's allies in the spring of 2002 as European politicians sharply questioned the US on a number of issues regarding the region. On 5 February 2002 the Spanish Foreign Minister, Josep Piqué, then holding the Presidency of the European Union (EU), became the first high-ranking European politician to insist that the European Union would continue trade negotiations with Iran despite the American accusations of Iran's sponsorship of terror,[96] and on 7 February 2002 French Foreign Minister Hubert Védrine sharply denounced the unilateral approach taken by the Bush administration. 'We are currently threatened by a simplified approach which reduces all problems of the world to the mere struggle against terrorism', he said in an interview with *France Inter*. 'This is an ill-considered conception which we cannot accept', he declared, and went on to say: 'The Americans are acting on a unilateral basis, without consulting anyone else, and their decisions are guided exclusively by their own individual views and interests.'[97] Chris Patten, the EU commissioner for foreign affairs, questioned Bush's 'unilateralist overdrive'.[98] In addition, the foreign ministers of all 15 EU member states assembled for an informal meeting in the Spanish town of Cáceres on 8–10 February 2002 and Javier Solana, the representative for EU foreign policy, joined those concerned about the possibility of the US disregarding the UN, cautioning the US against succumbing 'to the dangers of global unilateralism'.[99] In addition, the German Foreign Minister, Joschka Fischer, criticised Bush's thesis of an 'axis of evil', declaring this conception was 'not in accordance with our political ethos'.[100]

Nevertheless, despite this global concern, on his trip to Russia and Europe in May 2002, President Bush in effect raised the rhetorical barometer of his 'war on terrorism' even higher by calling Iraq a 'threat to civilisation' during his speech to the German Bundestag on 23 May 2002. Bush declared 'we are defending civilisation, itself' from 'regimes that sponsor terror', who 'are developing these weapons and the missiles to deliver them. If these regimes and their terrorist allies were to perfect these capabilities, no inner voice of reason, no hint of conscience would prevent their use.'[101]

Following his speech, Bush and the German Chancellor, Gerhard Schroeder, held a joint press conference at which they stated that they had no concrete plans to attack Iraq.[102] However, by then the US military and police forces had already been deployed in southern Iraq enforcing sanctions, in Afghanistan against the Taliban and al-Qaida, in Georgia,[103] in Yemen,[104] and in the Philippines against Muslim rebels,[105] and also in Pakistan,[106] Uzbekistan, Tajikistan and Kyrgyzstan.[107] Moreover, troops were also being based in Arab Gulf states in increasing numbers to defend US interests in the Middle East and Central Asia.[108] Iran had also come under increasing fire in the US public discourse on terrorism, and was named the principle sponsor of terrorism in the world.[109] As early as 31 January 2002, US Defense Secretary Donald Rumsfeld had explained that 'the real concern...is the nexus between terrorist networks and terrorist states'.[110] Although it posed no serious ideological or military challenge to 'American civilisation' (to paraphrase Bush), Iraq was an easy and important target to rally American public support for the administration, as Saddam Hussein had been the West's favourite villain since the 1990–91 Gulf War. Iran, on the other hand, posed a real ideological challenge to the American hegemony of Western civilisation and Israeli hegemony of the Middle East, represented a relatively successful model of indigenous political development and has already diversified its reserve currency by buying the euro and divesting itself of some US dollar reserves.

It is politically conceivable that, after installing an ally in Baghdad, the Americans will focus on protecting it by ensuring that bordering countries like Iran and Syria pose no challenge to this new American regime. The *Middle East Times* reported on 11 April 2003 that the Senate was planning to authorise $50 million for dissidents inside Iran, and was supporting training for the Iranian-American community and civil society groups in Iran;[111] in other words, internal subversion, à l'Americaine.

INVASION AND THE AFTERMATH

The American descriptions of the war were confusing, if not contradictory. The State Department asserted that it was 'liberating Iraq'; the military described the military operation as 'shock and awe', and the media commentary employed the phrase 'winning the hearts and minds of the Iraqis'. After the war officially ended on 1 May 2003, the conflict turned out to be an invasion; 'liberation' was the occupation of Iraq for an indefinite period of time; 'shock and awe' was further wanton destruction of the civilian infrastructure and 'winning the Iraqis' was seen in terms of increasing opposition to the Anglo-American occupation. The reality is that the invasion of Iraq was one more step in the Bush administration's setting the seal of American global domination.

In the geopolitical vision driving current US policy toward Iraq, the key to national security is global dominance over any and all potential rivals. To that end, and because the United States cannot project its military forces everywhere all the time, it must control key resources, chief among them oil, and especially Gulf oil. To the cabal which now sets the tone at the White House and the Pentagon, control of this region is crucial, not simply for its share of the US oil supply but because it allows the United States to maintain a grip on the world's energy lifeline and potentially deny access to its global competitors – i.e. the EU, China and Japan. The Bush administration 'believes you have to control resources in order to have access to them', says Chas Freeman, who served as US ambassador to Saudi Arabia under the first President Bush. 'They are taken with the idea that the end of the Cold War left the United States able to impose its will globally, and that those who have the ability to shape events with power have the duty to do so. It's ideology.' [112] Furthermore, controlling Iraqi oil as an instrument of global domination was implied by Paul Wolfowitz when he attended an Asian security summit in Singapore in early June 2003. Asked why North Korea, which possesses nuclear power, is treated differently from Iraq, he answered that 'economically we had no choice in Iraq; the country swims on a sea of oil'. His declaration came to underscore his statements reported in an interview in *Vanity Fair* in May, in which he said that 'for reasons that have to do with bureaucracy, we settled on one issue that everyone could agree on: weapons of mass destruction'.[113]

While the ramifications of the invasion spread at international and regional levels, the domestic theatre of Iraq suffered the immediate effects of the war.

The international level

The US military has initiated plans for the redeployment of forces from Germany, Turkey and Saudi Arabia into what is called the 'arc of instability' which encompasses a giant territory that extends from the Caribbean Basin through Africa to South and Central Asia and across to North Korea. What characterises the 'arc of instability' is that American military forces can be rapidly deployed to intervene in many of the countries in the arc, especially oil-rich countries like Nigeria, São Tomé and the Gulf of Guinea. Thomas Barnett of the Naval War College explains that the countries that lie in that 'arc' are disconnected from 'the trend of globalisation' and, therefore, pose a 'danger' to the 'seam states' (which are American allies) because they are perceived to harbour terrorist networks. This emerging military doctrine is reminiscent of Teddy Roosevelt's 1903 assertion of Washington's 'international police power, which intervenes against chronic wrongdoing or loosening of the ties of civil society'.[114]

As early as 1996, France and Germany set up a joint armament agency to award contracts on behalf of the two governments. Between 1999 and 2000 the German Daimler's DASA and the French Aerospace Matra, and later the Spanish CASA formed the largest European defence conglomerate to rival the Anglo-American joint military venture in providing weapons for NATO and the new Eastern states coming into the European Union, thus becoming a serious economic challenge to the US. In addition, the euro is becoming increasingly the dominant currency within the EU, thus competing with the dominion of the US dollar in armament and industrial contract sales in the EU, and for that matter, worldwide, from the Mediterranean to China.[115] By reinstituting the dollar as the currency for the sale of Iraqi oil, while occupying Iraq and dominating the oil-rich states in the Gulf, the US, for the time being, has ensured that the European Union, whose demand for oil will exceed that of the US by 33 per cent in two years, will use the dollar in oil purchases. By physically controlling the oil, the US can pursue, in the short run, an intensive policy of permeating and consolidating over-pluralism in the EU, which puts 'a premium on manoeuvre, policy and manipulation capacities of the European nations which thwart the emergence of a hostile coalition that could seek to challenge American primacy in Eurasia and the Middle East'.[116] From such a position of comparative advantage, the US can destabilise the economic objectives of the European military industries, thus creating a downward pressure on the euro.

The regional level

Early in May 2003, while Colin Powell was on his visit to Israel and the Occupied Territories, he met with Mahmoud Abbas, the (then) new Palestinian Prime Minister, and separately with a small group of civil society activists, including Hanan Ashrawi and Mostapha Barghuti. According to Barghuti, Powell expressed surprise and mild consternation at the computerised maps of the Israeli settlements, the eight-metre-high West Bank fence, and the dozens of Israeli Army checkpoints that have made life so difficult and the future so bleak for Palestinians. Powell asked for materials to take away with him and, and he assured the Palestinians that the same effort put in by Bush on Iraq was now going into implementing the 'Road-Map', which the UN, EU and Russia, along with the US had devised, probably with the intention of delinking the Palestinian issue from the Iraqi problem. Bush himself, in the course of interviews with Arab media, made a similar point in the last days of May although, as usual, he employed generalities rather than stating anything specific. He met with the Palestinian and Israeli leaders in Jordan, and earlier, with the major Arab rulers, excluding of course Syria's Bashar al-Assad. This now appears to be a major American push forward.[117]

The Road-Map, whose professed goal is to establish peace between Israel and the Palestinians, and therefore the Arabs at large, is no more than phases or stages, each of which declares a goal within a time frame. The modalities of execution and the details of each stage have never been declared, but left to negotiations.

By June 2003 Phase One was assumed to have seen the dismantling of the last 60 hilltop settlements (so-called 'illegal' outpost settlements established since March 2001), though nothing is said about removing the other settlements, which account for more than 200,000 settlers on the West Bank and Gaza, to say nothing of the 200,000 more in annexed East Jerusalem. Phase Two, which was slated to end in December 2003, focuses on the option of creating an independent Palestinian state with unspecified provisional borders and 'attributes of sovereignty', culminating in an international conference to approve and then 'create' a Palestinian state, once again with 'provisional borders'. Phase Three is to end the conflict completely, also by way of an international conference whose job it will be to settle the thorniest issues of all: refugees, settlements, Jerusalem, and borders. Israel's role in all this is to co-operate. However, the real onus is placed on the Palestinians, who must keep coming up with the goods in rapid succession, while the Israeli military occupation of Palestinian land remains more or less in place, although it has eased in the main areas invaded during the spring of 2002. No monitoring element is envisioned, and the misleading symmetry of the plan's structure leaves Israel very much in charge of the overall situation. As for Palestinian human rights, at present not so much ignored as suppressed, no specific rectification is written into the plan. Apparently it is up to Israel whether to continue as before or not. [118]

The Israeli Prime Minister, Ariel Sharon, has already added 14 conditions to the Road-Map. In addition to Israel's 14 conditions, they only accepted 'steps laid out in the Road Map', not the Road-Map in its entirety – and even that much barely survived a vote by the Israeli cabinet. The most striking of these conditions include the waiving of all rights of return on behalf of Palestinian refugees and the diaspora, as well as the complete disarming of the proposed pseudo-state of Palestine.[119] This disarming will not only include the complete dismantling of organised paramilitary resistance organisations, such as Hamas, Islamic Jihad, the Popular Front, the Democratic Front, Al-Aqsa brigades, and others, but it will also include a demilitarised state apparatus, with only police and internal security allowed. Furthermore, Israel refuses to discuss any settlements in Judea, Sumeria, or Gaza beyond the freeze on further settlement construction. Finally, while the Palestinian Authority, under new leadership approved of by the US and Israel, must educate for peace and dismantle any terrorist and resistance organisations, as in the other mutual frameworks, the Road-Map will not state that Israel must cease violence and incitement against the Palestinians.

Clearly, this array of conditions, if included in the negotiating details, could derail the Road-Map. Also, given the political stance of Ariel Sharon, and the fact that his cabinet includes extreme right-wing religious political parties, which typically support more settlements, the Palestinian militia, Hamas and the Islamic Jihad, did not initially accord credibility to Sharon's statements about his readiness to remove the 'illegal' settlements, and refused to lend support to the Bush proposal. The refusal is further supported by the fact that the invasion of Iraq confirmed the dominance of the pro-Likud hard-liners in the American Administration whose rhetoric, before and during the war, was that the American 'war on terrorism' and Israel's war on the Palestinian 'violence' were one and the same. Nevertheless, these militias later agreed to stop armed resistance for a period that ended in September 2003, most likely to test Sharon's real intentions as well as to gain enough time to be close to the American election campaign which could be sensitive to any re-emergence of violence in the occupied Palestinian land.

The insistence of President Bush on acting separately in negotiating the Road-Map with certain Arab allies in the Aqaba sea port first, and then with Sharon and Abu Mazen, the Palestinian Prime Minister, was a message to the world that the US would act unilaterally when the issue, or the region, constitutes strategic goals for the US: unconditional protection of Israel and a free trading zone in the Middle East, even though the so-called Road-Map was devised by multilateral powers. Some analysts argue that Sharon's consent to remove the 'illegal' settlements (the meaning of illegal is vague and open to interpretations) is no more than a tactical card lent to Mr Bush to support his re-election in 2004, and for the maintenance of the cabal in the administration for another term. This period should be long enough for the cabal, once and for all, to impose the Israeli agenda in the Arab world, including access to the cheap Iraqi oil instead of the expensive Russian oil that Israel imports at present.

The American discourse on transforming the Middle East into a free trade zone by 2013, as a component of the Road-Map, is not novel; it was an item on the agenda of the peace process that the US championed during the 1990s. This earlier plan finally collapsed in 1997 under Arab popular resistance that saw in it the centrality of the Israeli-American hegemony in the Arab region. The resurfacing of the same idea, when the American administration unequivocally backs Israel, seems menacing to the Arabs. The first American condition for the project to take place is full and complete normal-isation with Israel regardless of its non-monitored nuclear programme which Israel refuses to submit to inspection by the International Atomic Energy Agency; second is the macro-restructuring of the Arab economies in a manner calculated to diminish the sovereign role of the state, and to amplify the role of transnational corporations in the fledgling Arab economies; third is the integration of Israel in the Arab free trade zone from a competitively advantageous position by giving it preferential access to American advanced technology.[120] What is not stated in the American plan, though evident to some analysts, is that the plan results in dislodging the European Union from the Middle East after many EU countries have secured, through bilateral commercial agreements with certain Middle Eastern countries, a preferential position in the region, thus paving the way for the euro to gain more strength against the dollar. Consumption in the Middle East is growing exponentially, while American exports to the region are falling dramatically. Out of total Turkish imports, in 1993, the American share was 11.4 per cent, while in 2001 it was 7.9 per cent; the American share in total Moroccan imports in 1993 was 7.7 per cent, falling to 3.7 per cent in 2001; American exports to Tunisia went down from 5.7 per cent of total Tunisian imports in 1993, to 4 per cent in 2001.[121]

Iran seems to be suffering from the same American 'battle cry' that Iraq endured before the invasion and in all probability, Iran, not Syria is the next American target. This is because Iran, the world's third largest oil-producing country, has diversified its reserves to include the euro, and should Iran peg oil to the euro in its transactions with the EU, the ripple effects may spread to other oil-producing countries beyond American control. This will re-create the same economic threat that Saddam posed, but without the basis for the media hype that encouraged the use of military force. Second, Iran has long contiguous borders with Iraq, in addition to its influence on the Shi'ite south. Any regime in Iran which is not pro-American is also conceived to imperil American interests in the Middle East. Third, the political regime in Iran is anti-Israeli, and has all the resources to become a regional hegemony on its own, which neither Israel nor the US appear willing to tolerate. Fourth, geographically Iran is situated with long borders with Afghanistan. Consequently, it is in the interest of the US to have a pro-American ally in Iran to ensure that it will not destabilise the precarious existence of the American military in Afghanistan, and will not take the trans-Afghan gas pipeline political hostage.

The Iraqi domestic level

The Anglo-American military forces persistently presented their war aims as liberating the Iraqis, democratising the political system, assisting in the reconstruction of Iraq and giving the Iraqi people the wealth which Saddam Hussein had expropriated. Once Iraq had been occupied, the first political hurdle that the Americans had to remove was the economic sanctions multilaterally imposed on Iraq by the UN Security Council in 1990. Furthermore, the unilateralist posture of the US before the war had to accommodate itself to other powers in the UN, particularly Russia and France who enjoy veto power. What agreements were sealed behind closed doors are not yet known, but the Anglo-American coalition was successful in securing UN Resolution 1483 that lifted the sanctions, on 22 May 2003, before even verifying that Iraq no longer possessed WMDs, which had been the *raison d'être* of the sanctions in the first place. The resolution, while marginalising the UN in Iraq (after it had been central in the oil-for-food programme) increased the authority of the occupation forces. The domestic context in Iraq, as expected, is very fluid, but certain observations, nonetheless, can be made.

The fall of Baghdad on 9 April 2003 was followed by a violent frenzy, on an indescribable scale, that saw the looting of thousands of priceless artefacts from museums and archaeological sites. The looting was combined with the deliberate incineration of historical manuscripts and other state documents from the various ministries except for those of which the US Marines had already taken control. General Tommy Franks, the overall commander of the coalition forces, issued an order to unit commanders prohibiting them from the use of force against the looters. Several days later he was forced to modify his order, owing to mounting pressure from Iraqis who saw the persistent destruction of their civilian infrastructure as a travesty. According to the American Defense Secretary, Donald Rumsfeld, the looting and looters were the price of freedom, an opinion that begs the question as to why that should be so. The American forces guarded only the Ministry of Oil and the Ministry of the Interior: in the former the detailed inventory of the Iraqi oil reserves is kept, and in the latter the vast wealth of intelligence information on Iraq, the region and the world was archived by Saddam Hussein's *mukhabarat*.[122] The ransacking of the public buildings might, in fact, have had the politically desirable effect of destroying all documents that incriminated the US, and most European countries in the strengthening of the regime of Saddam Hussein. As Robert Fisk points out, it seems odd that the only Ministries saved from public looting and burning were the Ministry of Oil and the Ministry of the Interior. Fisk has counted 35 ministries ravaged by fires, noting that the looters arrive first followed by arsonists, 'often in blue-and-white buses'. There are important questions to be asked about the destruction of public infrastructure and whose interests this widespread destruction serves.[123] Clearly, it cannot be in the interest of Iraqis who suffer the consequences of the loss of electricity, clean water and other public services. However, the destruction of the cultural heritage of its Mesopotamian civilisation robs the nation of evidence of its national identity for future Iraqi generations.

The US has plans to station military forces in Iraq as part of its overall strategy to shore up its physical presence in the region. The American plan is based on using the geo-strategic position of Iraq to station air force combat squadrons in four bases, while reducing its military presence in Saudi Arabia and Turkey. The four bases are the Baghdad International Airport (which the coalition took intact), a second near Nasiriyah in the south, a third located in the western desert along an old pipeline, and the fourth in the Kurdish north. However, the plan is predicated on having a democratically elected government that is pro-American and will, therefore, approve of the plan, something that is not yet in place or even guaranteed.

On 15 March 2003 the *Washington Post* reported that Condoleezza Rice, the American National Security Advisor, had announced that the American plan for post-war Iraq was to establish, almost immediately, 'an Iraqi Interim Authority', which would be a group of Iraqis with administrative power under the authority of the occupying forces. How such Iraqis would be selected was left vague. After lifting the sanctions on 22 May, the American Administrator of Iraq, Paul Bremer, announced on 25 May that no 'Iraqi Interim Authority' was contemplated. However, in July 2003 a national conference was to be held to create such an 'interim Iraqi administration subservient to his authority'.[124] On 26 May the *Washington Post* reported that Bremer had announced that he was rebuilding the Iraqi economy on the free market model, without consulting any Iraqi group. The statement was no more than privatising the state-run economy by opening the door to foreign companies and capital without a national government to negotiate the terms of such commercial agreements. On 2 June the *Financial Times* reported that Bremer had abandoned the idea of the national conference in July in favour of directly appointing 25 Iraqis in an advisory council. On 8 June the *Washington Post* reported that Bremer had finally scrapped the idea of an interim government because the political parties, including the INC, whose role was significant in the march to war, lack any genuine constituency within Iraq. Public relations consultant John Rendon worked with INC leader Ahmad Chalabi extensively leading up to the invasion of Iraq, describing himself as an 'information warrior and a perception manager' guiding the INC in its effort to convince the American public to invade Iraq.[125]

However, the deteriorating security situation, and an increasingly restive and sullen Iraqi population, has brought about a new dispensation. The US chief administrator, Paul Bremer, unveiled, on Sunday, 13 July 2003, Iraq's 25-member governing council in Baghdad. The new council replacing Saddam Hussein's Ba'ath Party regime initially consisted of 13 Shi'ite Arab members (who form nearly 60 per cent of Iraq's 24 million population but who had for many years been excluded by the Sunni elite), five Sunni Arabs, five ethnic Sunni Kurds, who have lived in autonomous northern Iraq since 1991, one Turkoman and one Assyrian Christian. The council includes three women and some tribal leaders. The leadership of the council is rotating between the members, but it remains unclear as to how effective this will be. The council will have some political the power, e.g., to name ministers and approve the 2004 budget, but the occupying powers, the US-British Coalition Provisional Authority (CPA), which the United Nations essentially was forced to recognise through *force majeure*, will retain the ultimate power in Iraq until a constitution is drafted, approved and elections held.

However, the formation of the Iraqi Governing Council (IGC) has engendered some negative reactions across the Iraqi political spectrum. Interviews with Iraqi politicians, academics, members of political parties and unaffiliated Iraqi citizens has shown that virtually all Iraqis interviewed wish the Council success in its tasks, but doubt that success is possible.

Many reasons were given for these doubts. The council lacks democratic legitimacy by virtue of its creation and its non-representative nature. Its mandate and authority are sharply limited, with key powers reserved to the Coalition Provisional Authority. Further, it was formed without consultation with the technically skilled, scientific, and academic sectors of Iraqi society and, finally, the war, and subsequent occupation, has created such monumental difficulties that even the ideal governing body might not succeed.

Criticism of the formation process has come from many quarters. Professor Mohammed Jawad Ali, Director of the Centre of International Studies at Baghdad University, stressed that the very existence of the occupying authority, which appointed the Council, is illegal since it was imposed by unilateral US (or 'coalition') action, not by any international resolution. In addition, the mysterious and non-transparent way in which the Council was selected also provoked violent disagreement within academic and political circles in Iraq.

'Why didn't they ask our opinion?' Professor Wisal al-Azzawi, Dean of the College of Political Sciences of Nehrein University, wonders. 'What role has been given to scientists, technocrats, intellectuals, businessmen, unions? Because of the way it was secretly appointed, the Council appears very much an American creation imposed on the Iraqi people.' Professor Azzawi suggests that in a situation like that of Iraq, the sensible procedure is to appoint a committee of experts of the occupied country, from the scientific and professional community, to manage the country and fill the power vacuum until the political parties, including the newly-formed ones, have a chance to build a public base, put forward programmes, and prepare themselves for a general election. 'The democratic process does not happen in a day or two, and should not be connected to a handful of people who collaborated with the occupation.'

Although Iraq has been torn apart by ethnic, religious, and political/factional differences, and there is a very great need to safeguard both minority rights and adequate representation of the Shia majority, it is also true that the explicit inclusion of quota systems like that of the Governing Council has always been a standard part of an imperial 'divide-and-conquer' strategy. According to Professor Salman Al-Jumaily of the University of Baghdad's College of Political Sciences, the Americans have gone one step further than simply utilising the existing divisions; they have created a new one – a division between exile and indigenous political groups. According to Al-Jumaily, 'the unbalanced distribution of representation may well lead to a resurgence of factional consciousness and an entrenching of political differences, which in its turn could easily lead to open factional conflict'.

A political science professor who was part of the process of forming the council, and spoke only on condition that he remained anonymous, said that its members were appointed by the Americans as a reward for aiding the occupation. They immediately reciprocated by declaring the date of the fall of Baghdad (9 April 2003) a national holiday while simultaneously eliminating other national holidays like 14 July, the anniversary of the anti-colonialist uprising in 1958. He explained that the long-drawn-out political process, the meetings, the talks with different Iraqi political parties and formations were actually designed to test how much these groups would cooperate with US policies in Iraq and how closely they would align with long-term US policy goals. Accordingly, the level of co-operation was the 'only criterion for inclusion into or exclusion from the council'.

The limited mandate was another main criticism. It has been announced that the Council will hire and fire ministers, put forth a draft constitution, pave the way to the election, approve the 2004 budget, and see to basic services and policing. It is well known that the areas over which the Council has no authority are defence and 'national security' issues (including the basing of US troops), foreign affairs and the oil sector.

The same anonymous insider claims that Bremer does not take this Council very seriously, and does not consider its members to be important officials. In fact, members are afraid that, if there is conflict on some issue, Bremer will invoke the fact that they are not elected and that they do not represent the Iraqi people.[126]

American tactics in Iraq almost certainly represent political blunders and have created the perception of the Anglo-American forces as foreign occupying powers whose intention was to humiliate and exploit Iraq. Bremer reinforced this perception when he reinstituted the American dollar for Iraqi oil sales, disbanded the Iraqi army (300,000) and its civilian employees of 100,000 people without pay and censored the handful of Iraqi press that reported the unbecoming practices of the occupying forces.

While the framework of privatisation is expected in about a year,[127] the timetable for the election of a national government has not yet been dealt with. Furthermore, while resumption of oil production has been a priority, reparations and the reconstruction of the destroyed civil infrastructure has been very slow, thus prolonging and intensifying the staggering misery of the population. In the meantime the armed Iraqi opposition has been increasing to visible proportions, and assuming the tactics of guerrilla warfare. The result is that US/British casualties have been averaging more than one soldier killed every day. Interviews with Iraqis reveal that in the public perception, Bremer is essentially re-creating the oppressive conditions that existed under Saddam: unilateral decisions to isolate Iraqis, reneging on promises, parades and heavy security, twisted truths about improving living conditions, insensitivity to the daily suffering of the people, the disappearance of Iraqi civilians and press censorship.

On 23 July 2003 Amnesty International accused the US-led occupying forces in Iraq of failing to uphold human rights in their treatment of Iraqi civilians. The group is to present a memorandum detailing 'allegations of ill-treatment by coalition forces and inhumane detention conditions' to Paul Bremer. A team of eight Amnesty workers was in Iraq during July 2003 collecting testimonies from alleged victims of human rights abuses committed under the CPA. The allegations included the shooting of a twelve-year-old boy during house-to-house searches by US troops, and reports of Iraqis detained by coalition forces being subjected to torture.

In many cases it is alleged that people have been snatched from the street without warning and denied access to relatives and lawyers while in jail – a 'strong echo' of methods used by Saddam Hussein's regime, according to Amnesty. Former detainees related that Abu Ghraid prison in Baghdad – one of the most notorious jails under the old regime but now under CPA control – was overflowing with inmates. Researchers were told that many people were being held in tents in extreme heat and without sufficient drinking water. The head of Amnesty's delegation to Iraq, Mahmoud Ben Romdhane, said that after more than 100 days of occupation, the promises of human rights for all Iraqis have yet to be fulfilled. In addition, the legal reforms introduced by the occupying powers mean that Iraqi courts have no jurisdiction over coalition personnel in relation to civil and criminal matters.[128]

Amnesty spokesman Steve Ballinger told the *Guardian* that the team had collected 'scores' of testimonies in Baghdad and Basra in the last week, but that these were just the 'tip of the iceberg' and there would be further delegations to visit other parts of Iraq and collect more evidence. He said one of the main problems was a 'two-tier' legal system. 'If an Iraqi is dealt with in the Iraqi court system, they are given access to a magistrate who can review the case within 24 hours. If they are detained by coalition forces they might not see a magistrate for 90 days.'[129]

Reports from Iraq allude to the alarming conclusion that armed opposition is the only way left to deal with a malevolent force.[130] The actions of the occupying forces and the decisions they have made, in the absence of the promised freely elected government, have created a future dilemma for the US. Should a representative national government take office, it will have to either endorse the record of the occupying power, in which case it may incur the popular wrath that would perceive it to be a quisling government; or the government will act independently, review the record of the occupation negatively, and thus arouse the suspicions of the occupying Anglo-American forces, which in turn will intensify popular opposition to the occupation, and lend popular support to the national government. Either way, the government will be in a 'no win' situation.

CONCLUSION

The US has never declared its true motives for invading Iraq, which mounting evidence reveals to be the safeguarding of the hegemony of the US dollar and control of oil as a key instrument of global domination. While the cabal that dominates Bush's administration did formulate and act decisively on these strategic and military goals, they displayed no parallel global political capacity. More to the point, the Bush administration has failed to project a coherent vision of Iraq's future political order, other than in purely negative terms: that the Ba'ath shall not return, Iraqi exiles will not form a provisional government and that the US will not permit Iran to 're-make Iraq in its image'. In addition, the Coalition Provisional Authority, which Paul Bremer now heads, has created much uncertainty regarding its own structure and scope of authority, thus contributing to noticeable confusion within Iraq. Ambassador Tim Carney spent about seven weeks with the CPA and reported that the US officials were isolated from Iraqis.[131] The disbanding of the Iraqi army without pay has not only multiplied the huge list of the jobless, but also added strength to the organisation of guerrilla warfare that is becoming costly to the lives of the Anglo-American military. The rising cost of the military operations (identified as $3.9 billion a month by the Pentagon), and the increasing criticism of the Pentagon's administration of post-war Iraq, in addition to the fact that the occupying forces have not established any evidence of Iraq's weapons of mass destruction, which was the primary justification for the war, would make a winnable war in Iran before the next US election extremely unlikely.

During the Cold War era, the US dominated the Western world as the head of an alliance. Europe then understood the logic of the US Western Empire. Today, in contrast, the US is forced to react to the fact that its goals are no longer accepted. The sudden application of a ruthless US power, and circumventing of international law is hard to understand, much less so the US attempt to dominate a world that is far too complicated for a single power to control unilaterally. Furthermore, except for its weaponry, the US is suffering a diminishing share of global trade, making it vulnerable in both the short and the long term.

In military terms Iraq was an easy war to win. However, the Bush administration neglected its duty to think through properly a process to run and maintain the country during the occupation – for example, along the lines of the classic British model in India. The assumption of the cabal that the US can go to war, conquer and go home leaving behind puppet regimes without genuine allies among other states, or genuine popular support in the countries which the American army has conquered, is untenable.

American officials like Richard Perle, Paul Wolfowitz and Donald Rumsfeld, we would venture to suggest, freely converse in the 'arrogance of power', both in public and in private. For example, speaking for the administration, Vice President Dick Cheney asserted publicly that the Anglo-American invaders would be 'greeted as liberators' and that he anticipated a short military campaign.[132] Douglas Feith and Paul Wolfowitz led a group of policy-makers in the Pentagon that felt all along that the war in Iraq was going to be a 'cakewalk, it was going to be 60–90 days, a flip-over and hand-off, a lateral or whatever to Chalabi and the INC'.[133] It is clear from several sources that the Pentagon and the White House relied heavily on the INC for intelligence and strategy, but their over-reliance on what is essentially an American organisation meant that there was little contact with domestic Iraqi opposition groups. Richard Perle pointed out this mistake, arguing 'the answer is to hand over power to the Iraqis as soon as possible'.[134] Past military ventures in the Middle East and policy pronouncements indicate a willingness to engage precipitously in military operations in order to advance foreign policy objectives. The consequences are dangerous on two fronts: domestically it appears to be leading to the possible regimentation and militarisation of American society, while internationally it leads to the destabilisation of the international environment. In Europe the US has been trying to turn NATO into a world military police force in defence of US interests. It has gone even further to sabotage the European Union by driving a wedge between the new Eastern member states and its original members.[135] The agenda of the US administration is becoming clearer by the day, and today's allies of the US, like Turkey and Canada, have indicated that there are limits to American pressure despite the tempting offer. Turkey refused American access to its bases and land for the invasion of Iraq, thus sacrificing about $26 billion. Canadian Prime Minister Jean Chretien refused to take any part in the invasion, despite strong American pressure. When, after the conclusion of the war, it became clear that the Americans could not establish evidence of the existence of WMD in Iraq, Prime Minister Chretien was reported at the end of May 2003 to have said that he was relieved that he had not taken part in the invasion, and that Canada was thus vindicated.[136]

The manipulation of the Iraqi predicament in international affairs was complete and necessitated the need for war in Iraq. The media relied heavily on the intelligence of the INC which had a clear interest in ousting Saddam Hussein, and whose support from public relations officials allowed the INC to craft an acceptable message that the media readily reproduced. The fact that Canada's Jean Chretien feels vindicated is not necessarily the issue, but rather, the ability for false intelligence, special interests, and narrow ideological perspectives to guide American foreign policy, and all of this with the news media reneging on its role as the public critical eye. Journalist I.F. Stone once mentioned when speaking to a group of graduating journalism students that 'governments lie'. The role, Stone argued, for media was to always remember those simple words and question everything and accept nothing. It would seem that in the march to war in Iraq, these traditional roles got reversed: the media questioned nothing and believed everything.

4
UN Sanctions: Tools of Domination and Oppression

Since Iraq's fateful invasion of Kuwait in August 1990, the United Nations Security Council (UNSC) has played a decisive role in Iraq through the application of sanctions. Sanctions are a coercive diplomatic measure for enforcing compliance. By article 41 of the United Nations Charter: 'The Security Council may decide what measures not involving the use of armed force are to be employed to give effect to its decisions, and it may call upon the Members of the United Nations to apply such measures. These may include complete or partial interruption of economic relations and of rail, sea, air, postal, telegraphic, radio, and other means of communication, and the severance of diplomatic relations.' Article 41, in other words, empowers the Security Council to employ coercive diplomacy to enforce compliance. However, it should be noted that a Security Council resolution may or may not be mandatory. Where a resolution is mandatory, its legal weight is such that it demands universal observance and carries the power to even supplant existing treaties and obligations. In such circumstances, when the only global superpower is a permanent member of the Security Council, it can bribe or intimidate the Council into adopting resolutions that could shape the 'the character of international law'. That was the unique position of the US from 1990 to the present date. Additionally, a mandatory resolution is seldom a tightly written legal document – a fact which allows much room for interpretation that powerful states exploit as justification of unilateral actions. This is particularly true in the case of Iraq.[1] The US, in lobbying resolutions regarding Iraq, has been consolidating its expansion of hegemony over the Middle East, and has manipulated the UN in its pursuit of what is called 'full spectrum dominance': the American use of propaganda, as well as economic and military means to achieve the goal of global hegemony.[2] The application of sanctions went far beyond diplomacy to contain and limit Iraq's sovereignty on the one hand, and on the other to foster the empowerment of a tyrant over a population trapped in the quagmire of international politics. In the context of regional politics

Iraq from 1980 was the only Arab country that had the resources to become a regional hegemony, which both Israel and the US viewed with mounting alarm because they perceived in it a serious challenge to their interests in the region: oil, and the security of Israel.[3] This chapter examines the transformation of sanctions from tools of compliance to tools of domination and oppressive containment, in their application to Iraq.

TOOLS OF COERCION

In response to Iraq's 2 August1990 invasion of Kuwait, the United Nations Security Council passed a series of eleven sanctions against Iraq, as delineated in Table 4.1. The sanctions ranged in coercive capacity from condemnation to the most comprehensive economic embargo in this organisation's history. Beginning with Resolution 660, which condemned the Iraqi invasion of Kuwait and demanded Iraq's 'immediate and unconditional withdrawal', the Security Council acted with unprecedented co-operation amongst the permanent members to sanction Iraq. Under a strong diplomatic offensive led by the United States, the Security Council was challenged to act forcefully to contain aggression in what was being billed as the 'new world order'.[4]

Of the eleven resolutions, 661 and 665 were the most overtly coercive. UNSC Resolution (UNSCR) 661 imposed stringent sanctions on all trade to and from Iraq, and established a sanctions committee, the 661 Committee, to monitor the resolution's implementation and application.[5] UNSCR 665 imposed a maritime blockade on Iraq, and called for the use of 'such measures...as may be necessary' to enforce the maritime embargo. This resolution not only isolated Iraq from sea-borne commerce but also assigned the practical responsibility for monitoring compliance with the sanctions from the UN bureaucracy to the states imposing the naval blockade. By permitting states to use 'limited' naval force to ensure compliance with the economic sanctions, to ensure the stoppage of naval vessels, and to detain ships and their crews for the inspection of cargoes in the Gulf (one of the most heavily travelled corridors of commerce in the world), the United Nations allowed member states to dictate compliance, in effect establishing the modus operandi for transformation of sanctions from tools of coercive diplomacy to tools of coercion.

Another dimension of this transformation was UNSCR 666, which was passed in response to concerns voiced over the effect of the

Table 4.1   Sanctions as Tools of Diplomacy

UN Security Council Resolution	Date Passed	Terms of Reference
660	2 August 1990	Condemns Iraqi invasion of Kuwait and demands Iraq's immediate and unconditional withdrawal.
661	6 August 1990	Imposes comprehensive sanctions and establishes a committee to monitor them.
662	9 August 1990	Declares Iraq's annexation of Kuwait 'null and void'.
664	18 August 1990	Demands that Iraq releases 'third state nationals'.
665	25 August 1990	Imposes shipping blockade.
666	13 September 1990	Assigns responsibility of monitoring foodstuffs to UNSC.
667	16 September 1990	Protests the closure of diplomatic and consular missions in Kuwait.
669	24 September 1990	Asks sanctions committee to consider requests for aid by countries harmed through sanctions on Iraq.
670	25 September 1990	Clarifies embargo and states that it applies to aircraft as well.
674	29 October 1990	States Iraq's responsibility for any losses as a result of the invasion of Kuwait.
677	28 November 1990	Raises concerns about Iraq's treatment of demographic composition of Kuwait.

embargo on the population. In 666 the Security Council promised to 'keep the situation regarding foodstuffs...under constant review', and significantly gave itself the responsibility for determining when dire 'humanitarian circumstances' had arisen in Iraq. This left such recognition within the hands of the permanent members of the Security Council, and would prove decisive as a growing body of evidence emerged about the immense humanitarian crisis which was documented over the next twelve years, as is detailed in Chapter 4.

With increased international focus on the diplomatic efforts to avert hostilities, UNSCR 670 strengthened and clarified the embargo by confirming that it applied to commercial aircraft, and by also warning that unspecified 'measures' would be taken against states that evaded the sanctions regime.[6] Under traditional understandings of international law, the Security Council was only able to impose such measures against the state responsible for a breach of, or threat to, the peace. The expansion of the sanctions regime to third countries, directed primarily against Arab and Muslim states sympathetic with either Iraq's leadership or its people, raised concerns about the implications for the entire regional political economy.[7]

Through the first round of sanctions, the Security Council in effect appropriated the United Nations' role and responsibility for their implementation. This facilitated US preparations for war and provided them with an aura of international legitimacy.[8] On 29 November 1990 the Security Council passed Resolution 678 which authorised military action to be taken against Iraq by 'member States co-operating with the Government of Kuwait...to use all necessary means to uphold and implement resolution 660 (1990)', unless Iraq withdrew its forces and implemented 660 itself, on or before 15 January 1991. Western politicians' interpretation of the 'all necessary means' paragraph in Resolution 678 relied on creating the impression that 'all' logically means 'every' while dropping the adjective 'necessary'. The resolution did not clarify who it was could interpret or how to define 'necessary'. This looseness of drafting allowed the US, as a superpower, to force its own interpretation and justify a war against Iraq that has persisted until the present.[9] All efforts by the international community to forestall conflict were thwarted by the combination of Saddam Hussein's brinkmanship politics and George Bush's new world order policy.[10] US deployment of military forces at the head of an international coalition,[11] and its a priori rejection of compromise, accepting nothing less than unconditional Iraqi compliance with Security Council dictates, circumvented the implementation of sanctions as a tool of coercive diplomacy and used them instead to legitimate the initiation of war.[12]

At 6:30 p.m. EST on 16 January 1991 coalition forces launched offensive operations against Iraq with an aerial bombardment of Iraq and Iraqi positions in occupied Kuwait. After 43 days of offensive operations against an ever-expanding list of targets, a ceasefire was scheduled, and on 28 February 1991 the war was ended. Dubbed the 1100-hour war by the media,[13] aerial bombardment occupied the first 1000 hours. Ground forces entered the war theatre only in the last 100 hours. Aerial bombardment devastated not only Iraq's military forces in Kuwait but also Iraqi civilian infrastructure across the entire country. The most intensive and sustained bombing campaign in history was unleashed against a population of about 23 million people.

More explosives were dumped on Iraq in 43 days than were dropped on Europe in the whole of the Second World War.

UNSCR 686, passed on 2 March 1991, affirmed the independence, sovereignty and territorial integrity of Iraq and Kuwait and set the terms and conditions of a ceasefire. The resolution invoked chapter VII of the United Nations Charter, 'Action with Respect to Threats to the Peace, Breaches of the Peace, and Acts of Aggression' (articles 39–51).[14] Further, UNSCR 686 affirmed that all twelve resolutions would continue 'to have full force and effect' until 'Iraq implement[ed] its acceptance of all twelve resolutions [in] full compliance'. This was followed by UNSCR 687, the 'ceasefire' resolution, passed on 3 April 1991, which recalled the 'objective of the establishment of the nuclear-weapons-free-zone in the region of the Middle East'. The fact that this zone clearly included Israel was not acknowledged, not even with lip service. In the context of Resolution 687 the main issues to be settled were the delineation of boundaries, the elimination of Iraq's weapons of mass destruction (WMD), removal of the capacity to develop them, payment of reparations, and ending support for terrorism. According to paragraph 22, sanctions would be lifted once Iraq satisfied the Security Council on all such relevant matters. Of course, the question of who would be capable of deciding on the satisfaction of the Council when the US had such an unassailable position to impose its will still remained. This Resolution had ensured that the sanction war, as a weapon of mass destruction against the civil population of Iraq, was well placed to run for more than a decade.[15] Resolution 667 established the United Nations Special Commission on weapons (UNSCOM), and called on it to provide verification of both Iraq's compliance in destroying its nuclear, chemical and biological weapons, as well as its weapons-producing capacity.

The conduct of the Gulf War devastated Iraq's social infrastructure but left intact the political infrastructure of Saddam Hussein's dictatorship. The war's destruction of the former – especially water and sanitation – served to set off a complex humanitarian disaster – a catastrophe of such scope and magnitude that the very fabric of human life (structure, context and texture) is to this day still threatened by its lingering affects. Furthermore, the terms of the ceasefire maintained the original sanctions under the post-war conditions of civil devastation and deprivation. No measures were implemented by the Security Council to mitigate the impact of the maintenance of the sanctions regime on the civilian population following the war's devastation until agreement was reached with the government of Iraq nearly six years later. The isolation from the international community and external economies dramatically augmented the power of the regime over the population, leading to immense human suffering, as detailed in Chapter 5.

TOOLS OF DOMINATION AND OPPRESSION

It was in the post-war period that sanctions became a regime – a political system to administer the terms of the ceasefire. This regime functioned as a tool of domination and oppression, on the one hand facilitating the Security Council's domination of the state of Iraq and, on the other, the oppression of the Iraqi population by Saddam Hussein's dictatorship. At the outset of the post-war era, maintenance of the sanctions regime was ostensibly a means to ensure Iraq's compliance with the ceasefire resolution (UNSCR 687). Whatever the initial intention, however, with institutionalisation the sanctions regime took on a life of its own and domination became an end in itself. The sanctions regime, in other words, became entrenched and developed all the accoutrements of organisational life. The process of institutionalisation is reflected in the 49 Security Council resolutions passed between 5 April 1991 and 30 December 2002. These can be described in terms of three sequential stages of institutionalisation – weapons inspection, inspections with humanitarian aid, and aid without inspections. Table 4.2 identifies the resolutions in the first stage.

WEAPONS INSPECTION

In the first stage the Security Council resolutions reflect the concentration on weapons inspection. In this period the relationship between the government of Iraq and the Security Council witnessed an ongoing cat-and-mouse game between intrusive weapons inspectors acting with virtually unlimited authority on a mission to disarm Iraq's WMD programmes, and a defiant government of Iraq which viewed the inspectors as foreign agents intent on infringing on Iraqi sovereignty. The bombastic brinksmanship of both parties exasperated the domination–subordination relationship inherent in the sanctions regime. Contributing to the problem, conditions for the removal of the sanctions regime, as outlined in paragraphs 21 and 22 of the ceasefire resolution, and the inspectors' mandate, lacked clarity and definition.

Table 4.2   Security Council Resolutions, 5 April 1991 to 14 April, 1995

UN Security Council Resolution	Date Passed	Terms of Reference
687	3 April 1991	Declares ceasefire and establishes the UN Special Commission on weapons (UNSCOM). Extends sanctions.
688	5 April 1991	Demands an end to Iraq's repression of its civilian population.
689	9 March 1991	Approves the Secretary-General's report on the United Nations Iraq–Kuwait Observation Mission.
692	20 May 1991	Establishes the UN Compensation Commission.
699	17 June 1991	Approves the Secretary-General's plan for UNSCOM and the IAEA.
700	17 June 1991	Approves the Secretary-General's guidelines for an arms and dual-use embargo.
705	15 August 1991	Establishes a cap on Iraq's maximum compensation payments in relation to its exports.
706	15 August 1991	Allows for an emergency oil sale by Iraq to fund compensation claims, weapons inspection and humanitarian aid in Iraq.
707	15 August 1991	Declares Iraq to be in 'material breach' of UNSCR 687 and allows for UNSCOM and IAEA flights throughout Iraq.
712	19 September 1991	Limits Iraq's oil sales to a total of $1.6 billion.
715	11 October 1991	Approves the plans of UNSCOM and the IAEA, including long-term monitoring.
773	26 August 1992	Declares that the Commission is not reallocating territory between Iraq and Kuwait.
778	2 October 1992	Condemns Iraq for not implementing UNSCRs 706 and 712; takes steps to seize Iraq's overseas assets to pay for compensation and humanitarian expenses.
806	5 February 1993	Arms UNIKOM to prevent border incursions by Iraq.
833	27 May 1993	Concludes the work of the Boundary Demarcation Commission.
899	4 March 1994	Allows compensation for individual Iraqi's who lost assets in the boundary demarcation process.
949	15 October 1994	Condemns Iraqi military build-up near the Kuwaiti border.
986	14 April 1995	New 'oil-for-food' resolution.

Iraqi attempts to limit UNSCOM inspectors and circumvent the inspectors' authority constituted violations of the ceasefire agreement[16] and were repeatedly used as evidence by the United States and the United Kingdom of Iraq's belligerence, justifying retaliatory air strikes against Iraqi targets in unilaterally imposed 'no-fly zones'.[17] The lack of clarity provided by UNSCOM, and the United States' vacillation on the goals of the UN mission in Iraq, made the pursuit of weapons, weapons-production capability and potential weapons-production virtually unquantifiable, and no lifting of the sanctions appeared feasible. The increasing list of 'dual-use' goods denied to Iraq only further derailed Iraqi and UN reconstruction efforts. The absence of necessary items had a dramatic and wholly negative impact on the Iraqi people, thereby further aggravating the humanitarian crisis. Following the ceasefire, and inspired by calls from US President George Bush for an overthrow of the Ba'ath regime, a popular rebellion arose to oust it from power. The rebellion failed miserably, and as the regime regained and consolidated its power, human rights abuses were barbaric and widespread. In spite of the fact that coalition forces were in close proximity to much of the fighting, they did not intervene. The Security Council only later responded to Ba'athist repression by passing Resolution 688 on 5 April 1991. The resolution condemned 'the repression of the Iraqi civilian population' and demanded 'that Iraq...immediately end this repression'. It was at this point that sanctions became tools of oppression by allowing the Saddam Hussein regime to be the sole arbiter of the welfare of the population. Resolution 688 was not adopted under chapter VII of the Charter, and did not provide for the use of force to defend those being slaughtered by the forces loyal to the Ba'athist regime. The reason is that Resolution 688 was not mandatory, and therefore had no legal weight, much like Resolution 660, which demanded Iraq's withdrawal from Kuwait without authorising military action in case of non-compliance. Despite reaffirmation of the 'sovereignty, territorial integrity and political independence of Iraq' in Resolution 688, the US used it to establish illegally 'the no-fly zones' in the north and south to allow Western military planes to rove over large areas of Iraq, bombing and gathering intelligence.[18] The two no-fly zones were originally designed to protect these areas from Iraqi air strikes by banning all Iraqi military flights, but they had no precedent in international law and no authorisation from the United Nations. The UN/US tolerance of repeated incursions by the Turkish air force to attack Kurdish targets in northern

Iraq, as well as being a clear infringement of Iraqi sovereignty, undermined the claim that the US and UK maintenance of the zones was done for the protection of the Kurdish minority in northern Iraq. Furthermore, allied aircraft maintaining combat air patrol (CAP) over Iraq had consistently engaged in punitive strikes against Iraqi targets, which were justified by the presence of Iraqi forces in the zones, a presence not prohibited by any UN resolution.[19]

Resolution 689, passed on 9 April 1991, approved the Secretary-General's 2 May 1991 report on the United Nations Iraq–Kuwait Observation Mission (UNIKOM) which had been established by the Security Council to monitor the demilitarised zone along the Iraq–Kuwait border, deter border violations, and report on any hostile action to the Security Council.[20] Resolution 692 of 20 May 1991 established the UN Compensation Commission. The Commission would monitor and process claims against the Compensation Fund. It would then 'pay compensation for losses and damage suffered as a direct result of Iraq's unlawful invasion and occupation of Kuwait' from funds gathered, principally from the profits accrued from the sale of Iraqi oil through the Office of the Iraq Programme – the oil-for-food programme. Through July 2002 the overwhelming majority of individual claims (exceeding 2.6 million) filed with the Commission had been resolved. As of 23 July 2002 there were a total of 2,595,581 claims resolved, with 1,505,554 claims receiving a total of over US $42 billion. However, the claims still to be considered by the panels of commissioners include those with the largest asserted values. With some 6700 claims, the total dollar amount requested had been totalled at almost US$181 billion.[21]

UNSCR 699, passed 17 June 1991, approved the Secretary-General's organisational plan for UNSCOM, and for the weapons inspection regime to be conducted jointly with the International Atomic Energy Agency (IAEA). UNSCR 700, passed 17 June 1991, gave final approval to the Secretary-General's guidelines for the arms and dual-use embargo against Iraq, and called upon states to act consistently with its prohibition of sales of the designated goods to Iraq. The 661 Committee, taking on an ever-increasing role in shaping and conducting the relationship between the UN and Iraq, was made responsible for the ongoing monitoring regime. UNSCR 705, passed 15 August 1991, declared that 'compensation to be paid by Iraq...shall not exceed 30 per cent of the annual value of exports'. Following the war, and throughout 1991, accumulated reports pointed to a humanitarian tragedy of epic proportion, which the US faced with

Security Council Resolutions 706, 712 and 986. The political purpose of these resolutions was to maintain the ruthless sanction regime without the appearance of being vengeful or cruel. It should be recalled that these resolutions were meant to fund compensation payments to claimants, the UN costs in executing the tasks of Resolution 687 and the full costs of the other various activities of the UN from the revenue of Iraqi oil sale. Given the fact that contracts for humanitarian needs, but not for compensation payments, could be blocked in the sanctions committee, whatever the realised proportion from oil sales, it would inevitably be insufficient for food and medicine. When Resolution 706 was passed on 15 August 1991, a US official referred to it as a good way to maintain the bulk of the sanctions without being on the wrong side of a potentially emotional issue: the starving of the Iraqi people. With the weapons inspectors meeting resistance from the Iraqi government, the Security Council passed UNSCR 707 on 15 August 1991 which condemned Iraq's non-compliance on weapons inspections, and called on the Iraqi government to provide 'full, final and complete disclosure...of all aspects of its programmes to develop weapons of mass destruction'.

International humanitarian organisations and aid donors expressed alarm at the 19 September 1991 passage of UNSCR 712 which rejected the Secretary-General's suggestion that at least $2 billion in oil revenue be made available for humanitarian needs, and instead allowed for only $1.6 billion. The denial of funds raised questions within the aid organisations then working in northern Iraq, and those appraising the entire country, about the Security Council's commitment to averting the humanitarian disaster that had been predicted, and was by this time emerging. The setting-up of the humanitarian effort, outside the control of the Iraqi government and the increasingly successful UNSCOM inspections, saw the government of Iraq reject the proposed agreement on the basis that it infringed Iraqi sovereignty. Hopes were raised when the Iraqi government did agree to the monitoring system, including long-term monitoring, following UNSCOM's designation of Iraq being WMD-free, established by UNSCR 715 of 11 October 1991. UNSCR 773, passed 26 August 1992, responded to Iraqi claims that UNIKOM was reallocating territory along the Iraq–Kuwait border.

However, the impasse over the implementation of the Office of the Iraq oil-for-food programme continued, since without Iraqi agreement it could not begin operations in the country. The Security Council responded to Iraq's unwillingness to cooperate on 2 October

1992 with the passage of UNSCR 778, calling on the government of Iraq to recognise its responsibilities, especially as those outlined by UNSC Resolutions 706 and 712. In response to Iraq's unwillingness to sell oil to accrue the funds necessary for the increasing UN bureaucracy, including UNIKOM, UNSCOM and the Office of the Iraq Programme (in addition to paying the compensation claims against it for the invasion of Kuwait), the Security Council took measures to transfer funds confiscated from Iraqi assets held in foreign states. The funds were to be transferred into a UN escrow account, established at a Parisian bank, to pay for compensation and humanitarian expenses.

Tensions continued and the Security Council adopted Resolution 806 on 5 February 1993, arming UNIKOM in response to its reports of Iraqi incursions into the demilitarised zone between Iraq and Kuwait. Later that year, following the completion of UNIKOM's redrawing of the Iraq–Kuwait border, the Security Council passed Resolution 833 on 27 May 1993. The boundaries created by the Boundary Demarcation Commission were recognised and accepted as legitimate by both the Iraqi National Assembly and a presidential decree issued by Saddam Hussein on 10 November 1994. Both statements also recognised the territorial integrity and political independence of the State of Kuwait. As the stand-off over the implementation of the oil-for-food programme continued, the Security Council, in UNSCR 899 on 4 March 1994, expanded those eligible for compensation to include Iraqi citizens who had lost assets to the boundary demarcation process carried out by UNIKOM. Apparent Iraqi troop deployments near the border with Kuwait led to UNSCR 949 on 15 October 1994, which sternly condemned the deployments, demanded an immediate Iraqi withdrawal, and called for full Iraqi co-operation with UNSCOM.

Following five years and eight months of sanctions (three years and seven months after passing Resolution 712), the Security Council passed the oil-for-food resolution. Public concern at the humanitarian toll then being exacted, in large measure due to sanctions, forced the Security Council's hand, as the consensus required to maintain the embargo was increasingly coming under assault. UNSCR 986 passed on 14 April 1995 adopted the terms of reference for the oil-for-food programme. However, without the co-operation of the government of Iraq little could be accomplished, and no humanitarian assistance could be deployed within the 15 governates in central and southern Iraq still under the control of the Ba'ath regime. Negotiations were pursued, and the impasse was finally broken when a Memorandum of Understanding was signed on 20 May 1996 between the United Nations and the government of Iraq. The 'oil-for-food' resolution allowed for $1 billion in oil sales every 90 days, to be used to fund the humanitarian effort, weapons inspectors and all other UN operations in Iraq, with Phase I set to begin on 10 December 1996. The programme was intended by the Security Council to be 'a temporary measure to provide for the humanitarian needs of the Iraqi people', a temporary measure that lasted until the invasion of Iraq on 19 March 2003. Iraq agreed to Resolution 986 for two main reasons. First, the ration system that the government had established could not maintain all the Iraqi people, and thousands were dying from starvation and disease, which had increased dramatically under the US-initiated embargo. Second, the resolution increased the amount of oil sales, changed the distribution monitoring mechanisms, and increased the revenue proportion for humanitarian needs. Ironically, while the resolution reaffirmed the 'sovereignty of Iraq', Iraq itself was excluded from all the decisions that involved the management of its economy or the care of its population.[22] Perhaps not so inadvertently, the same pattern has re-emerged after the more recent invasion by Anglo-American forces.

UNSCR 986 marked the end of the first stage of the sanctions regime and initiation of the second. By the end of the first stage, a full-blown bureaucracy had emerged to implement the sanctions regime, as reflected in Table 4.3.

HUMANITARIAN AID

In the second stage, Security Council resolutions reflect the tension inherent in the sanctions regime between the geopolitical objectives of disarmament and humanitarian principles. This contradiction illustrates dramatically the predicament of people caught in the quagmire of world politics. This stage began with the institutionalisation of humanitarian aid[23] and ended with the termination of UNSCOM. Table 4.4 lists the resolutions encompassed in this period.

The implementation of oil-for-food reduced international pressure to alleviate the humanitarian crisis in Iraq, and the Security Council returned its full attention to disarmament issues. UNSCR 1060, passed 12 June 1996, strongly denounced Iraq's continued efforts to obfuscate the inspectors' efforts to locate WMD, WMD production facilities, and the infrastructure required to reconstitute Iraq's WMD capabilities.

Table 4.3 Select Committees Established to Implement and Administer UN Sanctions

Committee	Mandate	Membership	Terms of Reference
Sanctions Committee	SCR 661	All members of the Security Council	Pursuant to article 6, '(a) to examine the reports on the progress of the implementation of the present resolution which will be submitted by the Secretary-General; (b)to seek from all States further information regarding the action taken by them concerning the effective implementation of the provisions laid down in the present resolution'.
Multinational Interception Force	SCR 665	Pursuant to article 1, 'Member States co-operating with the Government of Kuwait which are deploying maritime forces in the area'	Pursuant to article 1, 'to halt all inward and outward maritime shipping in order to inspect and verify their cargoes and destinations and to ensure strict implementation of the provisions related to such shipping laid down in resolution 661.'
Fund and Compensation Commission	SCR 692	Constituted by the Secretary-General	Pursuant to article 9 of SCR 674 and section E of 687, to consider all claims for compensation arising out of Iraq's occupation of Kuwait, and to administer a fund established for this.
UNIKOM	SCR 689	United Nations Observer Unit	Pursuant to article 5 of SCR 687, 'to monitor the Khor Abdullah and a demilitarised zone; to deter violations of the boundary; to observe any hostile or potentially hostile action'.
Iraq–Kuwait Boundary Demarcation Commission	SCR 687	Constituted by the Secretary-General	Pursuant to article 3, 'to demarcate the boundary between Iraq and Kuwait'.
UNSCOM	SCR 699	Pursuant to articles 9b and 13 of SCR 687, the Director-General of IAEA and Special Commission constituted by the Secretary-General	Pursuant to articles 9, 10, 12 and 13 of SCR 687, destruction of Iraq's weapons of mass destruction; and monitoring and verification in perpetuity of Iraq's compliance with the monitoring and verification regime established under the resolution.
Office of the Iraq Programme	SCR 778	Pursuant to article 5, under the responsibility of the Secretary-General	Pursuant to article 5, '(a) to ascertain the whereabouts and amounts of [Iraqi petroleum products] and the proceeds of sale [of these products],...(b) to ascertain the costs of United Nations activities [in Iraq];' and to use the funds to pay for these activities.

Table 4.4   Security Council Resolutions, 27 March 1996 to 5 November 1998

1051	27 March 1996	Establishes a mechanism for the long-term monitoring of potential 'dual-use' items.
1060	12 June 1996	On Iraq's refusal to allow access to sites designated by UNSCOM.
1111	4 June 1997	Establishes Phase II of 'oil-for-food'.
1115	21 June 1997	Condemns Iraq for blocking inspection efforts and demands full compliance.
1129	12 September 1997	Alters the timing of Phase II of 'oil-for-food'.
1134	23 October 1997	Reaffirms Iraq's obligation to comply with inspection efforts and threatens a travel ban on Iraqi officials.
1137	12 November 1997	Rejects Iraq's demands to reduce the number of US inspectors and imposes travel ban on Iraqi officials.
1143	4 December 1997	Establishes Phase III of 'oil-for-food'.
1153	20 February 1998	Increases the cap on Iraqi oil sales.
1154	2 March 1998	Endorses Memorandum of Understanding and acknowledges Iraqi promises of compliance with weapons inspections.
1158	25 March 1988	Continues 'oil-for-food' under the provisions of UNSCR 1153.
1175	19 June 1998	Allows Iraq to import a limited number of oil industry spare parts.
1194	9 September 1998	Condemnation of Iraq's decision to halt all UNSCOM disarmament work.
1205	5 November 1998	Condemnation of Iraq's decision to halt monitoring.

UNSCR 1051, passed 27 March 1996, established mechanisms for the long-term monitoring of potentially 'dual-use' Iraqi imports and exports, institutionalising the mechanisms called for by UNSCR 715.

UNSCR 1111, passed 4 June 1997, initiated Phase II of the 'oil-for-food' programme. The continuing confrontation between UNSCOM and the government of Iraq over the mandate of UNSCOM and conduct of weapons inspections resulted in further condemnation of Iraq in UNSCR 1115, passed 21 June 1997. The resolution, once again, condemned the 'refusal of the Iraqi authorities to allow access to sites' and demanded 'that [they] cooperate fully' with UNSCOM. To penalise the Iraqi government, the resolution suspended the sanctions and arms embargo reviews – the reports by which measure Iraq could be verified as WMD-free – and therefore the mechanism by which sanctions could be lifted. Further, the resolution threatened to 'impose additional measures on those categories of Iraqi officials responsible for the non-compliance', believed to be a ban preventing the individual identified from being able to travel abroad or represent the government of Iraq abroad.

The Iraqi government, again arguing that the United Nations control over funds accrued from the oil sales amounted to an abrogation of its sovereignty, protested against delays in delivering supplies approved by the sanctions committee (the 661 Committee) and refused to sell oil beginning in September 1997 until the UN approved its Distribution Plan. The Security Council responded by passing UNSCR 1129 on 12 September 1997, which altered the timing of permitted Phase II oil sales. After a month of negotiations between the Secretary-General and the government of Iraq, the Security Council approved Iraq's pricing formula for oil exports, removing the legal hurdle for the resumption of oil sales under the oil-for-food plan.

Tensions between the inspection teams and the government of Iraq again led to Security Council retribution after Iraqi officials announced in September 1997 that 'presidential sites' would be prohibited to UNSCOM inspectors. The Security Council responded with Resolution 1134 on 23 October 1997, threatening a travel ban on obstructive Iraqi officials not 'carrying out bona fide diplomatic assignments or missions' if non-co-operation continued, and again delayed the sanction reviews. When the Iraqi government announced in November 1997 that it would no longer tolerate UNSCOM over-flights, and intended to prohibit weapons inspections unless the composition of UNSCOM teams was altered to limit the number of inspectors from the United States, the Security Council responded with Resolution 1137 on 12 November 1997. Iraqi officials retracted their demands when a travel ban was imposed on Iraqi government officials that was to be lifted only when full co-operation resumed. UNSCR 1143, passed on 4 December 1997, began Phase III of oil-for-food on 5 December 1997 and also welcomed the Secretary-General's intention to submit a supplementary report on possible improvements in the oil-for-food programme addressing the increasing calls critical of the limited impact of the programme in the face of the widespread destruction of Iraqi civilian infrastructure and the intransigence of the 661 Committee in holding and blocking dual-use items.

The cyclical passage of Security Council resolutions and punitive air raids by the US and the UK, along with the continuing humanitarian crisis in Iraq received increasing international condemnation at the beginning of 1998 from a growing number of Middle Eastern states, international NGOs and from within the United Nations itself. Allegations of UNSCOM working as spies for Western intelligence agencies further undermined their position as impartial arbiters. The combative tactics, and US and UK demands for unfettered access for inspections, increasingly created what came to be identified as the 'UNSCOM crisis'. UNSCR 1153, passed on 20 February 1998 during the initial stages of the crisis, again attempted to deal with international calls for a removal or a revamping of sanctions on thr grounds of the humanitarian toll they were exacting on the Iraqi people, by agreeing to increase the cap on permitted Iraqi oil sales to $5.256 billion per phase once the Secretary-General approved an 'enhanced distribution plan' for the new revenues.[24] Significantly, the resolution recognised – for the first time – the importance of infrastructure and project-based purchases, which were to be targeted with the beginning of Phase IV on 30 May 1998.

By the spring of 1998 the Security Council appeared badly divided, with three of its permanent members – China, France and Russia – opposed to military action by the two other permanent members, the UK and US. In an attempt to break the stalemates, both between Iraq and the United States and amongst the members of the Security Council, Secretary-General Kofi Annan visited Baghdad to negotiate a resolution to the impasse. On 23 February 1998 Annan and Iraq's Deputy Prime Minister, Tariq Aziz, signed a Memorandum of Understanding designed to enable UNSCOM to complete its mandate of weapons inspections without obstruction. Iraq dropped its two stated goals of limited inspections: regarding the presidential sites as off-limits to inspectors, and setting a time limit to the inspections regime (reported to be 60 days) that had now been ongoing for seven years. UNSCR 1154 was passed on 2 March 1998 in which the Secretary-General was commended for 'securing commitments from the Iraqi government to fully comply with weapons inspections', following his mission to Baghdad. With inspections again under way, the Security Council returned to addressing the humanitarian situation in an effort to stifle further criticism of the sanctions. UNSCR 1158 was passed on 25 March 1998 continuing Phase III under the enhanced provisions of UNSCR 1153. However, funding constraints imposed by the derelict conditions of Iraq's oil industry hampered any revamping of the humanitarian efforts underway in Iraq. Suffering under the sanctions, especially the holds on dual-use items, the eight years of neglect had taken their toll and slowed production levels. In response the Security Council passed Resolution 1175 allowing Iraq to apply to import up to $300 million of oil industry spare parts during Phase III. This was deemed sufficient to increase production levels to the cap set in UNSCR 1153.

The crisis deepened, however, owing to the continued brinkmanship of UNSCOM and Iraq. The international community and the UN Secretary-General became increasingly engaged in diplomatic efforts to avoid further hostilities. Iraq again refused to allow inspectors total freedom of action, including a denial of access to 'presidential sites' within Iraq. In response the US and British governments threatened to conduct punitive bombing raids to force Iraqi compliance with UNSCOM. On 31 October 1998, the government of Iraq halted work by UNSCOM, and the United States and Great Britain conducted a military build-up in the Persian Gulf. With military forces deployed in the Gulf, the UN Security Council condemned Iraq for violating the ceasefire agreement and called for a return to unfettered inspections on 5 November. On 11 November, UNSCOM withdrew its entire staff from Iraq, and other United Nations agencies removed non-essential staff in anticipation of a US-UK attack. Bowing to international pressure, reportedly with US bombers in the air and within minutes of attack, the government of Iraq agreed to allow UNSCOM to return on 14 November, and weapons inspectors to return a few days later. The relative period of calm saw the passage of UNSCR 1210 on 24 November 1998 that initiated Phase V of oil-for-food on 26 November 1998.

In spite of the return of UNSCOM and a return to the inspection process, the crisis continued, and on 8 December UNSCOM chief Richard Butler reported that Iraq was still impeding inspections. However, as several of the inspectors later made plain, after seven years the inspections had largely proven successful at removing the WMD stockpiles and productive capacities possessed by the Iraqi regime. Inspectors were now increasingly, if not solely, concentrating their efforts on the Iraqi government's capability to reproduce a weapons programme. This required an aggressive pursuit of individual Iraqi scientists and bureaucrats, and a focus on the paper trail of past Iraqi purchases, and recent activities to procure materials. This saw UNSCOM intrusions not only into the material records of the Iraqi regime regarding WMDs, but also into virtually any other records and files maintained by the Iraqi government. The sensitivity of such material which was directly related to the day-to-day operations of the Ba'ath regime threatened the sovereignty of the state of Iraq as well as its oppressive regime. The genuine independence and impartiality of UNSCOM and its inspectors, long recognised as critical to an internationally acceptable anti-proliferation effort, was now even more essential. However, following the longstanding confrontation between UNSCOM and the government of Iraq, the inspectors returned to Iraq under instructions to pursue Iraqi duplicity aggressively, while at the same time disguising the real purpose and time limits of its own mandate. Questions about the organisation's impartiality, about a recognisable horizon for an end to sanctions following seven years of inspections, and increasing fears about the bellicose threats to use force in an effort to topple the regime, created pressure to find evidence of Iraqi compliance or culpability within a compressed window of time.

Within weeks of UNSCOM's return, its chair, Ambassador Butler, again publicly berated the Iraqi government for hindering UNSCOM's efforts and, on the advice of the US government, on 15–16 December 1998 withdrew all UNSCOM personnel from Iraq to Bahrain.[25] Butler's public charges were then produced in a formal UN report accusing Iraq of a 'repeated pattern of obstructing weapons inspections by not allowing access to records and inspections sites, and by moving equipment records and equipment from one site to another'. The report was dated 15 December and, although it served as the ostensible basis for the punitive use of force, was not presented to the Security Council until after the US-UK attacks had begun the following day. Operation 'Desert Fox', as the attacks were code-named by the US, was allegedly aimed at Iraqi WMD. According to US Defense Secretary William S. Cohen, US 'forces attacked about 100 targets over four nights, following a plan that was developed, and had been developed and refined over the past year'.[26] However, target selection and identification would cause many to criticise the US government, both for the human casualties incurred in the attacks and for the large number of targets that did not correspond to locations UNSCOM wished to investigate, but instead were the private residences of the Ba'ath political leadership, the buildings housing the Ba'ath party apparatus, and the headquarters and offices of Iraqi military and intelligence agencies.

Throughout the 1998 period of confrontation and crisis Iraq had frequently accused UNSCOM arms inspectors of being conduits for American spying, and was often joined in these criticisms by the French and Russian governments. During the stand-off, Iraqi Deputy Prime Minister Tariq Aziz sent a letter to Kofi Annan, demanding an investigation into whether UNSCOM was being used by US and other intelligence agencies 'to carry out espionage on Iraq'. These allegations were reported as being largely speculative and dismissed outright by UNSCOM and the United States as Iraqi propaganda. However, press reports and unconfirmed speculation continued, rising to a crescendo as the year wore on. Following the four-day bombing campaign 'Desert Fox' (16–19 December 1998), the allegations were appearing as confirmed stories in Western news organisations, originating reportedly from leaks inside the United Nations. The Clinton administration's unwillingness to deny the spying allegations, now appearing as a series of damning articles in the *New York Times*, *Boston Globe* and *Washington Post* citing UNSCOM's use of equipment supplied by the Central Intelligence Agency (CIA) and Defense Intelligence Agency (DIA), was seen by many as an admission of guilt.[27] Prior to the collected data being analysed by UNSCOM, it had been in the possession of the US intelligence agencies, who were accused of using the information to attempt to overthrow the Iraqi regime as well as for the expressed purpose of targeting Iraq during the air strikes of Desert Fox. The *Washington Post* quoted advisers of Kofi Annan acknowledging that the Secretary-General was trying to put pressure on UNSCOM chief Richard Butler to resign in favour of a successor who would restore UNSCOM's credibility as an objective arbiter of the disarmament effort in Iraq. Throughout the seven years and nine months period (April 1991–December 1998), both sides repeatedly provoked confrontations and crisis situations in an effort to advance their agendas. In the process both parties ignored the consequences for the Iraqi people, especially the most vulnerable members of Iraqi society.

In the third stage of the sanctions regime, three new programmes were added to the regime's bureaucracy, two expanding and deepening inspections into perpetuity and one related to humanitarian aid, as detailed in Table 4.5.

AID WITHOUT INSPECTIONS

In the third stage of the sanctions regime, humanitarian aid essentially replaced inspections as the *raison d'être* of the sanctions regime, as reflected in Table 4.6 outlining Security Council resolutions in this period. Although the resolutions suggest that humanitarian issues occupied the Security Council's focus on Iraq, actually the stage ended with the United States initiating a unilateral pre-emptive war, the very thing the United Nations was established to avoid.

The progression from humanitarian aid to war was a product of the inherent tension between geopolitical objectives and humanitarian principles discussed earlier. In the Security Council the

Table 4.5   Committees Established during the Third Stage

Committee	Mandate	Membership	Terms of Reference
Baghdad Monitoring and Verification Centre	SCR 1051	Pursuant to articles 2 and 3 of SCR 715, UNSCOM and the Director-General of IAEA	Pursuant to article 9 of SCR 687, monitoring and verification of Iraq's compliance in perpetuity with the monitoring and verification regime established under the resolution.
Export/Import Monitoring Unit	SCR 1051	Pursuant to article 7 of SCR 715, the unit is established under the aegis of UNSCOM and IAEA	Pursuant to article 7 of SCR 715, the unit is 'a mechanism for monitoring any future sales or supplies by other countries to Iraq of items relevant to the implementation of section C of resolution 687 (1991)...'; so-called dual-use items.
Oil-for-Food Programme	SCR 1143	Pursuant to article 7 of SCR 986, appointed by the Secretary-General	Pursuant to article 7 of SCR 986, 'to establish an escrow account [from the proceeds of the sale of Iraqi oil]...used to meet the humanitarian needs of the Iraqi population', as well as other expenses incurred by the various UN committees operating in Iraq.

tension was reflected in terms of the emerging schism among the permanent members. The bombings of 1998 met with international condemnation and an increased aversion to further use of the UN Security Council as an aggressive means to censure Iraqi actions. The sanctions were now being recognised by a large number of regional and international governments, as well as international relief agencies, as having a deleterious effect on the Iraqi population and running counter to the Charter and civilised conduct in international affairs. The United States, with the support of the United Kingdom, however, refused to waver in its prosecution of the Security Council mandate to quantifiably disarm Iraq, and in its resolve to maintain the sanctions regime as the primary coercive tool against the dictatorial government of Iraq. Increasingly, discussions within the United States began to centre on regime change (which was not part of the UN mandate) as opposed to disarmament. The Iraqi regime, believing that weapons

Table 4.6   Sanctions as Tools of Control

UN Security Council Resolution	Date Passed	Terms of Reference
1242	21 May 1999	Establishes Phase VI of 'oil-for-food'.
1266	4 October 1999	Allows for additional oil sales to offset the deficits from previous phases.
1275	19 November 1999	Extends Phase VI.
1280	3 December 1999	Extends Phase VI.
1281	10 December 1999	Establishes Phase VII of 'oil-for-food'.
1284	17 December 1999	Replaces UNSCOM with UNMOVIC, demands Iraqi co-operation on prisoners of war, and changes the 'oil-for-food' programme.
1293	31 March 2000	Doubles permitted spare parts imports for the oil industry.
1302	8 June 2000	Establishes Phase VIII of 'oil-for-food', asks for the creation of 'green lists' for water and sanitation, and calls for the establishment on a commission to asses the humanitarian situation in Iraq.
1330	4 December 2000	Establishes Phase IX of 'oil-for-food'.
1352	1 June 2001	Extends Phase IX.
1360	3 July 2001	Establishes Phase X of 'oil-for-food'.
1382	29 November 2001	Establishes Phase XI of 'oil-for-food' and adopts a new 'goods review list' (GRL).
1409	14 May 2002	Extends 'oil-for-food' by six months and establishes a new procedure for imports.
1441	8 November 2002	Condemns Iraq for non-compliance with inspectors.
1443	25 November 2002	Extends the 'oil-for-food' programme.
1447	4 December 2002	Extends the 'oil-for-food' programme and calls for a review of the GRL.
1454	30 December 2002	Implements revisions to the GRL.

inspectors were instruments of Western intelligence agencies rather than impartial monitors to verify disarmament, refused to allow UNSCOM to re-enter Iraq. However, the Iraqi officials did permit IAEA inspections to continue.

In attempting to respond to the international humanitarian calls for action regarding the plight of the Iraqi people, the Security Council made efforts to alleviate the negative affects of sanctions, while making no alterations to the basic principles that hampered Iraqi access to basic goods. UNSCR 1242 was passed on 21 May 1999 and Phase VI of the oil-for-food programme began four days later. UNSCR 1266, passed 4 October 1999, provided for an additional increase in oil sales of $3.04 billion to offset deficits accrued during earlier phases of the programme, largely a result of Iraq being unable to produce sufficient quantities of oil through the lack of spare parts that were required to maintain production levels.

The Iraqi-UNSCOM crisis[28] affected oil-for-food with Phase VI extended initially to 4 December 1999 by UNSCR 1275 (passed 19 November 1999), and then again until 11 December 1999 by UNSCR 1280 (passed 3 December 1999). Finally Phase VII was initiated with UNSCR 1281, passed 10 December 1999, set to begin two days later. The delays in implementation of new phases of the oil-for-food programme were the result of considerable debate within the Security Council over a revamping of the sanctions regime that ultimately would result in UNSCR 1284. However, the delays in implementation caused delays in service delivery by the oil-for-food programme, and concerns about its ability to supply the increasingly dependent people of Iraq. Oil orders were cancelled as the delays precluded the contracting of Iraqi production, which was tied by UN decree to a process whereby prices were set not by the market, but by the tender at the end of each phase.

With the diplomatic manoeuvrings taking place in the Security Council, Iraq continued to refuse to allow UNSCOM inspectors to return, their impartiality having been compromised. This raised questions about UNSCOM's viability as an organisation. On 30 June 1999 Richard Butler completed his two-year tenure as Executive Chairman of UNSCOM, and with the negotiations to revamp both sanctions and the monitoring vehicle following UNSCOM's fall from grace, a successor was not appointed. Charles Duelfer, Deputy Executive Chairman, remained as officer-in-charge and submitted the final UNSCOM report to the Secretary-General on 8 October 1999.

UNSCR 1284, passed on 17 December 1999, replaced UNSCOM with the United Nations Monitoring, Verification and Inspection Commission (UNMOVIC), reiterated demands on the government of Iraq with regards to prisoners of war, altered the oil-for-food programme, and obscurely referred to the possible suspension of sanctions. With UNSCOM and later UNMOVIC, a complex bureaucracy emerged to administer sanctions as tools of disarmament. The scope and nature of this bureaucracy is indicated in Table 4.5. UNMOVIC was to continue UNSCOM's mandate to disarm Iraq of its weapons of mass destruction (chemical, biological weapons and missiles with a range of more than 150 km), and to operate a system of ongoing monitoring and verification to check Iraq's compliance with its obligations. Kofi Annan appointed Hans Blix of Sweden, a career diplomat with longstanding credentials as a disarmament expert, to be the Commission's Executive Chairman, a dramatic change compared to the bombastic Richard Butler. In line with other UN organisations and the UN Charter, UNMOVIC was profession-alised in the wake of the UNSCOM crisis. Further, unlike UNSCOM, the staff of UNMOVIC were to be employees of the United Nations. In addition, a 16-member College of Commissioners of UNMOVIC was appointed by the Secretary-General to provide advice and guidance to the chairman.[29]

However, the resolution failed to alter the basic dynamic of the relationship between the Security Council and the government of Iraq and, more important, that of the Security Council with the people of Iraq. The provisions dealing with the improvement of the humanitarian crisis of the Iraqi people failed to meet that recommended by the UN's own Humanitarian Panel, as well as earlier drafts of the resolution that had been leaked publicly during the long-drawn-out negotiations, and which concretely linked the measures designed to alleviate the suffering of the Iraqi civilian population to progress in negotiations between the Iraqi regime and the governments comprising the permanent members of the Security Council.[30]

In addition, the resolution failed to answer the major criticism of the Iraqi government, its allies, the international NGOs and UN member organisations dealing with the humanitarian crisis. This criticism was centred on the ambiguous standards by which the sanctions would be lifted. Such concrete definition of the parameters – how weapons monitors would conduct their efforts to certify Iraqi compliance; the conditions required for the lifting of the sanctions regime; and how Iraq would be reintegrated into the community of nations – would have answered these criticisms. Without any apparent benefits to be gained through co-operation, the government of Iraq was not encouraged to accommodate inspectors or negotiate with the US and UK governments. This position adopted through immense US lobbying in the Security Council ensured the maintenance of the stalemate, and firmly entrenched sanctions as tools of domination. Without an alteration in the US-UK position, or the removal of the Ba'athist regime in Iraq, sanctions would be maintained and the US veto in the Security Council would prevent any relief for the Iraqi people. In Britain the Campaign Against the Sanctions on Iraq (CASI) at Cambridge University judged that the resolution had 'deliberately obscured what is required of the government of Iraq and what benefits

Iraq can expect'.[31] In May 2000 a newsletter issued by CASI said that the humanitarian situation in Iraq would not likely improve because the resolution required Iraq to trust that the US would generously and beneficently interpret the vague terms of the resolution.

UNSCR 1293, passed 31 March 2000, doubled the permitted oil-industry spare part imports for Phases VI and VII, allowing Iraq to spend up to $1.2 billion to upgrade its oil industry infrastructure. Independent oil industry experts had reported that Iraq would need to rehabilitate its pumping stations if it wanted to continue exporting crude through the UN programme.[32] The United States had been under increasing criticism for its policy of withholding the parts needed for repairs for the Iraqi oil industry by placing on hold in the UN sanctions committee (the 661 Committee) more than $1 billion in contracts for spare parts and other equipment. Relenting under this pressure, the US sponsored the resolution to deflect criticism of its tough line on Iraq, which was under increasing disapproval internationally, and even within the United States. UNSCR 1302, passed 8 June 2000, began Phase VIII of oil-for-food. In an effort to address almost a decade's continued lack of construction of new infrastructure following its destruction in the Gulf War, the resolution asked for water and sanitation 'green lists', and extended the oil spare parts permission of UNSCR 1293. The attempt of the resolution to circumvent the 661 Committee as a result of its longstanding rejection of items crucial to the refurbishment of the water and sanitation systems within Iraq raised hopes that the Office of the Iraq Programme and other UN agencies could be equipped with the tools necessary to effect an improvement in Iraq's humanitarian condition, but these hopes were largely dashed as efforts were dependent upon Iraqi cooperation for their success.

Nowhere was this more evident than in paragraph 18 of UNSCR 1302, which called for the establishment of a team of independent experts who were to prepare a comprehensive report and analysis of the humanitarian situation in Iraq by 26 November 2000. The report was simply a vehicle chosen by the US and UK to placate international condemnations of the humanitarian crisis, as the report was tasked to merely assess the situation in Iraq and report back to the Security Council. The implication was that the large volume of reports and evidence produced by UN member agencies and international NGOs on that issue were somehow tainted or inaccurate. It adroitly attempted to shift the focus of blame, which was at that time squarely on the Security Council, to the government of Iraq. However, the impasse reached between the government of Iraq and the Security Council precluded the required co-operation, and thus no such report was ever produced. UNSCR 1330, passed 4 December 2000, commenced Phase IX of the oil-for-food programme. The Resolution allocated a further $600 million to oil-industry spare parts and reduced Compensation Fund deductions to 25 per cent. UNSCR 1330 further requested both electricity and housing 'green lists' to aid in stalled reconstruction efforts and expressed 'a readiness to consider' paying Iraq's UN membership dues out of oil-for-food revenues.

Unable to escape the ever-increasing condemnation of the sanctions regime, and their deleterious effects on the Iraqi people, US and UK policy-makers shifted the debate to the adoption of new measures under the name of 'smart sanctions'. On 21 February 2001 the *Guardian* reported that Downing Street was reconsidering the mixture of sanctions, military posture, oil revenue and the enforcement around the borders in order to realise a clear-cut sanction policy that would focus on the Iraqi regime, and on Saddam's attempts to acquire weapons of mass destruction (WMD), removing sanctions that were harmful to the Iraqi people. The *Guardian* also quoted Brian Wilson, the Foreign Office minister in charge of Iraq, as having said that: 'The first stand in British policy is to minimise the human impact of the sanctions and the second is to maximise the inability of Saddam to wage war on his people, the region and the world.'

The shift in sanctions policy at that particular junction was, according to the *Daily Telegraph* on 21 February 2001, a required change of presentation to engage domestic and international attention on Saddam, because, according to *The Times* on 21 February 2001, the Anglo-Americans were the villains of the piece in the eyes of the Arab world, which American Secretary of State Colin Powell was about to visit. Following Powell's tour, on 26 February 2001, *The Times* quoted a British official source as commenting that: 'We have lost the propaganda war with Saddam. The perception today is that the sanctions are responsible for the death of the children in Iraq.' In fact, to imagine the possibility of preparing exhaustive lists of 'innocent' items that the civilian infrastructure in Iraq needs (the notion of smart sanctions) is sheer insanity because a modern economy involves hundreds of thousands of humanitarian items that are essential to a working society. How the Office of the Iraq Programme could scrutinise tens of thousands of contracts where every sock and shoe, toothbrush and toothpaste, every nut and bolt and every sheep and cow must be reviewed, approved, stored and distributed is inconceivable. To operate with any degree of consistency would require a bureaucracy of unparalleled magnitude. Furthermore, this ridiculous notion of 'smart sanctions' was not to the liking of the pro-Israeli faction in the Bush administration. In March 2001 Donald Rumsfeld, the US Secretary of Defense, revealed that he would prefer to fund anti-Saddam terrorism and bomb the Iraqi regime out of existence.[33]

UNSCR 1352, passed 1 June 2001, extended Phase IX of the oil-for-food programme by one month only. The Security Council agreed that more time would be required to review the UK's draft resolution and its annex, which were intended to change the spirit and the manner in which sanctions would be implemented. The Iraqi government, increasingly emboldened by calls in the Arab world, the international NGO community and the international community outside the Security Council to end the sanctions, threatened to halt oil production if smart sanctions were implemented, and unless a clear set of guidelines were produced to allow for the lifting of the sanctions regime. From May to July 2001 negotiations among Security Council members ended with an absence of consensus on future sanctions. With no agreement reached, UNSCR 1360 was passed on 3 July 2001 extending the oil-for-food programme by an additional 150 days to begin Phase X. On 1 December 2001 the continued debate at the Security Council and an apparent lack of support for the US-UK position saw the government of Iraq once again halt oil exports. When the Security Council dropped its proposed overhaul of the sanctions and agreed to the five-month extension of oil-for-food, the government of Iraq agreed to resume oil sales a mere two days later, thus scoring a diplomatic victory which owed much to Russia's willingness to veto the new scheme.

However, the hard-line position adopted by the US and UK governments saw the passage of UNSCR 1382 on 29 November 2001, scheduled to take effect on 30 May 2002. Critically, the resolution provided a new 'goods review list' (GRL), that would bar the items contained within the lists provided in UNSCR 1051, as well as those listed in a new 150-page annex to resolution 1382 created by the government of the United States. The proposal appeared simple. All applications to import goods into Iraq were to be reviewed by UNMOVIC and the UN Office of the Iraq Programme to determine if the proposed imports contained items on the GRL. If an item were on the list, it would be denied; if not on the list, it would be allowed.

However, the fact that no list of banned items was in any way exhaustive opened the door for 'further refinement' through deliberation and consultation, which continued the bureaucratic delays that had been typical of the Office of the Iraq Programme. It soon became clear that Resolution 1382 would effect little improvement on implementation, and practically none on Anglo-American obstructionism, while the civilian population of Iraq would continue to suffer the genocide inflicted by the sanction apparatus.[34]

However, with the passage of UNSCR 1409 on 14 May 2002 the new import procedures contained in the GRL implemented a wide-ranging series of import restrictions. Prior to the passage of UNSCR 1284 in December 1999, the Iraq sanctions committee of the Security Council maintained control over all imports to Iraq. The mandated green lists of items, contained in 1284 and implemented in 1409, that could be imported without further approval from the Sanctions Committee, began a movement towards more rigidly focused import controls. Although the United Nations would still need to approve all purchases made by the Iraqi government and UN inspectors would still oversee all imports into the country, the 1382 proposal was promoted as more people friendly on the basis that it would end import controls on all items except those explicitly listed as being associated with weapons, and weapons-development programmes. However, the proposed dual-use lists represented a considerable broadening of the original dual-use lists outlined within the scope of UNSCR 1051. The new list(s) referred to military technology more generally and in a much broader manner, while the 1051 lists had been organised around those weapons systems prohibited by the Security Council under the ceasefire resolution (nuclear, biological, chemical and missiles with ranges of over 150 km). In addition, as OIP, UNMOVIC and the IAEA were all now required to review purchases, instead of just the 661 Committee, there was every likelihood that the mechanism co-ordinating these three organisa-tions in overseeing the 661 Committee would prove unworkable. Lastly, the resolution dropped some of the major contentious issues debated amongst members of the Security Council throughout 2001: namely, regional smuggling of illegal exports of Iraqi oil and the importation of banned substances, as contravening the embargo had proved untenable to Iraq's Arab neighbours and their allies at the United Nations.

US policy, however, was not driven simply by a desire to adopt a higher moral position and avoid charges that it was responsible for the humanitarian crisis in Iraq. Rather, US manoeuvres ensured that the sanctions regime remained in place during a period when international calls for their abrogation were near-unanimous. While the US propaganda position remained 'sanctions relaxed to help Iraqi civilians', an informed observer, like Denis Halliday, the former head of the UN Humanitarian Programme in Iraq, could comment:

> The new smart sanction regime...is dangerously misleading...The reality is that we will continue to punish the innocent populace...As intended, the UN hands will look cleaner as the children of Iraq continue to die from the ongoing loss of fundamental human rights due to the Security Council.[35]

Through its diplomatic efforts on the Security Council the US was able to maintain the illusion that sanctions were an internationally supported effort to contain the WMD threat posed by the Iraqi regime. As a result, it was able to deflect attention from the more aggressive US policy focused on bringing about regime change. The US was forced to move diplomatically thanks to Iraqi efforts to establish a more transparent set of guidelines regarding sanctions and weapons verification at the United Nations. In March and early May of 2002 UN Secretary-General Kofi Annan was engaged in discussions with Iraqi Foreign Minister Naji Sabri to negotiate the resumption of weapons inspections. At the talks held in New York Sabri had posed a series of 17 questions to Annan, including whether the US threat of military action for Iraqi non-compliance with inspections was legal under UN resolutions, the legality of the US-UK no-fly zones, and whether a timetable for the lifting of sanctions would not bring about a more agreeable climate between Iraq and the inspectors. Annan was forced once again to address the issue of the unilateral co-opting of the UN effort to disarm Iraq, while maintaining pressure on the Iraqi regime to live up to its obligations under the ceasefire agreement. The US policy, however, put the UN in the unenviable position of having to convince the Iraqi government of the benefits of compliance, while American statements and diplomatic signals seemed to indicate that the US veto in the Security Council would keep sanctions in place even if they were to comply with WMD inspections or were found in compliance by UNMOVIC.[36]

On 8 November 2002 the Security Council unanimously passed Resolution 1441, ordering Iraq to comply with UNMOVIC and IAEA inspections, and to provide a complete list of all WMD programmes and dual-use items within Iraq by 8 December 2002. In addition, UNSCR 1441 provided inspectors with complete authority to access even the most sensitive of Iraqi sites without advance notice. However, the resolution, drafted under threats of an American invasion and through US bare-knuckle diplomacy in the Security Council, contained no reference within the document towards the lifting of sanctions if the inspectors found no evidence of ongoing WMD programmes. Right after the issuance of the resolution, legal observers believed that it was meant to justify the US military take-over of Iraq. Paragraph 8 states that: 'Iraq shall not take or threaten hostile acts directed against any representative or personnel of the United Nations or of any Member State taking action to uphold any Council resolution'. The resolution further declares that 'false statements or omissions in the declarations submitted by Iraq' and 'failure by Iraq at any time to comply with, and co-operate fully with the implementation of this resolution shall constitute a further material breach of Iraq's obligations'. The US could, as it has in the past, take it upon itself to judge whether Iraq had complied with this provision, in spite of the Security Council's exclusive authority to declare when a country is in material breach.

Iraq responded to Resolution 1441 by denying it had weapons of mass destruction, indicating its intention to co-operate with the weapons inspectors, and stating it would later issue an analysis of why this resolution violates the United Nations Charter, prior Security Council resolutions and other provisions of international law.

It would be very difficult for any sovereign nation to comply with Resolution 1441, which in effect authorises the occupation of Iraq. A particularly onerous provision grants weapons inspectors the unrestricted right to interview all Iraqi officials and all other persons inside or outside Iraq. That provision would give inspectors power to act as de facto asylum for officers and to transport anyone, including high-ranking Iraqi officials, with or without their permission.

Finally, in a direct invitation for non-compliance, the resolution set a 30-day deadline for Iraq to declare not only its weapons programmes, but also all chemical, biological and nuclear programmes unrelated to weapon production. Even Hans Blix, Executive Chairman of UNMOVIC, told the Security Council that this was an unrealistic deadline.

The invasion of Iraq was likely to take place even without further authorisation from the UN, however. Indeed, Colin Powell said on CNN's *Late Edition* that if the UN was not willing to authorise the use of 'all necessary means' to disarm Hussein, 'the United States, with like-minded nations, will go and disarm him forcefully'.[37]

Iraq allowed the inspectors back into Iraq on 25 November 2002. Iraq's readiness to comply was further exemplified by the admission of inspectors into one of the presidential palaces, al-Sajoud, on 3 December 2002 in what was considered by the *New York Times* to be a symbolic display of power on the part of the UN.[38] For whatever reason the palace was chosen, it served temporarily to cool the guns of the American regime.

However, the first hurdle emerged when the US and Britain claimed that the report submitted by Iraq was incomplete and had serious omissions that constituted a 'material breach', therefore justifying military intervention. France, Germany and Russia, on the other hand, all contended that, despite the problems with the Iraqi statement and even issues with the level of Iraqi governmental co-operation, there was a drastic improvement and there existed ample evidence that the inspections and disarmament process was working. This position was generally reinforced by the statements of the weapons inspection teams, especially that of Mohammed El-Baradei, the head of the IAEA, who asserted in his statement of 27 January 2003 that the process had thus far achieved encouraging results and that a continuation of inspections would be most prudent in resolving the concern over Iraq's nuclear weaponry potential. He asked that the inspection be allowed to continue and 'run its natural course.'[39] Hans Blix, although significantly more concerned over the level of Iraqi compliance with UNMOVIC inspection teams, made no allusion to any 'material breach' on Iraq's part.

In an attempt to garner international support for war, the US and Britain released intelligence material that they felt proved conclusively that Iraq was in 'material breach' of UNSC Resolution 1441 and posed a threat to world security. This attempt to convince the world of the failure of the inspections regime culminated in US Secretary of State Colin Powell's lengthy address to the United Nations on 5 February 2003, in which he presented the American government's proof that Iraq was indeed in 'material breach' of Resolution 1441. This included a slideshow of alleged links between al-Qaida and the Ba'ath party, satellite photos of what the Bush administration considered to be Iraqi mobile chemical and biological weapons facilities, and phone recordings of Iraqi officials attempting to hide evidence of illegal agents from the weapons inspectors.[40] Altogether, the US and British intelligence seemed wholly speculative and failed to produce the proverbial 'smoking gun'. Significant members of the UNSC, and most notably France, Germany and Russia, were highly sceptical of the attempt and suggested that the evidence provided did not build a case for war but rather a strengthened inspections regime. The French Foreign Minister, Dominique De Villepin, announced: 'With the choice between military intervention and an inspections regime that is inadequate for lack of co-operation on Iraq's part, we must choose to strengthen decisively the means of inspection.'[41]

With the second set of reports released by Blix and El-Baradei on 7 March 2003, the case put forth by the US and Britain was further weakened. Mohammed El-Baradei's report specifically addressed two of the major concerns voiced by Washington – the importation of high-strength magnets and high-strength aluminium tubes for development of nuclear weaponry. He asserted that, following examination of these specific issues, 'there is no indication that Iraq has attempted to import aluminium tubes for use in centrifuge enrichment. Moreover, even had Iraq pursued such a plan, it would have encountered practical difficulties in manufacturing centrifuges out of the aluminium tubes in question' and that, 'although we are still reviewing issues related to magnets and magnet production, there is no indication to date that Iraq imported magnets for use in a centrifuge enrichment programme'.[42] Additionally, Blix reported that Iraq's co-operation with inspectors had improved and in terms of longstanding open disarmament issues the Iraqi government could be seen to be handling the situation in a 'proactive' manner.[43]

The reports strengthened the position of Germany, Russia, France and China in their opposition to a war solution to the Iraq disarmament issue. The majority of the permanent Security Council members maintained that a military venture was unnecessary if the inspections were working. The US and the UK who, having submitted a draft resolution declaring that Iraq having 'failed to take the final opportunity afforded it in resolution 1441 (2002)', demanded immediate military intervention, found themselves at an international impasse, with both France and Russia suggesting that they would employ their vetoes to stop the resolution. In a last-ditch diplomatic effort to convince the anti-war group, the US and Britain, now joined by Spain, presented the UN with a new draft resolution on 7 March 2003, the same day that the new inspection reports came out. The draft resolution gave Iraq a deadline of 17 March to comply fully with UNSCR 1441. However, France, Russia and Germany maintained that there was no case for war and saw no need for a second resolution.

Nevertheless, the US government maintained throughout the entire debate over resolutions that it had the ultimate right to defend its interests against any threat, and that unilateral action, although not preferred, was legitimate. US Defense Secretary Donald Rumsfeld even indicated on 12 March 2003 that the US was willing to engage in unilateral action even without its ally Britain if Prime Minister Tony Blair's political crisis escalated.[44]

All the while the UN seemed unable to provide a clearly defined set of guidelines for the lifting of sanctions. Furthermore, what goals existed were continuously obfuscated by the US government's adherence to the idea that Iraq posed a direct threat to their national security. This doctrine has been consistently reiterated throughout the Bush administration's public addresses and in the National Security Strategy of September 2002 in reference to the threat posed by 'rogue states'. Interestingly, the idea that the US itself may be considered a 'rogue state' was even alluded to by Thomas Friedman in an editorial for the *New York Times*, but has never seriously been considered by the American mass media or the public at large.[45]

The 'moving goal posts' and the continuous obfuscation by the US government suggest that there may well be an ulterior agenda motivating US policy. One of the most dominant theories put forward by critics of the US government's foreign policy is that American concerns in the Middle East are motivated primarily by its need to ensure dominance over the region's vast oil reserves. During the First World War Henry Berenger, the French Commissioner General for Oil Products, stated, 'who has oil has empire'.[46] This observation, made at the turn of the last century and reinforced by history, has since been adopted as a basic assumption in debates regarding the national security of states. US foreign policy since the 1960s, when the United States became more dependent upon foreign sources of oil, seemed to recognise the necessity of this factor and was heavily influenced by efforts to limit any other world powers' influence over oil resources, while at the same time attempting to bolster its power in the Middle East.

With 'the world's second-largest proven oil reserves after Saudi Arabia',[47] Iraq has made itself potentially one of the greatest allies or enemies of any state wishing to exert economic, political and military global dominance. According to prominent Canadian business journalist Deborah Lamb: 'If Iraqi oil flows from western hands, it will counter-balance Saudi Arabia's huge power in OPEC.'[48] The ability of the United States government to undermine the power of OPEC would shift control over world oil prices directly back into the hands of the industry giants, the majority of whom maintain headquarters within the US and have significant ties to the second Bush administration. The presence of key figures from the petroleum industry within the Bush administration (which includes Vice President Dick Cheney, Condoleezza Rice, and George W. Bush himself) would seem to indicate that the prominence of oil concerns in American foreign policy has not diminished, but rather increased. Additionally, the strategic negotiations amongst UNSC members, in which the US essentially threatened dissenters with withdrawal of access to conquered Iraqi oil reserves, lends further credence to the notion that oil was at the forefront of the Bush administration's push for war.[49]

As many expected, the Anglo-American forces commenced the invasion of Iraq on 19 March 2003 without authorisation from the Security Council, and in defiance of the international community. George W. Bush declared the end of war on 1 May 2003, and from then onward the US had been trying to obtain a resolution to lift the sanctions and legitimise the invasion without even verifying the destruction of the WMD, the pretext which had caused the imposition of the sanctions in the first place.

According to the *Guardian* of 10 May 2003, the US and Britain laid out their blueprint for post-war Iraq in a draft resolution to the United Nations security council, naming themselves as 'occupying powers' and giving themselves control of the country's oil revenues. The French president, Jacques Chirac, intimated on 9 May 2003 that there was room for negotiation: 'I can confirm to you that France's will [is] to undertake discussions on the future of this country in an open and constructive spirit.'

Russia, which has considerable economic interests at stake, was less emollient. Russian ambassador, Sergei Lavrov, warned that he would pose 'lots of questions' to US ambassador, John Negroponte. In a further sign of the confusion over the US role in Iraq, Defense Secretary Donald Rumsfeld said on 9 May 2003 that a one-year timeline attached to the presence of US and British forces in Iraq was probably 'just a review period' in the overall post-war plan. 'Anyone who thinks they know how long it's going to take is fooling themselves', he said. 'It's not knowable.'

Outside the UN, the proposals provoked a vociferous response from the European Union's Commissioner for Aid and Development, Poul Nielsen, who accused America of seeking to seize control of Iraq's vast oil wealth. Mr Nielsen, a Dane who had just returned from a three-day fact-finding mission to Iraq, said the US was 'on its way to becoming a member of OPEC'. 'They will appropriate the oil', he told the Danish public service DR radio station. 'It is very difficult to see how this would make sense in any other way. The unwillingness to give the UN a genuine, legal, well-defined role, also in the broader context of rebuilding Iraq after Saddam…speaks a language that is quite clear.' Eager to avoid another bitter transatlantic diplomatic row, the commission headquarters issued a swift rebuttal, saying Mr Nielsen's views did not 'reflect the opinion of the commission as a whole'.

Iraqis also responded frostily to the plans, praising the lifting of sanctions but calling for the UN or an Iraqi interim government to take charge of the nation's oil wealth. 'It is a good initiative that should have taken place a long time ago', said Ragheb Naaman, 43, who works for Iraq's military industrialisation commission in charge of developing weapons. 'But we don't accept that the revenues be controlled by the United States and Britain.'

The blueprint, which was 'hard' and 'in your face', defines the US and Britain as 'occupying powers' – a legal designation apparently aimed at reassuring council members that America would adhere to its obligations under international law. A former State and Defense Department official told the *Wall Street Journal* that occupying power status meant the US could not give all reconstruction contracts to American companies and 'it can't choose the political leadership of the country'.[50]

Between the official end of the war and the issuance of UNSCR 1483 on 22 May 2003, which lifted the sanctions, the US made some 'cosmetic' concessions to reduce opposition to the initial draft, which Russia, France and Germany championed. In effect, the French and Russians decided that their self-interest outweighed any of the principles of international law that they had been invoking, and so collaborated with the resolution.

The resolution passed unanimously and gave the US and Britain a mandate to 'occupy' Iraq and rebuild it. The roles of other organisations, such as the UN, the IMF, the World Bank and the Arab Fund for Social and Economic Development, have been marginalised, leaving control of Iraqi oil sales as well as the Development Fund for Iraq to the Anglo-American occupying forces. On 23 May 2003, the *New York Times* reported that international experts, such as David Phillips, a senior fellow at New York's Council on Foreign Relations, saw in the implications of the Resolution an Anglo-American authority 'far beyond that envisioned for occupying powers in existing international treaties. Instead of power-sharing with the UN agencies, the coalition authority will be able to do as it sees fit.' The UN Secretary-General, Kofi Annan, would appoint a Special Representative, whose job description was limited to co-ordination, with no mention whatsoever of executive powers over the occupation regime. Kofi Annan has since appointed to this post Sergio Vieira de Mello, the United Nations High Commissioner for Human Rights, who would undertake the task for four months. It is reported that he is an unusually strong-minded individual by UN standards, which left observers curious as to why the US lobbied hard for him. (De Mello was killed in the 14 August 2003 terrorist attack on UN headquarters, Baghdad.)

The French had asked for a 'sunset' clause ending the resolution in a year. Instead, the US conceded that the Security Council would review it in twelve months but, typically, the US could veto any attempt to actually change it. The Russians were insisting that the UN weapons inspectors declare Iraq disarmed before sanctions were lifted, as previous resolutions had demanded. Nevertheless, they went along with a promise in 1483 to review the functions of UNMOVIC and the IAEA in a few months, and the fact that the latter were mentioned at all was in the category of a little victory – the only size of those on offer in fact – something to grasp at.

The 'sideshow' over the inspectors was highly revealing about the motivations and the powers involved. The British wanted to see the UN inspectors in, since they realised that the refusal to admit them would make nonsense of their entire legal case for the war. They were also aware that, in the unlikely case that any WMD would be found, no one would believe it unless the UN was involved. (Three months after the end of the war, the Anglo-American army of 160,000-strong men still had not found any substantial evidence of WMD.) The Pentagon, however, did not seem to forgive Hans Blix for his stance regarding the weapons in Iraq. If UNMOVIC had been allowed back into Iraq, it would not likely have been headed by a figure of Blix's personal stature.

Reality did prevail, however, in the prolonging of the time for disbanding the UN oil-for-food programme from the proposed four to six months. There is considerable doubt about whether the Coalition Provisional Authority (a self-proclaimed title for occupation) is in a position to feed the vast majority of Iraqis, which depends on the UN's organisation of the food supply. Even there they did not make allowances for the semi-autonomous arrangement which the

Kurdish provinces have had with the UN. The programme immediately handed over $1 billion to the Iraq Development Fund, whose spending is at the complete discretion of the occupiers, on condition, of course, that it is spent on the welfare of the people of Iraq. While that would be monitored by an allegedly independent board, which would include representatives from the UN, the IMF, the World Bank and the Arab Fund for Development, 1483 does not specify how many other representatives the Authority can appoint. In any case, the fund, and any subsequent Iraqi government, will still have to pay 5 per cent of oil revenues for reparations to Kuwaiti and other claimants from the last Gulf War. While the resolution calls for the 'bringing to justice' of all Iraqi leaders against whom crimes are alleged, it does not mention international involvement in any judicial process for any Iraqi leaders accused of crimes, which is somewhat ominous in view of reports about the preparation of a Death Row in Guantanamo Bay.[51]

With the invasion legitimised by Resolution 1483, the US placed its personnel in control of the Iraqi society. The *Washington Post* on 27 May 2003 reported that on the top of the power hierarchy (the Coalition Provisional Authority) is Paul Bremer, who reports to Donald Rumsfeld and his top aides, who in turn firmly control the reconstruction of Iraq. Walter B. Slocombe, a Democrat in the Clinton administration, is in charge of the defence ministry; Peter McPherson, a friend of Vice President Dick Cheney, is a financial co-ordinator; trade and industry is given to former US ambassadors Robin Ralph and Timothy Carney; David J. Dunford, a former ambassador to Oman, is in charge of foreign affairs; and Philip J. Carroll, a former executive of Shell Oil Company, is selected to take charge of Iraq's oil industry. The substance of Resolution 1483 has left Iraq in American power ad infinitum. Further, the legacy of the sanctions regime in Iraq has produced this unique scenario, which ravaged the entire Iraqi general population for over twelve years and paved the way for Anglo-American forces to become the de facto masters of this oil-rich and now socially, economically and politically impoverished country.

5

Social Deconstruction: Social Development under Siege

(co-authored with Shereen T. Ismael)

The concept of social development generally refers to a society's investment in the development of a system of programmes, benefits, and services that help people meet their basic health, education and welfare needs (food, clothing and shelter) in the context of a modernising economy. In what was called the Third World in the aftermath of the Second World War and the decolonisation it entailed, a major portion of the population was rural and met their basic needs at the level of subsistence economies. As an integral part of nation building and economic modernisation, post-colonial governments assumed primary responsibility for the development of social infra-structures of health, education and welfare. In the Arab world social development was a high priority of nation building in the political ideologies in the post-Second World War era. The development of a social infrastructure figured prominently in Nasserist, Arab Nationalist Movement and Arab Ba'ath Socialist programmes. With the collapse of the Soviet Union in 1991 and the hegemony of the neo-liberal model of development, public investment in social programmes dropped off the public agenda; and throughout the non-Western world, national social development programmes came about under financial siege by the International Monetary Fund's (IMF) structural adjustment agenda. However, the deconstruction of Iraq's social infra-structure came under military siege, first by the state and then by the international system. The purpose of this chapter is to relate the story of this siege, in both the first and second instances.

SOCIAL DEVELOPMENT BEFORE THE 1990–91 GULF WAR

Between 1927 and 1977, a span of just 50 years, Iraq's population increased four-fold, from just under 3 million to just over 12 million. Social, political and economic changes in this period were as dramatic as the population explosion. From a primarily rural, agricultural society with a quasi-feudal, quasi-tribal social structure in 1927, by 1977 Iraq had been transformed into a modern urban-based society.[1] In 1977, largely thanks to its immense oil wealth, Iraq's GNP per capita was $1594. This can be compared to a world average GNP per capita of $1838, with the developed world's $5853, and the developing world's $548.[2] Basic social indicators reflected the level of public investment in the social well-being of the population. Life expectancy had increased from less than 37 years in 1927 to 55 in 1977. By 1977, 76 per cent of the Iraqi population had access to safe drinking water (well above the world average of 53 per cent and the developing world average of only 39 per cent); 60 per cent of school-age children were enrolled in school (compared to the developing world average of 50 per cent and the developed world average of 69 per cent).[3]

Financed by the expansion of government oil revenue, from 6 million dinars in 1950 to 69 million dinars in 1956, Iraq's monarchy initiated rapid economic development in the 1950s.[4] As an indicator of the emphasis on economic development in this period, electricity consumption increased from 117 million units in 1950 to 506 million in 1956, almost a five-fold increase.[5] In contrast, social development indicators averaged less than a two-fold increase. The number of hospital beds, for example, increased from 5000 in 1950 to 9000 in 1956. Similarly, the number of primary school students enrolled in government schools increased from 170,000 in 1950 to 333,000 in 1956.[6] A military coup in 1958 brought republican rule to Iraq and unleashed ideological competition between nationalist and socialist groups for a new development model that emphasised ideas of social and political modernisation. As a spin-off from this competition, and a result of increasing oil revenues,[7] Iraq experienced an even more rapid social development in the 1960s and 1970s. Reflecting this, by 1976 the number of hospital beds in general hospitals alone increased to 14,493.[8] Similarly, the number of primary students enrolled in government schools in 1976 increased to 1,947,182.[9]

Within this period in Iraq, alongside the construction of a comprehensive social infrastructure in health, education and social welfare, the seeds of its deconstruction were at the same time being sown. The seeding and sowing metaphor is used here to summarise the complex and convoluted relationship between the international political economy of oil and the national political economy of Iraq.[10] There are two facets of this relationship that relate to the construction–deconstruction metaphor: first, the Ba'ath Party took power in Iraq in 1968;

second, Iraq's oil revenues increased phenomenally, from about $800 million in 1970 to $8.2 billion in 1975.

From its assumption of power in 1968, the Ba'ath government initiated an assault on the human rights of Iraqis. Islamists, communists, humanists, and intellectuals of all political persuasions were targeted and eliminated. In a sustained campaign of terror and purge, the Ba'athist regime attempted systematically to annihilate any suspected or potential opposition to its absolute authority. Following Saddam Hussein's assumption of the presidency in 1979, ethnocultural cleansing was added to the litany of violations in regime's human rights record. An ethnic cleansing campaign involving genocide against the Kurds of northern Iraq was initiated in the 1980s in the infamous Anfal Campaign in which 4000 Kurdish villages were destroyed and tens of thousands of Kurds disappeared. With the initiation of the Iraq–Iran war in 1980, the ethnic cleansing campaign expanded to include Iraqis of Iranian descent with the forced expulsion of over 300,000 Iraqi Shi'ites.[11] This was all undertaken in the full view of the international community. In fact, the major powers gave tacit approval and assistance to the Ba'ath's emergence as a 'republic of fear',[12] and to Iraq's development of weapons of mass destruction.[13] Thus, the process of deconstruction of the welfare state was rooted in the inherent chauvinism/militarism of the ruling Ba'ath's nationalist/socialist ideology, buttressed by the great wealth accruing to it from oil revenue which Saddam Hussein's regime lavished on the purchase of intelligence apparatus and military equipment (largely from the West), as shown in Table 5.1.

The table shows that Iraq's expenditure in 1977 on health represented only 6 per cent of its expenditure on the military – far lower than any other OPEC state; indeed, far lower than the average of 30 per cent in the developing world. In addition, its expenditure on education represented 40 per cent of its expenditure on the military, also lower than all the OPEC states except the United Arab Emirates (UAE); and lower than the average of 210 per cent for the developing world. In the 1980s, with the onset of the Iraq–Iran war, social expenditure declined even further. In 1987 expenditure on health represented less than 1 per cent of GNP while military expenditure represented 30 per cent; and education, only 4.6 per cent. By comparison, public expenditure on the military in the developing world in 1987, on average, represented 5.2 per cent of GNP.[14]

What this reflects is that social policy in Iraq under the Saddam Hussein regime played a marginal role at best in public policy. The marginality of this role is reflected in Table 5.2, which provides a comparison of Iraq's resource commitments under Saddam Hussein regime with the state's commitments in 1960.

Table 5.1   Public Expenditures Per Capita on Selected Areas, 1977, OPEC Members

| | MILITARY | EDUCATION | | HEALTH | |
	$	$	E/M*	$	H/M**
Iraq	138	56	40%	9	6%
Iran	222	118	531%	33	14%
Kuwait	659	520	79%	231	35%
Libya	125	350	280%	84	67%
Qatar	1257	2131	169%	235	19%
Saudi Arabia	939	561	597%	125	13%
UAE	822	288	35%	264	32%
Venezuela	43	142	330%	74	172%
Algeria	28	93	332%	12	42%
Gabon	29	138	475%	42	144%
Indonesia	8	259	324%	2	25%
Nigeria	28	23	82%	7	25%
Ecuador	26	37	142%	8	30%

*E/M: The ratio of education to military expenditures.
**H/M: The ratio of health to military expenditures.

Source: Sivard, R.L. (1980). *World Military and Social Expenditures*, Leesburg, VA: World Priorities.

Table 5.2   Iraq's Public Expenditures as a Percentage of GNP, 1960, 1987 and 1990

	1960	1987	1990
Health	1.0	0.8	0.8
Education	5.8	4.6	5.1
Military	7.3	30.2	27.4

Source: Sivard, R.L. (1991, 1993). *World Military and Social Expenditures*, Leesburg, VA: World Priorities.

Table 5.2 reflects the relative stability of social spending as a proportion of GNP over three decades and the dramatic increase of military spending under the Saddam Hussein regime. What it does not reflect is the substantial increase in GNP from about $15 billion in 1960 to $31 billion in 1987.[15] By comparison, average GNP in the developing world increased from $740 million in 1960 to $3 billion in 1990.[16] While education and health care programmes benefited from the substantial increases in spending that the oil wealth made possible, the increases were marginal in comparison with military spending which greatly increased in both relative and absolute terms. Writing on social policy in Iraq in the late 1970s, Jacqueline Ismael observed 'the subordination of social policy to political and economic objectives' and noted that this was 'consistent with Ba'ath ideology'.[17] In fact, they were subordinated to the militarisation of Iraq and occurred against a backdrop of flagrant human rights abuse and in the context of the support of the US and its Western allies. The militarisation of Iraq should, however, be appraised against the facts that Iraq was involved in military action, from the early 1960s to 1975, with the Kurdish revolt that had been financed by Iran, Israel and the US. Furthermore, Iran, much like the Ba'ath, was an ideology-driven state that not only posed an ideological Shi'ite threat to Iraq but was also the regional hegemony appointed by the US.

SOCIAL DE-DEVELOPMENT AFTER THE 1990–91 GULF WAR

With the implementation of sanctions in 1990 and the destruction of Iraq's social infrastructure wrought by the 1991 Gulf War, the situation of the people of Iraq deteriorated precipitously and continued to decline throughout the decade. During the 1991 war the US dropped the equivalent of seven Hiroshima atomic bombs on Iraq, in addition cluster bombs (flesh shredders), fireballs (equivalent in effect to napalm) and other massive explosives that caused perhaps 200,000 Iraqi casualties.[18] A 1999 United Nations report on Iraq warned, 'the humanitarian situation in Iraq will continue to be a dire one in the absence of a sustained revival of the Iraqi economy, which, in turn, cannot be achieved solely through remedial humanitarian efforts'.[19] The report, prepared for the president of the Security Council, detailed the complete devastation of Iraqi social infrastructure following the 1990–91 Gulf War and the imposition of Security Council economic sanctions. Before the war Iraq's social and economic indicators were generally above the regional and developing country averages, with Iraq's GDP in 1989 standing at 26.9 billion for a population of 18.3 million people. GDP growth had averaged 10.4 per cent from 1974 to 1980, and by 1988 GDP per capita totalled $1,756. The report stated that

Iraq's GDP may have fallen by nearly two-thirds in 1991, owing to an 85 per cent decline in oil production and the devastation of the industrial and services sectors of the economy. Per capita income fell from $2,279 US dollars in 1984 to $627 in 1991 and decreased to less than $700 in 1998. Other sources estimate a decrease in per capita GDP to be as low as $450 dollars in 1995.[20]

With oil accounting for 60 per cent of the country's GDP and 95 per cent of foreign currency earnings, Iraq's economy was heavily dependent on the external sector and sensitive to oil price fluctuations. In the early 1980s Iraq was producing about 3.5 million barrels per day (bpd), but that amount had declined to 2.8 million by 1989. The report found that, although Iraq was exporting more oil than ever since the initiation of the 1996 'oil-for-food' programme, 'revenue remains insufficient due to a negative correlation linking low oil prices, delays in obtaining spare parts for the oil industry and general obsolescence of oil infrastructure'.[21] In addition, Iraq's production infrastructure continued to decline and, owing to sanctions, Iraq was unable to repair lost production facilities to allow increased production. Consequently, Iraq's production capacity was unable to meet the amount of money demanded by the 'oil-for-food' programme in order to meet the needs of the Iraqi population, as well as its international obligations. A panel of oil industry experts, convened by the Secretary-General, found that it would take approximately '$1.2 billion US to ensure a gradual and sustainable increase in the production of crude oil in Iraq so as to allow for production levels to reach 3,000,000 barrels per day; the full rehabilitation of Iraq's oil industry', they argued, 'would require several billion dollars' of investment.[22]

In spite of reconstruction efforts by the Iraqi government and international NGOs following the 1990–91 Gulf War and the oil-for-food humanitarian programme, begun in 1996, the economic and social conditions of Iraq's population continued to deteriorate. As summarised in the next section, numerous surveys and reports conducted by the government of Iraq and UN agencies since the 1990–91 Gulf War detailed the continuing deterioration in specific areas – such as health, nutrition and child and maternal mortality. The 1999–2000 Report of the UNDP Iraq Country Office summarised the situation accordingly:

Iraq's economy has been in crisis since the imposition of economic sanctions in 1990. Despite the Oil-for-Food programme, the country continued its decline into poverty, particularly in the south. Food supplies continue to be inadequate in the centre and south of the country; the prevalence of general malnutrition in the centre and south has hardly changed. Although the rates have stabilised, this happened at 'an unacceptably high level'. In the area of child and maternal health, in August 1999, UNICEF and the Government of Iraq released the results of the first survey on child mortality in Iraq since 1991. The survey showed that under-five child mortality had more than doubled from 56 deaths per 1000 live births in 1984 to 131 deaths in the period 1994–1999. At least 50 per cent of the labour force is unemployed or underemployed; a shortage of basic goods, compounded by a drought, has resulted in high prices and an estimated inflation rate of 135 per cent and 120 per cent in 1999 and 2000 respectively...Most of the country's civil infrastructure remains in serious disrepair. GDP per capita dropped to an estimated US $715 [from US $3508 before the Gulf War], which is a figure comparable with such countries as Madagascar and Rwanda.[23]

Food production and availability were major factors in exacerbating the problem of increasing morbidity and mortality in Iraq under the sanctions regime. Prior to 1990 domestic food production represented only one-third of total consumption for most essential food items, with the balance covered by imports. Thanks to its oil-endowed prosperity and focus on industrial development, agricultural development was virtually ignored, and increasing consumption was satisfied through increasing imports. Thus, although domestic development in agricultural production did not advance, food consumption increased. The implementation of the embargo drastically curtailed the importation of food, resulting in serious food shortages. The UN found that dietary energy supply had fallen from 3120 to 1093 kilocalories per capita/per day by 1994–95, with women and children singled out as the most vulnerable members of Iraqi society. Against a UN target of 2463 kilocalories and 63.6 grams of protein per person per day, the nutritional value of the distributed food basket did not exceed 1993 kilocalories and 43 grams of protein. Prior to the start of the oil-for-food programme, the government of Iraq had been distributing 1300 kilocalories per day.[24]

The prevalence of malnutrition in Iraqi children under five almost doubled from 1991 to 1996 (from 12 per cent to 23 per cent). Acute malnutrition in the centre and south regions rose from 3 per cent to 11 per cent for the same age bracket. Indeed, the World Food Programme (WFP) indicated that, by July 1995, average shop prices of essential commodities stood at 850 times the July 1990 level. While the humanitarian programme in Iraq successfully staved off starvation, the level of malnutrition within Iraq remained high and contributed directly to the morbidity and mortality rates.[25] In March 2000 Kofi Annan acknowledged in his report that the prices of the necessary food items were beyond the reach of most Iraqis. As early as January 2000 the value of food applications under the food handling and food processing sub-sector, which the US and Britain placed on hold, was $185.5 million. In the same year egg production fell to less than 10 per cent of the target, which meant about ten eggs per person in a year in 15 governorates in southern and central Iraq while the US and Britain blocked 90 agricultural contracts the value of which was worth $175.3 million. In November 2000 the UN Secretary-General announced that the food and health situation had become very serious. Of estimated malnourished children 24 per cent were under five years of age. The number of underweight children increased from 9.5 per cent to 13.4 per cent; and acute malnutrition jumped from 1.8 per cent to 4.1 per cent. Ninety per cent of raw sewage was being pumped into the rivers and streams and, because there was not enough electric power to operate water plants, Iraqis were forced to drink contaminated water from the rivers with all attendant serious health risks. Worse still, none of the public health centres or 68 community childcare units had any vehicles to distribute nutrition supplies, let alone ambulances whose contract Washington had blocked, as it had for fire engines, forklift trucks and agricultural and sanitation equipment.[26] Together with malnutrition, the devastation of the national infrastructure of health care, sanitation and water purification resulted in estimated Iraqi deaths after the imposition of sanctions exceeding 2 million people over and above the number of predicted deaths before the imposition of the sanctions.[27]

Thus, it is in the destruction of the infrastructure in areas of education and health care provision, water purification and sanitation – essential services that the Iraqi government was largely successful in providing prior to 1990 – on which UN reports place much of the blame for the humanitarian crisis. From its inception in 1996 the oil-for-food programme provisionally increased in size and complexity.

By 2000 relief goods no longer made up the major portion of the programme's distribution effort as items directly related to infrastructure rehabilitation were required to stave off humanitarian disaster. The devastation of the national electrical grid during the 1991 Gulf War continued to hamper development efforts in all areas. By August 2000 much of the central and southern area was left without electricity for 18 hours a day. In the Kurdish north, Sulaimaniyah received no more than two hours of power per day, while Erbil had no central grid power at all.[28] Without electrical power, hospitals were forced to abandon modern technology, medicines had to be destroyed through lack of refrigeration, water purification plants could not prevent untreated water from entering the water supply, and industrial plants were forced to abandon economic production. In an effort to ameliorate the shortage the government of Iraq, the UNDP and the United Nations Department of Economic and Social Affairs (UNDESA) established a joint venture focusing on the electricity sector. In the 15 governates of central and southern Iraq it aided in the implementation of the government's electricity rehabilitation programme.[29] Although the amount allocated in the oil-for-food programme for the rehabilitation of the national electrical grid increased, becoming second only to the allocations for food, the gap between supply and demand could not be reduced.[30]

In spite of their obvious importance in any efforts to rebuild Iraqi society and improve the social infrastructure of the country, electrical goods needed to repair and rebuild the national infrastructure had the highest value of holds imposed by the 661 Security Council Committee. The number of holds in this sector reached US$500 million by the end of June 2001. In denying the requested purchases, the sanctions committee undermined any positive lasting effects of the oil-for-food programme. Daily power cuts have become common, and the continued decline of power stations has reduced the safety of the system itself.[31]

Infant and child mortality rates are widely accepted as the most sensitive indicators of poverty, inequality and inequity. Comparative infant and child mortality rates reflect varying standards of living and social well-being. A direct correlation between post-neonatal and child mortality and standards of living has been well established in the literature. While ostensibly health statistics, these mortality rates have their roots in socio-economic and political developments and provide direct indicators of the standard of living of a population at any given point in time. The main source of data for a discussion of mortality in Iraq should be UNICEF's 1999 Child and Maternal Mortality Survey.[32] It reported that Iraq's infant mortality rate (deaths under one year of age) had climbed from 47 deaths per 1000 live births in the period 1984–89 to 108 deaths per 1000 live births in the period 1994–99. Similarly, the child mortality rate (deaths under five years of age) had increased from 56 in 1984–89 to 131 in the period 1994–2000. The report concluded that

if the substantial reduction in child mortality throughout Iraq during the 1980s had continued through the 1990s, there would have been half a million fewer deaths of children under five in the country as a whole during the eight year period 1991 to 1998.

This is the only independent, comprehensive study carried out, and supersedes previous estimates. It is important to note that, while the UNICEF report does not make any conclusions about causality, there was a section of the survey that included records of the 'cause of death' of individual samples, although this part of the study has not been released. The dramatic increase in infant and child mortality rates in Iraq since the imposition of sanctions does indicate a direct causal link with socio-economic and political conditions in Iraq in which sanctions played a significant part. A UN Food and Agriculture Organisation (FAO) report concluded that the continued high incidence of malnutrition 'supports UN findings that infant and child mortality have more than doubled since the end of the 1980s'.[33] Also, in the words of the 1999 humanitarian panel report:

Even if not all suffering in Iraq can be imputed to external factors, especially sanctions, the Iraqi people would not be undergoing such deprivations in the absence of the prolonged measures imposed by the Security Council and the effects of war.[34]

In June 2001 9000 Iraqis, of whom 6000 were children under five years, died as a result of the sanctions regime and the Anglo-American holds on contracts for humanitarian needs. In July 2001 black fever broke out in the south and the centre of Iraq because the supply of medical provisions was delayed. In September 2001, 10,000 Iraqis died from causes relating to the sanctions, as Table 5.3 shows.[35]

Table 5.3   Causes of Death

Cause of Death	September 1989	September 2001
Children under 5 years		
Diarrhoea	123	2932
Pneumonia	96	1594
Malnutrition	67	2354
Adults over 50 years		
Heart disease	106	638
Diabetes	73	557
Cancer	260	1701

ASSESSMENTS OF THE HUMANITARIAN IMPACT OF SANCTIONS ON IRAQ

Operation Desert Storm completely destroyed Iraq's social infrastructure but left intact the political infrastructure of Saddam Hussein's dictatorship. The United Nations and international NGOs since the end of the war have monitored the impact of sanctions on the civilian population of Iraq. The devastation of Iraqi society in 1991, made worse as a result of sanctions, was made plain to the international community, which was fully apprised of the situation by UN member agencies and international NGOs. Table 5.4 identifies a selection of the major reports released between the ceasefire in April 1991 and August 2002 describing the humanitarian situation in Iraq. Of the almost 50 Security Council resolutions adopted on Iraq since its fateful invasion of Kuwait in August 1990, 25 were adopted in response to the complex humanitarian disaster that was unfolding in Iraq as a direct consequence of the war and sanctions.[36] At best these efforts are only token responses that have given the appearance of responding, but actually they have contributed only marginally to disaster relief. They did, however, serve to legitimate the continued maintenance of the sanctions regime, even in the face of the deepening humanitarian disaster. In Iraq, as James Orbinski, vice president of Médecins Sans Frontières International Canada observed, speaking about other complex humanitarian disasters, the Security Council used humanitarianism 'as a substitute for legally defined political and military obligations under international law'.[37] The duplicity of the so-called humanitarian sanctions was brought to the fore when Hans von Sponek, Humanitarian Co-ordinator for Iraq, questioned the unwillingness of the Security Council to create a mandate – prior to the call for such an assessment in UNSCR 1302

Table 5.4 Selected Reports on the Impact of Sanctions on Iraq, April 1991 to June 2002

Date	Issuing Agency	Title	Author (and publication information)
20 March 1991	United Nations	Report to the Secretary-General on Humanitarian Needs in Iraq in the Immediate Post-Crisis Environment	Martti Ahtisaari (Document S/22366)
February 1991	WHO/UNICEF	Joint Report: A Visit to Iraq, 16–21 February	Harvard Study Team
May 1991	Harvard School of Public Health	Public Health in Iraq After the Gulf War	
15 July 1991	United Nations	Report to the Secretary-General on Humanitarian Needs in Iraq	Sadruddin Aga Khan (Document S/22799)
1991	London School of Economics	Hunger and Poverty in Iraq, 1991	Jean Dreze and Haris Gazdar (subsequently published in *World Development*, Vol. 20, No. 7, 1992)
21 September 1992	*New England Journal of Medicine*, Vol. 327, No. 13.	The Effects of the Gulf War on Infant and Child Mortality in Iraq	Ascherio et al.
April 1993	UNICEF	Iraq: Children, War and Sanctions	
March 1996	World Health Organisation	The Health Conditions of the Population in Iraq since the Gulf Crisis	Eric Hoskins (photocopy) WHO/EHA/96.1
October 1997	Food and Agricultural Organisation and World Food Programme	FAO/WFP Special Report of Food Supply and Nutrition Assessment Mission to Iraq	www.fao.org/giews/english/fs/fs9710/pays/irq9710e.htm
November 1997	UNICEF	Nutrition Status Survey	Gopher://gopher.unicef.org:70/00/.cefdata/.prgva97/
August 1999	UNICEF	1999 Iraq Child and Maternal Mortality Surveys	www.unicef.org/reseval/pdfs/irqncont.pdf
December 1999	Human Rights Watch	World Report 2000, Iraq	www.hrw.org/wr2k/Mena-05.htm
September 2000	FAO	Assessment of the Food and Nutrition Situation: Iraq	www.fao.org/WAICENT/FAOINFO/ECONOMIC/ESN/Iraq.pdf
September 2000	FAO	Child Malnutrition in Iraq 'Unacceptably High' as Drought, Lack of Investment Aggravate Food and Nutrition Situation.	www.reliefweb.int/library/documents/iraqnutrition.pdf
October 2001	WHO	Health Situation in Iraq – WHO Roles and Responsibilities	www.unicef.org/iraq/library/join-2/health/helth.pdf

on 8 June 2000 – to authorise a 'comprehensive report and analysis of the humanitarian situation in Iraq'. Von Sponek recalled that:

> every attempt that I made with the United Nations in New York to get an agreement to prepare an assessment of the human condition in Iraq was blocked. All I was allowed to do was to carry out an assessment of the oil-for-food programme. There was a bigger picture that needed to be portrayed...and I was not allowed to do that. It was blocked at different levels...including the Sanctions Committee.[38]

In November 2001, Denis Halliday and Hans von Sponek, who both resigned their UN humanitarian commissions in protest of the sanctions, said in a joint article that the West was holding the Iraqi people hostage to ever-shifting demands, and that the governments of the US and the UK were blocking $4 billion of humanitarian needs, which was the greatest constraint on the humanitarian programme.[39]

Nevertheless, international aid agencies, NGOs, member organisations of the United Nations and concerned members of international civil society have compiled a compelling, well-documented library of reports and evidence of the disastrous experience of the people of Iraq since the imposition of sanctions on Iraq. As Tom Nagy (Professor at George Washington University) documented, that sanctions would exacerbate the predictable humanitarian disaster brought about by the deliberate targeting of Iraqi infrastructure by coalition forces during the Gulf War was well understood by those who were responsible both for the attacks in 1991 and also the sanctions regime over the ensuing twelve years (see Ismael and Haddad 2000). The aggressive position taken by the Security Council, especially the representatives of the governments of the United States and the United Kingdom, in the imposition and maintenance of the sanctions regime ignored the overwhelmingly catastrophic effects they inflicted on the civilian population of Iraq. UN agency reports, the chief public source of reliable information on Iraq's humanitarian situation, make up the bulk of this examination. Foremost among these are the reports filed every 90 days by the UN Secretary-General at the mid- and end-points of each phase of the oil-for-food programme.

With the cessation of hostilities in Iraq, the Secretary-General of the United Nations, Javier Perez de Cuellar, responded to growing international concern about an anticipated humanitarian crisis by dispatching Finnish diplomat, Martti Ahtisaari, to Iraq in March

1991.[40] The Ahtisaari report (1991) returned with an emotive portrayal of the desperate situation then existing in the country:

> nothing that we had seen or read had quite prepared us for the particular form of devastation that has now befallen the country. The recent conflict has wrought near-apocalyptic results upon the economic infrastructure of what had been, until January 1991, a rather highly urbanised and mechanised society. Now, most means of modern life support have been destroyed or rendered tenuous. Iraq has, for some time to come, been relegated to a pre-industrial age, but with all the disabilities of post-industrial dependency on an intensive use of energy and technology....It will be difficult, if not impossible, to remedy these immediate humanitarian needs without dealing with the underlying need for energy, on an equally urgent basis.[41]

Ahtisaari was the first UN official to indicate the disastrous human consequences of the strategic bombardment of a modern society.[42] Worse, Iraq, as a country largely dependent upon imported technology, could not maintain or restore its own infrastructure from indigenous stores of natural or human resources, or industrial capabilities. In April and May 1991 an independent organisation of ten public health specialists, physicians and lawyers, travelled to Iraq to 'report on the effect of the Gulf crisis on the health and health care of Iraqi civilians'. Dubbed the Harvard Study Team, they published a portion of their findings in the *New England Journal of Medicine*.[43] The public exposure of their work brought to the world's attention the unfolding humanitarian crisis then underway in Iraq. Control of, and denial of access to, the international media by coalition forces during the Gulf conflict had allowed the level of destruction and its impact on the civilian population to go largely unreported during the euphoria and triumphalism following the cessation of hostilities. The Harvard Study Team's investigation, however, found that power generation had been devastated by coalition air attacks. Thirteen of Iraq's 20 power stations had been damaged or destroyed during the first days of allied bombing, and through the cannibalisation of spare parts from other plants the Iraqi government had managed to return generation capabilities to only a quarter of pre-war capacity in the months following the ceasefire. Running at maximum they could produce 40 per cent of pre-war output, but with frequent interruptions in service, and no husbanding of spare parts for future breakdowns. The loss of electrical power generation had a direct impact on Iraq's water purification and distribution infrastructure, including hospitals, and hampered relief operations, since food stores and medicines could no longer be refrigerated in sufficient quantities. The team also found that the loss of electricity had caused Baghdad's two sewage treatment plants to stop working, spilling raw sewage into the streets of Baghdad, as well as into the Tigris river. This led to epidemics of water-borne diseases like cholera, typhoid and gastro-enteritis. However, the exact scale of the problem went unrecorded, as the equipment required to make clinical diagnoses was often lacking. The Harvard report noted that most of the hospitals visited lacked even basic medical supplies such as vaccines, antibiotics, anaesthetics and syringes. These supplies had already been exhausted over the course of the previous months. Severe forms of malnutrition, and a lack of vaccines resulting from the embargo and a shortage of refrigeration led to a resurgence of preventable childhood diseases such as measles, polio, marasmus and kwashiorkor – conditions unseen for more than a generation by Iraqi physicians.

Concern raised by these reports saw de Cuellar dispatch a larger UN delegation, led by Sadruddin Aga Khan in July 1991, to conduct a further needs assessment. While the Ahtisaari delegation had been limited to central Iraq owing to the internal unrest and general destruction, the Aga Khan's delegation visited 16 of Iraq's 18 governorates. The Aga Khan's report[44] made very clear that Iraq's population was in considerable need, and called on the Security Council to respond. The Security Council did so by passing UNSCRs 706 and 712. Resolution 706 agreed with the Aga Khan's recommendation that oil sales be used to fund Iraqi humanitarian imports, and Resolution 712 fixed a limit on oil sales. The level established in the resolution limited the amount to considerably less than what was recommended, even for the 'greatly reduced services' synopsis in the Aga Khan's report, and that advocated by the Secretary-General during the discussions surrounding the drafting of the resolution. Additionally, in spite of the dire humanitarian condition then clearly becoming evident in Iraq, 30 per cent of this already reduced figure was to be deducted for a compensation fund. The government of Iraq protested, calling for a higher ceiling of exports to raise the funds necessary to pay for the humanitarian and recovery effort. This proved fruitless and Iraq decided not to accept the resolutions. Without Iraqi support, the UN humanitarian relief operation was stifled, and without a higher level of exports the Iraqi government felt that the relief effort was not minimally sufficient to meet the basic minimum needs of the population.

In August 1991 a larger group of independent researchers, supported by UNICEF, the US MacArthur Foundation, the John Merck Foundation and Oxfam-UK, visited Iraq. Dubbed the International Study Team, it visited Iraq's 30 largest cities in all 18 governorates. It was composed of 87 researchers in agriculture, child psychology, economics, electrical engineering, environmental science, medicine, public health, and sociology.[45] The team's findings again evidenced dramatic increases in disease, and a deepening crisis resulting from the destruction of the previously existing social infrastructure.

Though the International Study Team found that electricity generation had returned to two-thirds of its pre-war levels, it was believed that this was temporary, as the spare parts and other implements needed to achieve this level were now depleted. In addition, only one of the 18 water plants inspected by the team was working at full capacity. The team found that this was the result not so much of the bombing and subsequent civil uprisings, but of a lack of spare parts and chlorine. This was the first publicly reported link between the impact of ongoing sanctions and the declining public health situation in Iraq. Raw sewage flowed through streets and into water supplies, contaminating an estimated half of the public drinking water supply. Increasing outbreaks of hepatitis, meningitis, typhoid, cholera and gastroenteritis were observed, approaching epidemic proportions in many regions. The stores of off-the-shelf medicines had been depleted, resulting in older patients without access to anti-angina medication facing an increased risk of heart attack, diabetics lacking insulin, and in a dramatic increase in cancers such as treatable leukaemia which went untreated due to the embargo on anti-cancer drugs.

However, the most significant problem in the 29 hospitals and 17 community health centres visited was child and infant mortality. In an effort to gauge the situation, the International Study Team interviewed all women between 15 and 49 years old in 9034 randomly selected households throughout Iraq. Fewer than 50 women declined to participate in the interviews, producing a sample of households representing 16,076 children. Moreover, 2902 children under five were randomly drawn from this household sample and measured. The team found 25 per cent were stunted, 3.6 per cent wasted, and 14 per cent underweight. On the basis of this, they inferred that

900,000 children under five were malnourished and 118,000 at increased risk of death. Child mortality rates were also calculated based on the interviews with the mothers. The International Study Team estimated that an additional 47,000 children under five had died in the year since sanctions were imposed.

One of the strongest impacts made on the public recognition of the humanitarian impact of sanctions resulted from the report of a UN Food and Agriculture Organisation (FAO) team that visited Iraq from July to September 1995.[46] Its goal was to assess 'the nutritional status of the population...and...the crop and food availability situation which prevails after the imposition of the embargo in 1990'. The FAO report found that the agricultural sector had been given high priority by the government, to ensure food security, but that in spite of Iraqi efforts, output had declined. The report also investigated the public health infrastructure, and conducted a nutrition and mortality survey in Baghdad with the Nutrition Research Institute of the Iraqi Ministry of Health. The mortality survey, which interviewed 768 mothers, found that mortality rate for children under five years of age had increased nearly five-fold since 1990.

These results were then published in the British medical journal, the *Lancet*, where its authors, Zaidi and Smith-Fawzi, extrapolated some further figures to demonstrate the FAO's mortality findings.[47] Zaidi and Smith-Fawzi converted the mortality rates to deaths, and extrapolated the Baghdad figures to the rest of Iraq, estimating that 'since August 1990, 567,000 children [under the age of five] in Iraq have died as a consequence' of sanctions. Their findings prompted an infamous response from the US government. On 12 May 1996 CBS News reporter Lesley Stahl, on one of the most prestigious news programmes in the United States, *60 Minutes*, asked Madeleine Albright, then US ambassador to the UN, about the claims of child deaths. Stahl asked, 'We have heard that half a million children have died. I mean, that's more children than died in Hiroshima. Is the price worth it?' Albright responded, 'I think this is a very hard choice, but the price...we think the price is worth it.' The Albright comment raised widespread alarm internationally, and drew increased levels of media and activist attention to the plight of Iraqis in the face of the ongoing embargo. Although Albright's answer sounded brutal, it honestly conveyed a subtle message, which few observers interpreted as telling the world that in American foreign policy there was nothing too valuable to be expendable in the march to American control of the oil as an instrument for world hegemony. However, the increased pressure on the Security Council was one of many factors that led to the diplomatic manoeuvres that finally saw the implementation of the oil-for-food programme at the end of 1996.

A report prepared by the World Health Organisation (WHO) in March 1996, but not released until 27 April 1998, documented the mounting scale of the crisis in terms of quantum leaps in infant and child mortality, in the incidence of infectious disease, and in malnutrition.[48] The report's conclusions were unequivocal about the role of the Security Council's sanctions in Iraq's complex humanitarian disaster and are quoted here in their entirety to document how the UN's role in had effect become a process of internationally mediated genocide:

> In an attempt to assess the impact of the United Nations sanctions on the quality of life of the population in Iraq, the following facts should serve as constant reminders in drawing overall conclusions regarding the humanitarian aspects of the sanctions:
>
> 1. The six-week war in 1991 resulted in the large-scale destruction of military and civilian infrastructures alike. In general, civilian populations were subsequently more affected by the consequences of much destruction than the military populations, the latter of whom have tended to be more protected against the daily hardships ensuing since enforcement of the sanctions.
> 2. The sanctions imposed on Iraq and related circumstances have prevented the country from repairing all of its damaged or destroyed infrastructure, and whenever attempts have been made, these have been incomplete. This applies to electricity generating and water purification plants, sewage treatment facilities and communication and transportation networks. This has affected the quality of life of countless Iraqi citizens, especially those belonging to the mid and lower economic levels of the country's total population of 20 million, who do not have alternatives or options to overcome the effects of these ravages.
> 3. Iraq is an oil-rich country, which prior to the 1991 war was almost totally dependent on the import of two vital requirements for a healthy life – food and medicine. More than 70 per cent of food requirements of Iraq, prior to 1991, were imported and the bulk consisted of staple cereals, legumes,

cooking oils, sugar and tea, which are the major items in the daily diet of the average Iraqi citizen. *Financial constraints* as a result of the sanctions have prevented the necessary import of food and medicine.

4. Other items of the daily diet, especially animal products such as dairy products, chicken and beef, in which the country was almost self-sufficient, are now being sold on the open market at 'sky-rocketing' prices, which only those at the highest income level can afford. The average Iraqi citizen depends on rationed foods, which supply one-third of the daily minimum caloric needs. Iraq has a disciplined rationing system, which, so far, has prevented a major famine. Animal products on the free market, due to their high prices, are not available to infants and children in most families, which is a source of protein they urgently need.

5. The vast majority of the country's population has been on a semi-starvation diet for years. This tragic situation has tremendous implications on the health status of the population and on their quality of life, not only for the present generation, but for the future generation as well.

6. The reduction in the import of medicines, owing to a *lack of financial resources*, as well as a lack of minimum health care facilities, insecticides, pharmaceutical and other related equipment and appliances, have crippled the health care services, which in pre-war years were of a high quality. Assessment reports rightly remarked that the quality of health care in Iraq, due to the six-week 1991 war and the subsequent sanctions imposed on the country, has been literally put back by at least 50 years. Diseases such as malaria, typhoid and cholera, which were once almost under control, have rebounded since 1991 at epidemic levels, with the health sector as a helpless witness.

7. Very rarely has the impact of sanctions on millions of people been documented. Severe economic hardship, a semi-starvation diet, high levels of disease, scarcity of essential drugs and, above all, the psycho-social trauma and anguish of a bleak future, have led to numerous families being broken up leading to distortions in social norms.

8. The impact of this unfortunate situation on the infant and child population in particular in Iraq needs special attention. It is not only the data on morbidity and mortality that tell the story, but equally important are the crippling effects of many of these

morbidities which are often forgotten. The psychological trauma of the six-week 1991 war and the terrible hardships enduring with the sanctions since then, can be expected to leave indelible marks on the mental health and behavioural patterns of these children when they grow to adulthood. This tragic aspect of the impact of the war and conditions surrounding the sanctions is rarely articulated, but the world community should seriously consider the implications of an entire generation of children growing up with such traumatised mental handicaps, if of course, they survive at all.

The disastrous effects outlined by the WHO report were driven home in September 1998 with the resignation of the oil-for-food director Denis Halliday. A 34-year veteran of the United Nations, Halliday resigned from his post as UN Humanitarian Co-ordinator for Iraq to protest the continuation of economic sanctions against the country, calling the sanctions 'genocidal'. Following his appointment in August 1997, Halliday became an outspoken critic of sanctions, and after witnessing little change in the widespread malnutrition, mortality and social decay that afflicts the country, he stepped down in spite of the Security Council's doubling the size of the oil-for-food programme in February 1997. In a paper to the Madrid Conference, in January 1999, Halliday noted:

the de facto genocidal impact of the economic sanctions on the Iraqi people violates the legal instruments that are fundamental to the credible continuation of the United Nations. The UN needs the protection of an oversight of devices in regard to the output of the dangerously out-of-control Security Council. In the meantime, men and women of conscience, with moral posture and integrity, will continue to demand the termination of crimes against humanity, indeed genocide, in respect of Iraq.[49]

In February 1999, two further resignations – that of Halliday's successor, Hans von Sponek, and Jutta Burghardt, head of the UN World Food Programme (WFP) in Baghdad since January 1999 – further undermined the legitimacy of the oil-for-food programme. Hans von Sponek said after his resignation: 'How long should the civilian population of Iraq be exposed to such punishment for something they have never done?' In the same vein, Jutta Burghardt said that she could not tolerate what was being done to the Iraqi people. Such testimonies of UN officials gave credibility and support to observers claiming that the US and Britain were involved in a criminal conspiracy to commit protracted extermination of the civilian population of Iraq.[50]

In April 1998, UNICEF undertook its first effort to provide comprehensive data on the humanitarian situation in Iraq.[51] The 1998 report examined a broad range of factors influencing the humanitarian situation and provided a survey of the existing literature on Iraq's socio-economic development. The principle obstacle to tackling the humanitarian crisis for UN agencies remained the restriction on oil sales, which then stood at $2 billion per 180-day phase. This amount was well below the amount called for by UN agencies to complete even the most limited level of relief and it was not all devoted to those most in need. In the end only 53 per cent were devoted to humanitarian needs in South and Central Iraq, with the rest distributed to the Compensation Fund (30 per cent) and northern Iraq (17 per cent). In its examination of the results of oil-for-food's first year in Iraq, the UNICEF report highlighted the situation of children in Iraq. It noted that 'malnutrition was not a public health problem in Iraq prior to the embargo', but that it became an apparent concern in 1991, and had increased greatly since that time. In examining food availability, the logical impediment to children receiving a sufficient diet, the report commented on the continued decline in cereal production in Iraq since 1990. Shortages continued in spite of the concentration of government resources in efforts to make Iraq self-sufficient in grain, in order to possibly ameliorate the consequences of the embargo. According to *Pravda* on 7 March 2003, the consistent decline in the Iraqi agricultural output was eventually attributed to the agro-pests that the US has released in Iraq. In July of 1999, even before Pravda's news release, Iraq was complaining to the UN about the US dropping eggs of agro-pests as part of a biological attack against Iraqi agriculture.[52]

Following the December 1998 bombing of Iraq by the US and the UK (Operation Desert Fox), tensions among the members of the Security Council resulted in an active debate within that body which resulted in the establishment of three panels to investigate various aspects of the dispute with Iraq: disarmament and monitoring, humanitarian issues, and Kuwaiti claims (people and property). UN agencies then operating in Iraq had been limited to studying only their own individual efforts. The second panel was seen as 'a unique and invaluable opportunity to assess the overall humanitarian situation of the Iraqi people'. This opportunity resulted in a collection of reports that were then presented to the humanitarian issues panel.[53] The information presented by the UN agencies led to the completion of the panel report. It answered the concerns over the data reliability finding that: 'data made available to the panel were considered generally reliable, as they were undersigned either by UN agencies or other credible sources.' Important, in lieu of the political nature of the situation, the report stated:

> The gravity of the humanitarian situation of the Iraqi people is indisputable and cannot be overstated. Irrespective of alleged attempts by the Iraqi authorities to exaggerate the significance of certain facts for political propaganda purposes, the data from different sources, as well as qualitative assessments of bona fide observers and sheer common sense analysis of economic variables, converge and corroborate this evaluation.[54]

The report attempted to provide historical perspective, and contrasted Iraq's social indicators prior to the Second Gulf War with those afterwards. In so doing, it ventured to isolate the impact of sanctions, and other external factors, and their role in the humanitarian crisis in Iraq. The panel report noted that Iraq had 'experienced a shift from relative affluence to massive poverty', and now had infant mortality rates that were among the highest in the world.

UNICEF's 1999 survey of child mortality in Iraq was the first independent national study on this issue since 1991.[55] This report was paramount in importance as UNICEF surveyed women in a total of 40,000 randomly selected households across Iraq, with 24,000 households in south/central Iraq and 16,000 in Iraqi Kurdistan. In south/central Iraq, it was found that in children under five years of age, child mortality had more than doubled since the imposition of sanctions. It was the section of the preliminary report entitled, 'Iraq – under-five mortality' which maintained that 'if the substantial reduction in under-five mortality during the 1980s had continued through the 1990s, there would have been half a million fewer deaths of children under-five in the country as a whole during the eight-year period 1991 to 1998'.

The response from the US and British governments to the UNICEF findings consisted of denials or disagreement with UNICEF's estimate of an additional half-million child deaths. Both governments, however, used the report's findings that conditions were markedly better in

Iraqi Kurdistan as further evidence of the Ba'ath regime's malfeasance. Such claims were unwarranted and in fact were addressed directly by a UNICEF briefing document entitled 'Questions and Answers for the Iraq Child Mortality Surveys', which explained the discrepancy between the south/centre of Iraq and the north accordingly:

> The difference in the current rate cannot be attributed to the differing ways the Oil-for-Food Programme is implemented in the two parts of Iraq. The Oil-for-Food Programme is two and a half years old. Therefore it is too soon to measure any significant impact of the Oil-for-Food Programme on child mortality over the five-year period of 1994–1999 as is reported in these surveys. We need to look at longer-term trends and factors including the fact that since 1991 the north has received far more support per capita from the international community than the south and centre of Iraq. Another factor may be that the sanctions themselves have not been able to be so rigorously enforced in the north as the border is more 'porous' than in the south and centre of Iraq.[56]

In addition, unlike previous studies, UNICEF's methodology and data have not been challenged in spite of the general derision with which they were greeted by spokesmen of the US and UK governments.[57] Examinations by Professor Richard Garfield,[58] an epidemiologist at Columbia University, and also by Colin Rowat, an economist who completed a review of the materials for the Campaign Against Sanctions on Iraq (CASI), found that the assumptions UNICEF had adopted were in fact 'non-conservative but reasonable'. In Rowat's estimation three assumptions underpin the UNICEF estimate:

> The first assumption is that the counterfactual child mortality rate would have continued its 1980s average decline linearly over the 1990s. This assumption may be 'non-conservative', but is reasonable for two reasons. First, Iraq's child mortality rate was still high enough in 1990 to allow a continued linear decline. Second, Iraq's mortality rate began to decline more quickly after the First Gulf War's end in 1988. As the decade's average gives more weight to the war years, it might make the linear decline assumption more reasonable as a peacetime counterfactual. The second assumption is that Iraqi fertility has not declined. The fertility rate allows estimation of the total number of under five-year olds; if their mortality rate is known, total deaths can be estimated. This is also

a non-conservative assumption as evidence suggests that Iraqi women under sanctions are marrying later and having fewer children, dropping the fertility rate. The third assumption is that the national under five mortality rate was 50/1000 in 1990. The IST [International Study Team] estimates of 43.2/1000 for 1985–89 and 27.8/1000 for early 1990, which Garfield uses in his own work, may be more accurate. Their use would increase considerably the excess deaths estimate.[59]

In September of 2000, the FAO released a report that found:

Since the implementation of SCR 986, market prices of food products such as wheat flour, rice, vegetable oil and sugar, which are part of the food ration, dropped...However, market prices of commodities not included in the ration continued to be high and above the reach of a large section of the population with low purchasing power....In addition] the collapse of personal incomes and very low salary levels...has [had] serious consequences for the nutritional well being of the population, especially for children and other vulnerable population groups....The food industry has been in decline since 1991 when most of the factories were closed due to lack of hard currency to import new machinery, spare parts, raw materials and other supplies.[60]

In addition, the report maintained that distribution was erratic due to sanctions on the transportation sector:

Upon its inception, SCR 986 distributions were erratic, covering about 80 per cent of the planned items in the ration in the first half of 1997. Since mid-1997 up to Phase VII, monthly distributions improved to cover about 95 per cent of the target. However despite improvements in performance in covering the government of Iraq monthly requirements, food basket targets were fully met in only 6 out of the 38 monthly distribution cycles.[61]

The report highlighted problems of distribution and the lack of spare parts to revive indigenous industry required for food production:

Delays in clearance and finalisation of international procurement contracts have been an important reason for delay in the rehabilitation of food-handling facilities such as railway rehabilitation and milling facility reconstruction. The rehabilitation of mills was aimed to ensure that the minimum requirements for wheat flour production were met. However, the delivery of spare parts has not been adequate to address the extreme deterioration of 70 per cent of the mills that need to be replaced. With regards to transportation capacity, some 4,000 vehicles over 15 years old need to be replaced to ensure reliable and efficient distribution of food commodities. Under phases IV to VI, contracts for the procurement of 850 trucks...were approved, of which 447 trucks had arrived....the value of food contracts put on hold exceeds US $192 million.[62]

The level and diversity of 'holds' was becoming an increasing concern as:

The mechanisms and procedures for the contracting, screening, approval, and distribution of humanitarian supplies under SCR 986 have been protracted and cumbersome...Large numbers of contracts, for example for health supplies, often remain 'on hold', or have long delivery lead times thus creating shortages. While holds on food deliveries from the 661 committee are rare, delays in delivery are common, and quality control is often inadequate.[63]

In addition, the FAO confirmed what many UN reports had already stated:

SCR 986 food rations do not provide a nutritionally adequate and varied diet...the ration is lacking in vegetables, fruit, and animal products and is therefore deficient in micronutrients. With only 1/4 of the planned ration of pulses distributed due to important gaps in the submission of applications for procurement, the protein quality of the diet has also been poor. Adequate amounts of items such as meat, milk and vegetables are too costly for families to purchase to supplement their diet given the parallel decline in the economy and the effects of the current drought on the availability of crops and horticultural products. Consequently a significant portion of the population requires special attention, particularly the most vulnerable population groups whose coping strategies are quickly being eroded. The magnitude of the nutritional problems requires a proportionate response but current levels of assistance are largely inadequate.[64]

DEPLETED URANIUM IN IRAQ

Shortly following the second Gulf War, concerns were raised that the health and environmental problems experienced in Iraq may be linked to weapons used by US and British forces. Weapons and munitions utilising depleted uranium (DU) were used for the first time during the Gulf War as the US-led coalition drove Iraqi forces from Kuwait.[65] DU is a radioactive by-product of the enrichment process used to make nuclear fuel rods and nuclear bombs. Due to its high density, which is about twice that of lead, and other physical properties, depleted uranium is used in munitions designed to penetrate armour plate. It also reinforces military vehicles, such as tanks. Allied forces fired an estimated 300 metric tons, littering the battlefield with residue that could remain radioactive for millions of years.[66]

When depleted uranium is blown up, it burns at high temperatures and is altered into uranium oxides – tiny, hard particles that are a micrometre in size. They can stay airborne as aerosols, being blown around by the wind and falling as dust and, being microscopic, can easily be inhaled or ingested allowing organs, bones and body fluids to be directly exposed to the long-term radioactive properties of the particles.[67] Possible health consequences to combatants and populations residing in conflict areas where depleted uranium munitions were used have raised many important environmental health questions. The contaminated battlefields of southern Iraq, the location of much of the heavy fighting that saw the United States and its coalition allies destroy hundreds of Iraqi tanks and military armoured vehicles was – and has remained – home to Iraqi civilians who grow vegetables near contaminated areas, breath air and drink water that could be polluted with the radioactive particles.

The sanctions regime imposed by the UN Security Council in the aftermath of the war has made a clean-up of the hazardous by-products of the war virtually impossible. Growing health problems in Iraq, including a dramatic rise in cancer and birth defects and other diseases associated with exposure to radiation, have been evident, especially in children. Cases of lymphoblastic leukaemia have more than quadrupled, with other cancers also increasing at an alarming rate. In men, lung, bladder, bronchus, skin and stomach cancers show the highest increase. In women, the highest increases are in breast and bladder cancer, and non-Hodgkin's lymphoma. Diseases such as osteosarcoma, teratoma, nephroblastoma and rhabdomyosarcoma are also increasing, with the most affected being children and young men.[68] Exacerbating the crisis, UN sanctions have also devastated the Iraqi medical system. Requested radiotherapy equipment, chemotherapy drugs, and analgesics had been consistently blocked by the Security Council's 661 Committee. The basis for withholding such life-saving drugs and technology were charges that the chemical agents making up such drugs could be converted into chemical or biological weapons.[69] In spite of such dramatic outbreaks, the United States and United Kingdom governments have repeatedly denied there are any links between depleted uranium and cancer. They have commissioned studies of the existing literature that have found little or no effect, debunked preliminary research conducted by independent researchers and foreign governments, and stated that the issue was a propaganda tool of the Hussein regime.[70]

However, the US Army expressed concern about the use of DU in July 1990, some six months before the outbreak of the Gulf War.[71] Significant concerns about health and environmental risks were included in the appendix of a report comparing the effectiveness of tungsten alloy and DU in armour-piercing ammunition.[72] While the scientific basis for health and environmental concerns were largely ignored, the report kept from public consideration concern that the use of DU weapons might cause public controversy. Such 'controversy' and the political and potential legal ramifications are sufficient motivation for the issue receiving a full public review. However, some of the illnesses observed in Iraq have also been seen in Persian Gulf War veterans in many countries including the United States. Investigations examining the link between depleted uranium and 'Gulf War Syndrome' were expanded when the government of Italy – following the deaths from leukaemia of at least seven of its Balkan veterans – asked NATO to conduct its own investigation. Finally, in 2002, a World Health Organisation (WHO) delegation visited Iraq to study the possible health effects of depleted uranium.[73]

Isolating depleted uranium as the sole cause of any illness is difficult because the battlefield in southern Iraq was exposed to a toxic soup of dangerous pollutants including munitions used by the opposing forces, oil fires from Kuwait and possibly the use or destruction of Iraq's store of chemical and biological weapons. Although current research indicates that the risks of DU to the general population are small, the research is based on relatively short-term exposure of adults. It is insufficient to conclude that Iraqi citizens residing in or near contaminated areas could not suffer from chemically toxic effects associated with long-term uranium radiation exposure or poisoning. The US removed the small number of its armoured vehicles that had been struck by 'friendly' DU munitions and either decontaminated or buried them. Iraqi vehicles have been left in place for over a decade.[74]

What is certain, however, is that on 4 March 1998, journalist Robert Fisk, in the *Independent*, reported the nightmarish epidemic of leukaemia and stomach cancer that devastated the lives of thosands of Iraqis who lived near the war zone. Dr Jawad al-Ali, an oncologist in Basra, reported the escalation of cancer incidence and expressed his fear that he too might have contracted it. Faisal Abbas, a ten-year-old boy, bled to death from leukaemia in a cancer ward. Another child, Ahmed Faleh, started bleeding from the mouth, nose, ears and rectum, and took two weeks to die in excruciating pain. All that was taking place because the sanction regime was denying drugs to Iraqi civilians. Even the unborn could not escape the violation of abnormalities. According to Dr Jenan Ali in Basra, many babies were born without a brain or had no limbs, no face or eyes, and the radiation level in the region was alarming.[75]

PEOPLE IN THE QUAGMIRE:
'...A MINOR POINT IN THE HISTORY OF...WAR'[76]

As the Security Council debated the US threat of renewed warfare against Iraq in early March 2003, the Under-Secretary-General for Humanitarian Affairs, Kenzo Oshima, outlined the potential for a humanitarian catastrophe in the event of war in terms of the already fragile condition of Iraq's vulnerable population. One million children under five were chronically malnourished; 5 million Iraqis lacked access to safe water and sanitation; 80 per cent of average household income depended on food provided by the oil-for-food programme and 60 per cent of the population relied solely on the food basket from the oil-for-food programme to meet all household needs.[77] Highlighting the level of vulnerability of the population, 50 per cent of pregnant women in Iraq were anaemic because of protein and iron deficiency and 30 per cent of infants were underweight.[78] In planning for the humanitarian consequences of a war, the Under-Secretary noted that a conflict 'would severely disrupt critical infrastructure and the Iraqi Government's capacity to deliver basic services and relief, including the food ration' (which amounted to 460,000 tons per month, almost four times the highest amount delivered during the Afghanistan crisis).[79] Reporting on the humanitarian calamity that would be caused by war, the New York-based Center for Economic and Social Rights pointed out that, after twelve years of sanctions, the Iraqi population had been reduced to a state of dependency on government and international aid and as a result was far more vulnerable in 2003 to the shocks of war than it had been in 1999. The CESR cautioned that 'Iraq's public health and food distribution system would collapse in the event of a military intervention there, causing a humanitarian crisis far beyond the capacity of the United Nations and relief agencies.'[80]

On 18 March 2003 all international staff were evacuated from Iraq and the oil-for-food programme suspended. On 19 March 2003 the United States opened the war on Iraq with an aerial bombardment on Baghdad. Within days the US initiated its threatened 'shock and awe' strategy of air and missile bombardment of Baghdad, and US ground forces crossed the Kuwaiti border into Iraq and commenced ground fighting. With the outbreak of hostilities, the magnitude of the impending humanitarian catastrophe was predicted by international humanitarian agencies. For example, World Health Organisation spokesperson Fadela Chaib appealed for 'the most vulnerable citizens of Iraq – the elderly, women and children, and people with disabilities. With Iraq's vital infrastructure already devastated, the most basic human rights to clean water or to basic health care cannot be met.'[81] Similarly, UNICEF spokesperson Geoffrey Keele expressed deep concern:

> Disease spreads rapidly during war, when safe water supplies are disrupted, people are displaced from their homes, and sources of food and medicine are compromised. When you factor in the loss of education and the psychosocial trauma, there is no question that war takes its greatest toll on children. And we should all remember that children make up half of Iraq's population.[82]

By 24 March humanitarian agencies were reporting the beginnings of a nightmare scenario of humanitarian catastrophe. Hospitals in Baghdad were without water. Basra, Iraq's second largest city, was without potable water for three days. WHO reported that teams from the International Committee of the Red Cross had managed to restore service to about 40 per cent of the population, but UNICEF estimated that at least 100,000 children under five were at risk due to the additional threats of diarrhoea and dehydration.

> There must now be a threat of disease as tens of thousands of people in their homes, hospitals and care institutions attempt to cope and find what water they can from the river and other sources. Unfortunately, the river is also where sewage is dumped.[83]

The public health consequences of war go far beyond the direct casualties caused by weapons. Water, for example, is essential to prevent health problems including malnutrition, gastrointestinal infections and other communicable diseases. Without access to safe water sources, the civilian population, especially children, are at risk. Therefore Protocol II of the Geneva Conventions explicitly states:

> It is prohibited to attack, destroy, remove or render useless objects indispensable to the survival of the civilian population, such as foodstuffs, agricultural areas for the production of foodstuffs, crops, livestock, drinking water installations and supplies.

The pre-war UN *Likely Humanitarian Scenarios* report had already warned that damage to the electricity network would affect water supply and sanitation giving rise to the need for some 39 per cent of the population to be provided with potable water. It added that a high number of indirect casualties might materialise because the outbreak of diseases in epidemic proportions was very likely.[84]

Most civilian casualties in armed conflicts are the result of the destruction of civilian infrastructure that is essential for people's health. This was also the case for the first Gulf War that, according to the first post-war UN mission, had caused 'apocalyptic damage' to the infrastructure and had reduced the country to 'the pre-industrial age'.[85]

THE INVASION ATTACKS ON INFRASTRUCTURES

Basra was the first city to suffer a humanitarian crisis because of US-British belligerence. On 21 March air raids destroyed high voltage lines and knocked out Basra's electrical power. That in turn disabled Basra's water and sanitation systems, including the Wafa' Al Qaed Water Pumping Station, which pumps water from the Shatt al-Arab river to five water treatment plants that supply piped water to over 60 per cent of Basra's 1.5 million residents.[86]

After three months from the war water shortage was still severe and water was reportedly sold on the black market at US$1 per 1.5 litre bottle. The International Committee of the Red Cross (ICRC) successfully restored running water to some of the population on 2 April 2003 and continued to supply water trucks. At the end of April water and electricity supplies in Basra were still at only 60 per cent of their pre-war levels.

Apparently, the power and water supply of other cities were also targeted by the attacks. By 31 March half the 1.2 million people in the beleaguered city of Basra lacked water. People reported that they were reduced to drinking 'garden water' normally used for irrigation, which is not safe to wash in, let alone drink. Humanitarian agencies warned that the population of Basra, especially the young and the weak suffering the effects of economic sanctions, could be at risk of potentially fatal disease from drinking contaminated water (according to Amnesty International).[87]

On 2 April the ICRC reported that 'entire towns and suburbs have now been without piped water for about a week, including several district towns north of Dhi Qar and Najaf but also towns south of Basra such as Al-Zubayr and Safwan'. In Nasiriyah, the water treatment plant was reported to be working only six hours a day as of 20 April and water treatment chemicals were in short supply.[88]

On 4 April 2003 the *Washington Post* reported that on 3 April, power to 90 per cent of Baghdad was cut because of the damage to the Al-Doura power station during the American capture of Saddam International Airport. One week later, after the capture of Baghdad by US troops, the ICRC reported that power cuts had continued ever since. At that time, major water treatment plants in the city were operational at about only 40–50 per cent of their normal capacity. After the damage resulting from military operations and waves of vandalism and looting, the Baghdad water authorities reported the loss of all their assets and warehouse materials, including all spare parts, vehicles and other equipment.

Agence France-Presse released news that a spokesperson of the World Health Organisation had already warned on 6 April that Iraq was facing the risk of an outbreak of cholera or other infectious illnesses, as clean drinking water was scarce and hospitals were overwhelmed.[89] UNICEF echoed this same assessment on 21 April when they reported a huge increase in child diarrhoeal cases in

Baghdad. Although water was being supplied to most parts of Baghdad by the end of April, the sanitation situation remained extremely critical and threatened public health.

TARGETING AMBULANCES AND MEDICAL INFRASTRUCTURE

Medical infrastructure and personnel enjoy protection under the rules of war as laid down in the Geneva Convention. Article 12 of Protocol II states: 'Medical units shall be respected and protected at all times and shall not be the object of attack', while article 15 adds that 'Civilian medical personnel shall be respected and protected.' Article 21 extends the protection also to medical vehicles, including ambulances.

On 9 April doctors Geert Van Moorter and Harrie Dewitte were at the Saddam Centre for Plastic Surgery, which was operating as a frontline hospital for the war-wounded. They witnessed how one of their ambulances that had left to transport patients to another hospital returned two minutes later after being fired on by US troops. Two of the patients it transported were dead and the driver and his co-driver had gunshot wounds.

When Dr Van Moorter went up to one US officer to complain about the attack, the officer answered that 'the ambulance could contain explosives'.[90]

A similar justification for targeting civilian and medical vehicles alike was reportedly given by Colonel Bryan P. McCoy, the commander of the Third Marine Battalion of the 4th Regiment. According to *Le Monde* on 13 April 2003, when soldiers complained that they were uncomfortable shooting at civilians, the colonel countered that the Iraqis were using civilians to kill marines, that soldiers were being disguised as civilians, and that ambulances were perpetrating terrorist attacks.

Several hospitals sustained severe damage in air raids. On 2 April 2003, for example, US aircraft hit a building opposite the Red Crescent maternity hospital in Baghdad and the blast was so strong that the hospital's roof collapsed. The maternity hospital is part of a Red Crescent compound that also includes their headquarters and a surgical hospital.[91] Patients and at least three doctors and nurses working at the hospital were wounded.[92]

The damage to health infrastructure outside the major urban centres is still not fully assessed but is probably considerable. Members of the Iraq Peace Team reported that a hospital in Rutbah, near the border with Syria, was bombed on 26 March 2003. The anti-war activists who were leaving the country, according to Associated Press on 31 March, said that they saw no significant Iraqi military presence near the hospital or elsewhere in the town. In Nasiriyah the Primary Health Care Department and Department of Health warehouses were reported to be destroyed by a missile. These warehouses held a six-month stock of health supplies including high-protein biscuits.[93]

THE PLIGHT OF HOSPITALS UNDER US OCCUPATION

Whatever the involvement of the occupying forces in the widespread looting and destruction, they were responsible for the medical infrastructure in the territories under their control. As soon as Baghdad was under US control on 9 April 2003, the medical system of Baghdad had virtually collapsed, according to the ICRC.[94] The Medical City complex, which consists of four hospitals, was in total chaos. The triage and emergency units were completely disorganised and there was no ambulance service. No new patients were being admitted. Only a few surgeons and one or two nurses were present in the hospitals, each with 600 beds. Administrative, cleaning or kitchen staff were not existent, while there were still 300 patients to care for. Three days earlier, the ICRC medical co-ordinator had visited this hospital's triage and emergency centre, which could handle 100 patients at any one time, and found 'that the complex was a perfect example of mass casualty management'. Al Kindi hospital, which was still working efficiently on 8 April, was in total chaos under the occupation forces. There was only one medical doctor present and no surgeons. Some patients were found lying on the floor. Medical and other supplies were scattered all over the place.

On 12 April the ICRC team reported that the Yarmouk hospital, which had been treating patients at a rate of 100 per hour during the invasion of Baghdad, was working only as a first-aid post.[95] A rocket had hit the third floor, which was totally destroyed, and two of the three generators were damaged. Corpses were piled in the entrance hall before being buried in the hospital grounds. The doctors and staff had been able to salvage half of the equipment while looters were carrying off furniture. Al Karama hospital, with 500 beds, on the other hand, had been protected from looting by the civilian population, and its staff were even able to recover whatever equipment and supplies that were left at the Al Khark hospital for safekeeping on their premises. The 125-bed Alwiya children's hospital, the main paediatric medical facility in Baghdad, had been protected from looting by the presence of armed medical staff living in the hospital. The wards were closed, but some 100 consultations per day were being performed for the outpatients. In Ibn Nafis hospital, one of the few hospitals still functioning in Baghdad, the existing team had been increased in number by several surgeons from looted hospitals. Non-medical services such as cleaning, however, were very poor. The Al Numan hospital was intact and had been very well protected by the civilian population. Although the surgical staff was still on the site, the prevailing insecurity made access very difficult for patients. The Ibn Al Haythem eye hospital and Abduker military hospital were closed after being looted. However, at Rashad and Ibn Rushd psychiatric hospitals, no treatment was available for patients.[96]

On 17 April 2003 the ICRC was still reporting the dire situation in Baghdad's hospitals. In Al-Rashad psychiatric hospital, for example, waves of looters had descended on the facility, burning everything that was not stolen. The hospital director reported that some patients had even been raped. The 1050 patients fled the hospital and only 300 patients had returned, but their living conditions were dismal.[97]

On 19 April the Adnan specialist hospital was forced to shut down the only five of its 25 operating theatres which were then still working after running out of oxygen and anaesthetics. Dr Haifa Mohammed Ali, senior anaesthetist at the hospital, testified that the US troops refused to protect the hospital against looters. A small contingent of marines eventually showed up after the worst part of looting was complete, but they were withdrawn a few days later.[98]

According to UNICEF on 21 April, only 7 per cent of the Al-Salam Primary Health Care Centre's staff were working. They were assisted, however, by volunteers from the local community. The hospital was experiencing a shortage of water, anti-diarrhoeal drugs and injectable and oral antibiotics and suffered from bad sewage drainage. Because other hospitals in the area were not operational, it had to serve more than 100,000 people – more than double its normal coverage.[99] At the Saddam City hospital in northern Baghdad, the morgue was reported to be full and there was not enough power to preserve the corpses already piled inside.[100]

Only on 22 April did UNICEF finally report that health services were no longer deteriorating and the situation had started to stabilise. However, its spokesman, Geoffrey Keele, warned that the situation had stabilised at a very low level which left the most vulnerable section of Iraqi society, its children, at great risk.[101]

The inaccessibility of the few medical facilities that were still open was not only the result of the population's alleged lawlessness. The American forces reportedly prevented patients from seeking treatment and the health personnel from moving freely. On 11 April 2003 Dr Geert Van Moorter reported from Baghdad that

> Medical personnel do not even dare to ask permission from American checkpoints to bring the wounded to the hospital, as any Iraqi who approaches US soldiers risks to be shot. They would rather ask us, the foreigners, to negotiate with the US-troops for patients to be allowed to pass.

Amnesty International illustrated the inability of ambulances and other vehicles to move freely in one report, claiming that 'on April 10, around 20 bodies, including those of children, were still strewn on the road between al-Doura and the airport, days after they were killed. At that time, the road was already controlled by US forces'.[102]

In the city of Fallujah on 28 April it was also reported that the US troops shot the medical crews that tried to retrieve the injured after the American troops killed 13 protesters. This was confirmed by Dr Ahmed Ghanim al-Ali, director of the Fallujah general hospital.[103] Ironically, the US forces that claimed to be liberating the Iraqis from Saddam's criminal regime were committing worse crimes in violation of the Geneva Convention, article 15 of Protocol II, which states that 'the occupying power shall afford civilian medical personnel in occupied territories every assistance to enable them to perform, to the best of their ability, their humanitarian functions'. Moreover, they should give health personnel access 'to any place where their services are essential'.

Equally alarming was a report by the *Christian Science Monitor* on 15 April that US and British troops treated humanitarian aid as a propaganda exercise when they set up a 'photogenic playground' for children that were dying from the effects of the sanction regime and compounded by the war. This raises concerns of the effectiveness and appropriateness of military involvement in the aid programmes, which jeopardises aid workers, including many health professionals. The *Jordan Times* reported on 31 March 2003 of its fears that the military's humanitarian efforts would be ineffective because 'Iraqis know well that, if it weren't for those very US-British forces, they wouldn't be in need and wouldn't find themselves in want of food, water and medicine in the first place.' The ICRC therefore rejected any direct involvement of military forces in relief operations 'as this would or could, in the minds of the authorities and the population, associate humanitarian organisations with political or military objectives that go beyond humanitarian concerns'.[104] The ICRC's concern, according to the *Guardian* on 27 March 2003, is grounded in reports that the military involvement in relief operations in occupied areas confirmed that they were conducted in a hostile atmosphere. *Arab News* war correspondent Essam Al-Ghalib described how, during one of these relief operations in Najaf 'a soldier was pointing at the crowd ordering them away from the fence separating the food distributors from the hungry crowd. Every time the soldier passed an order on to the civilians or those arriving in vehicles, he aggressively pointed his 50-caliber truck-mounted machine gun at them, lowering his head to see as though taking aim.' When the reporter approached the soldier and asked why he was pointing his machine gun at unarmed civilians he answered that they might be suicide bombers.[105]

Even before the war, the US had already stated its intention to subject civilian humanitarian efforts to military authority. Its Office of Reconstruction and Humanitarian Affairs (ORHA), which is in charge of the reconstruction of Iraq, reports to the Department of Defense. It includes a Kuwait-based Humanitarian Operations Centre (HOC) staffed by American, Kuwaiti and British military staff. The Pentagon requires aid agencies to co-ordinate with the HOC and to wear identification tags issued by the military authorities. Many relief and aid agencies, including health NGOs, have already complained that the dangers faced by relief workers in the field were multiplied by the American insistence that NGOs work under Department of Defense jurisdiction.[106]

GALLANTRY OF SELFLESS IRAQI HEALTH WORKERS

The Iraqi health workers' commitment to ensuring health care despite the war contrasts sharply with the carelessness of the occupying forces. The WHO stated it was 'extremely impressed by the level of dedication the Iraqi health staff brought to their work, even in these circumstances'. WHO spokesperson Fadela Chaib said that the dedication of doctors, nurses and support staff, including cleaners, cooks, maintenance workers and drivers, was saving lives.[107] In Basra, Dr Dahham Falih al-Musa, a senior house officer at the Basra teaching hospital, said that there was a great team spirit among the medical staff. Even during the height of the fighting, the hospital remained operational although it director, Dr Akram Abid Hasan, had lost ten family members including two sons, two daughters, his mother, brother and a sister when a bomb or missile struck his home. Two senior doctors at the hospital also lost children and wives in the war.[108]

The high esteem of the UN for the Iraqi health workers was shared by several journalists. Robert Fisk, in the *Independent* described his meeting with Dr Khaldoun al-Baeri, the hospital director and chief surgeon of Adnan Khairallah Martyr hospital in Baghdad:

> Dr. Baeri speaks like a sleepwalker, trying to describe how difficult it is to stop a wounded man or woman from suffocating when they have been wounded in the thorax, explaining that after four operations to extract metal from the brains of his patients, he is almost too tired to think, let alone in English. As I leave him, he tells me that he does not know where is family is. 'Our house was hit and my neighbours sent a message to tell me they sent them away somewhere. I do not know where. I have two little girls, they are twins, and I told them they mustn't cry because I have to work for humanity. And now I have no idea where they are.' Then Dr. Baeri choked on his words and began to cry and could not say goodbye.[109]

According to the Amnesty International AI Index: MDE14/085/2003, millions of people in Iraq face grave dangers to their health, with many hospitals unable to cope with the number of war casualties and the sick. In addition, there are indications that serious water-borne diseases such as cholera are on the rise owing to the scarcity in some areas of clean water. Humanitarian agencies have reported that access to healthcare and medicines is increasingly difficult as medical stocks are running low and disorder in the streets prevents the movement of health workers and ambulances. UN Humanitarian Co-ordinator for Iraq David Wilmhurst asserted that 'with the breakdown of law and order in Iraq, the situation now is extremely critical, the longer the situation remains out of control, the more difficult it will be to start humanitarian relief operations'.[110]

On 6 April UN relief agencies warned that a health crisis faced the 5 million inhabitants of Baghdad, with hospitals overwhelmed and the infrastructure devastated. World Health Organisation (WHO) and ICRC officials confirmed that the capital's hospitals were struggling to cope. The ICRC reported that some areas of Baghdad had no water at all. An official in UNICEF said they were particularly worried about the impact on Baghdad's children, who are almost half the city's population. UNICEF also said that 100,000 children in Basra were threatened with serious illness because the water treatment plant had stopped functioning.[111]

The same day the ICRC reported that emergency services were not being provided by the hospital in Umm Qasr and that patients could not travel safely to Basra for treatment. It also said that the water situation in Umm Qasr remained a concern, and that there was no fuel available for pumps. On 7 April, matching Amnesty International reports, WHO officials warned that Iraq was facing an outbreak of cholera and other infectious diseases as clean drinking water was scarce. On 8 April an ICRC spokeswoman told a news briefing that hospitals had reached their limit, and that the main surgical hospitals and water treatment plants were relying solely on back-up generators. She described it as 'an untenable situation'. On the same day the ICRC reported that in Saddam City the flow of tap water was cut by half, and that lack of water and electricity supplies had badly affected Saddam Medical Centre. It also reported acute water shortages in Kerbala, Najaf and Basra. The UK's Department for International Development said that it understood there were water shortages in other parts of central Iraq as well, including Abu Ghraib, Mahmudiya, Al-Hilla and Al-Anbar. In Nasiriyah, residents were reportedly out on the streets searching for water. The ICRC said it was maintaining some water supplies to hospitals and other areas in particular need.[112]

By 9 April the ICRC was describing the humanitarian situation in Baghdad as 'critical', particularly as health, power, and water workers could not reach their workplaces safely, and many medical centres lacked water and electricity. On 10 April the ICRC resumed work in the capital, but reported that Al-Kindi hospital in Baghdad had been ransacked and that street violence and looting had forced the closure of others.[113] Agence France-Presse reported that US troops had been called in when looters stole two ambulances and medications from the hospital, but that they answered that they had no orders to intervene. WHO officials said they were 'extremely concerned that the apparent lack of law and order in Baghdad will have a very serious impact on health and healthcare in the Iraqi capital'.[114]

On 1 June the *Observer* reported that at least 10,000 unexploded cluster bombs were lying in cities, farmlands and on the main roads, and that this posed a serious threat to millions of children, adults, and humanitarian aid workers.[115] This revelation stands in contrast to Tony Blair and George Bush's pre-war claims that 'post-conflict Iraq would be a safer place than it was under Saddam'.[116] According to the Australian News Agency, the Reverend Neville Watson, one of twelve so-called Peace Team members still in Iraq, said that Baghdad hospitals were strewn with the mutilated corpses of civilians, stating:

> Corpses, horribly mutilated by blast and fire, litter the hospital corridors, while dismembered and badly injured children lie in beds. Distraught mothers identify their children in the morgue, and death and destruction are everywhere to be found.[117]

'The accuracy of bombs and missiles is over-rated, and when they go astray they cause terrific damage', he reiterated.

'If people generally saw the mangled and burned bodies of innocent women and children they would demand a stop to war', Rev. Watson added, saying that the bombing remained terrifying and that Baghdad had been in a lock-down situation. 'What we in the Iraq Peace Team are trying to do is identify with the suffering of the Iraqi people and apologise for our part in it.'[118]

THE TRAGEDY OF IRAQIS CONTINUES

On 8 August 2003 the *Middle East Times* reported that around 20,000 civilians were wounded in the Iraq war, and that the US-British occupiers are ignoring their suffering.[119] Likewise, on Thursday, 7 August 2003, the Iraq Body Count (IBC) website said, 'the maimed Iraqi civilians have been brushed under the carpet'.[120]

'A sizeable if as yet unknown proportion of Iraqi families will contain a relative whose life was ended or put on hold by the US or British forces', a research group of academics and peace activists said in a report seen by Reuters prior to publication on its website, www.iraq-bodycount.net. The report, entitled 'Adding Indifference to Injury', said that the IBC had calculated civilian casualties known so far as between a minimum of 16,439 and a maximum of 19,733. Incomplete information about casualties meant that the maximum figure was likely to be closer approximation to the real total, and might itself be an underestimate. The IBC's figures were based on media reports and counting projects from independent investigators up to 6 July 2003.[121]

The IBC insisted that the US and British military's reluctance to calculate the number of civilian wounded was inexcusable: 'there is indeed a possibility that not every death can be accounted for. Injuries are another matter. The injured are alive, perhaps receiving treatment, and the cause, nature and extent of their injuries will appear in medical, official, and informal records.' The IBC said that 20,000 injury compensation claims at $10,000 each would cost the occupiers $200 million – less than what the United States spends every two days on the occupation (the monthly cost of occupation had been estimated at $4 billion). However, with respect to compensation, Lieutenant Colonel Cassella, a Pentagon official, was reported by the *Guardian*, 13 June 2003, to have said: 'Under international law the US was not liable to pay any compensation for injuries or damages occurring during lawful combat operations.'[122] This is the same international law which the US violated when it invaded Iraq without any UN authorisation, and the same law which it ignored when it destroyed the Iraqi civil infrastructure. Security Council Resolution 1441, which authorised the return of UN weapons inspectors into Iraq, did not explicitly permit use of force in removing weapons of mass destruction (which have never, as yet, been found). That is why the US and Britain sought fervently another UN resolution that would mandate the use of force, but failed against the opposition from the members of the Security Council despite American pressure tactics and intimidation. In addition to this opposition, street demonstrations of hundreds of thousands of protesters, all over the world, including the US and the UK, against the looming invasion signalled the anti-war position of the international community. However, the US, being the sole superpower of global military reach, ignored the world community, brushed aside its traditional allies, ignored the UN as the embodiment of international law, along with the Geneva protocols about protecting non-combatant civilians, and proceeded unilaterally to invade a sovereign state pursuing its imperial grand strategy of domination.

CONCLUSION

The US and Britain proclaimed victory in Iraq, but wars, unlike sporting events, do not end with the blow of a whistle. The war rendered Iraq a land without peace, a land where the war continues between military occupation and a resistance cemented by national pride. The invasion has compounded the shattering effects of the sanctions that literally decimated the child segment of Iraqi society. Every day, shooting between the population and the occupation forces takes place, leaving a profound sense of uncertainty and fear, which is further exacerbated by the inadequate supplies of electricity, lack of potable water and impoverished access to healthcare and medications. The invasion has turned Iraq into a kind of prison, where people lack food, where they do not have safety, and where women cannot walk alone. From the Iraqis' perspective, this has been the cost of the freedom brought to Iraq by the Anglo-American forces.

6
Russia and the Question of Iraq

Russian and Soviet-Iraqi relations have been generally part and parcel of Russia's relations with the Third World countries and their national liberation movements, particularly Arab nationalism, which for both historical and geo-strategic reasons has been especially important for Moscow. However, at the same time, particularly between 1958 and 1990, some special features have marked Soviet-Iraqi relations, setting them in marked contrast with Soviet links with other Afro-Asian nations and even some states of the Arab Middle East.

First, Iraq was the nearest of all Arab countries to the Soviet borders and the threat of Soviet expansion might have been seen as being much more real by its leaders than by the leaders of the other Arab states.[1] Second, unlike the other Arab states of the Mashreq, Iraq, from its independence in the 1920s, contained a very substantial non-Arab ethnic minority with specific constitutional rights, which had been granted in 1925 as a condition for the incorporation of the largely Kurdish populated Mosul region into its national borders.[2] The Kurdish people, who also live in Turkey, Iran and Russia, have never entirely submitted to this division of their nation and the resulting denial of their national self-determination, and this has led to a consistent demand for national autonomy within Iraq since 1961. Their aspirations, towards which the Soviet Union could not remain indifferent, were, however, putting the Soviet government in the awkward situation of having to make a choice between its recognition of Kurdish self-determination and its general support of Arab nationalism and the friendly Iraqi government.

Third, the Iraqi Communist Party (ICP), which was founded in 1934, was one of the most effective and socially influential Marxist organisations in the region. Although it was never strong enough to take power by itself, it nevertheless represented a by-no-means negligible political force in the country. After 1958 it proved both a valuable asset and an embarrassment in the Soviets dealings with the anti-imperialist and 'progressive' but viciously anti-communist Iraqi government. Last but not least, Iraq's economic potential and relative wealth, especially after the 1973 October War and the subsequent rise of oil prices, made it a financially attractive partner and customer for Moscow. These economic aspects, which had never been absent in the past, have acquired additional importance since the collapse of the USSR and the emergence of Russia as a separate and pro-capitalist nation.

Post-Soviet Russia, rejecting Marxist ideology, the ideological support of Communist parties in the rest of the world and the national liberation movements of the Third World peoples, was, nevertheless, still interested in co-operation with Iraq and since 1994 until the outbreak of the new war in Iraq in March 2003 had been supporting Baghdad politically against the US-imposed punitive economic sanctions regime and the US military intervention. As the authors want to show, the history, geopolitics and economics, at both regional and global levels, have been inextricably interwoven into the process of shaping Russian attitudes and foreign-policy decisions towards Iraq. Therefore, although the main focus of the chapter is post-Soviet Russia after December 1991, the previous Soviet period needs to also be taken into account and analysed in order to find the elements of continuity and transformation evident in the present policy formulation.

SOVIET BACKGROUND

Soviet relations with Iraq evolved through a relatively long and complex history. Diplomatic relations between the two countries were established for the first time on 9 September 1944 at the end of the Second World War.[3] The monarchic regime in Baghdad, though staunchly anti-communist, established relations with Moscow largely thanks to its dependence on Britain and the British-Soviet alliance that existed during the war. In January 1955, with the onset of the Cold War, relations were broken off after the Soviets criticised the Iraqi government's decision to join the Baghdad Pact.[4] When the pro-Western monarchy was overthrown by a military coup on 14 July 1958, the new leader of the country, General Abd-al-Karim Qasim, immediately re-established diplomatic ties with Moscow and began to purchase Soviet arms.[5] This initiated more than 30 years of Soviet-Iraqi co-operation which was both intimate and multifaceted and, for most of the period, was even officially identified as a 'strategic partnership', until the onset of Mikhail Gorbachev's perestroika in the late 1980s. However, this did not mean that during this period the two states' mutual relations were always friendly and without tangible political differences. As an American scholar has indicated, Soviet support for national liberation movements saw a number of important Third World countries, such as Iraq, 'declare their friendship for and improved relations with the USSR and sided with it on a number of international problems'. In no instance, however, did their leaders 'compromise their own national interests or become Soviet stooges'.[6] Baghdad's interest in co-operation with Moscow 'was based on the need for a powerful patron in its [Iraq's] efforts to shed all the remnants of Western colonialism and to establish Iraq as an autonomous member of the world order of nation states'.[7] At the same time, however, the Iraqi ruling elite had shown stubborn resistance towards anything that could be regarded as an intrusion into the country's internal affairs or as an infringement upon Iraq's sovereignty over its international policies.[8]

When, on 8 February 1963, Qasim's regime was overthrown and the Ba'ath party came to power in Baghdad, its persecution of the Iraqi Communist party and what the Soviet Union then described as its 'policy of genocide towards the Kurds'[9] caused a sharp deterioration in Soviet-Iraqi relations. However, relations improved again after a second military coup on 18 November 1963 and during the ensuing Arif brothers' rule, which lasted until July 1968. The visit to Moscow by Iraqi Prime Minister Abd al-Rahman al-Bazzaz in July–August 1966 was a 'milestone in the process of improving Soviet-Iraqi relations'.[10] The Soviet Union welcomed the Iraqi government's statement of 29 June 1966 on the recognition of Kurdish national and linguistic rights, and in July 1967, following the June 1967 Arab-Israeli War, Iraqi President Abd al-Rahman Arif and Algerian President Houari Boumedienne visited Moscow as representatives of the Cairo Arab summit conference.[11] The friendly relations and further co-operation in military, economic and political spheres continued and even increased after the Ba'ath party's return to power on 17 July 1968. In retrospect, the 1968–75 period could be seen as 'the high tide of Soviet influence in Iraq'.[12] Its apogee was the Treaty of Friendship and Co-operation between the USSR and the Iraqi Republic signed on 9 April 1972. The treaty, which was concluded as a result of an Iraqi initiative,[13] stressed the need for 'concerted action in the international field to ensure world peace and security and to develop political co-operation between Iraq and the USSR' (article 7).[14] Both parties also declared that 'it will not enter into any international alliance or grouping or take part in any actions or undertakings directed against the other' (article 10).[15] However, the treaty did not include any direct military obligations and stopped short of a true military alliance.

The late 1970s and early 1980s brought some cooling of the mutual relations and a weakening of the co-operation between the two states. Iraq's growing financial resources after the 1973 rise in oil prices created the basis for its widening links with the West and the extent of the Soviet and Eastern European participation in the country's economy during this period of economic growth declined steadily. With this decline, the differences between the parties 'resurfaced, producing visible strains in the 'strategic alliance' between Moscow and Baghdad'.[16] In the late 1970s the difference postons on issues such as the Palestinian question and the Arab-Israeli dispute, where Iraq was questioning Soviet recognition of the State of Israel in the pre-1967 War borders, Iraq's treatment of the ICP, the Kurdish national movement and Soviet support for Ethiopia against Somalia and Eritrea, grew further apart after the Iranian revolution and even more so with the Soviet invasion of Afghanistan on 27 December 1979. On 6 January 1980 Saddam Hussein called the Soviet invasion 'unjustifiable, erroneous behaviour that could cause anxiety for all freedom-loving and independent peoples',[17] and Iraq voted for the resolutions condemning Soviet intervention both in the UN General Assembly and the Islamabad (Pakistan) Conference of Islamic States.[18] When, on 22 September 1980, Iraq attacked Iran, starting a war which would last for almost eight years and which proved to be devastating to both countries, the USSR did not outwardly condemn Iraq's aggression, but immediately stopped its military aid and adopted a neutral stance.[19] At all stages of the conflict the Soviet leaders described it as 'tragically senseless' and directed against 'the fundamental national interests of both countries'.[20] In a speech on 30 September 1980 Leonid Brezhnev called both the states of Iraq and Iran 'friendly to the USSR' and stressed that: 'We are in favour of Iran and Iraq settling their outstanding problems at the negotiating table.'[21] From the Soviet point of view, the situation when the two 'anti-imperialist regimes...were cutting each other's throats' was truly deplorable.[22] When, in the summer of 1982, the war began to be fought on Iraqi territory and Iraq promised to withdraw to the international border on 10 June 1982, Moscow renewed arms supplies to Baghdad.[23] However, it still supported all attempts at finding a mediated settlement between the belligerents.[24] The Soviet's balanced and cautious policy resulted in a marked improvement in its relations with Iran, which would be of particular importance for the future.[25]

Despite these tensions and even serious political disagreements, Soviet-Iraqi relations remained on fundamentally friendly terms for this entire period prior to the end of the 1980s, with mutual co-operation continuing without major disturbances. Condemning the Soviet invasion of Afghanistan, Saddam Hussein nevertheless declared that: 'Iraq would not change the trends of its general policy in its relations with the Soviets.'[26] The Treaty of Friendship and Co-operation of 1972 has never been suspended and up to 1990, in the implementation of its goals, 50 more specific treaties have been concluded.[27] According to a Russian scholar: 'In spite of some problems, Soviet–Iraqi relations might have been characterised as very stable and fruitful, opening great perspectives for the future.'[28] When the Egyptian government of Anwar Sadat turned Egypt towards an openly pro-American position with the Camp David Accords and the Islamic Revolution in Iran proved to be anti-communist and anti-Soviet, Iraq's importance for Soviet regional policies only increased. For the USSR it became one of the few remaining efficient instruments of influence in the region.[29] However, Iraqi leaders were well aware of Soviet difficulties and in exchange for political loyalty and even verbal acceptance of socialist ideas, constantly demanded economic support and a continued supply of arms.[30] Iraq was receiving about half of all Soviet exports to the region and the total value of the Soviet contracts with Iraq amounted to US$37.4 billion.[31] During the 30 years of co-operation, the Soviet specialists built more than 80 large factories in Iraq,[32] and prior to 2 August 1990, some 8000 Soviet citizens were in Iraq.[33]

Soviet-Iraqi relations started to change from the late 1980s. As a Russian scholar indicates:

> The basic changes in Russian foreign policy took place before the Soviet Union's collapse, still under the rule of the Communist Party of the USSR with Gorbachev's team coming to power and the so-called *perestroika*, which in its turn brought about a fundamental breakdown of the previous political orientation.[34]

Following the so-called 'new political thinking' and trying both to bring an end to the Cold War with the American superpower and alleviate Soviet economic problems, Gorbachev and his advisors looked for improved Soviet-Israeli relations and limited Soviet support for the more radical Arab regimes including Iraq. All Soviet policy towards the Middle East now became geared towards the major goal of close co-operation with the West – especially the US[35] – and the Russian national interests previously advanced in the region, which were by and large consistent with Arab interests, became 'blatantly ignored'.[36]

This became evident with the diplomatic manoeuvres following the Iraqi invasion of Kuwait in August 1990. Although Russian sources indicate that Gorbachev himself originally hesitated and did not want to condemn outright the Iraqi invasion and thereby follow US policy designs, he changed his mind under pressure from his foreign minister, Eduard Shevardnadze, a Georgian who was staunchly pro-American and pro-Israeli who had threatened to cause a scandal and resign.[37] Almost immediately after the invasion on 2 August 1990, what was still the Soviet government issued a statement condemning it as an act of aggression which contradicted the new positive developments in international affairs. The statement also demanded the 'immediate and unconditional withdrawal of Iraqi forces from Kuwaiti territory' and 'the re-establishment of the sovereignty, national independence, and territorial integrity of Kuwait'.[38] On 3 August 1990 a meeting between Shevardnadze and US Secretary of State James Baker fully confirmed Soviet support for the US position, regardless of the pre-existing Soviet-Iraqi Treaty of Friendship and Co-operation (particularly its article 10),[39] and the multitude of common links and enterprises between the two states.[40] The American side was understandably very pleased[41] and the joint Shevardnadze–Baker declaration condemned once more the 'rude and illegitimate invasion of Kuwait by the armed forces of Iraq'.[42] Although there was no lack of outspoken domestic Soviet opposition to the pro-American and anti-Iraqi policy,[43] Gorbachev's 9 September 1990 meeting in Helsinki with US President George Bush again demonstrated his administration's further development of its new Iraq policy. According to a Russian scholar, although 'officially there was no change in the positions developed earlier,...the political meaning was new' and the meeting 'marked a watershed in the policy of the two powers'.[44] In spite of all his domestic opponents, Gorbachev decided to support 'every crisis-related action of the United States, thus giving Washington a free hand on military matters'.[45] The USSR also voted for the 29 November 1990 UN Security Council Resolution 678 which called for 'all necessary means' to be used to end the occupation of Kuwait.

As generally understood, this implied the use of military force, although the US agreed not to mention it explicitly in order to enable the Soviet Union to support the resolution and for China to abstain.[46] The improved relations between the superpowers also allowed the United States to transfer a large amount of NATO's military power from Western Europe to the Gulf, assuring their swift victory over the Iraqi army.[47] However, the negative reactions of various groups in Soviet society, including Muslim circles in the country, against the new Middle Eastern policy[48] did not go without having some impact. On 20 December 1990 the main representative of the pro-American foreign policy in Gorbachev's administration, Eduard Shevardnadze, was forced to resign 'as a result of extreme pressure'.[49] A move to save the remnants of the 'special relations' with parts of the Arab world generally, and the remnants of the mutual 'credit of trust' with Iraq in particular, was committed to a prominent Middle Eastern expert, Evgenii Primakov. Although supportive of the general goals of Gorbachev's perestroika, Primakov had opposed Shevardnadze from November 1990, calling for a more independent policy in the Middle East and the protection of Soviet relations with the Arab world.[50]

Moscow's lack of influence on US political decisions was indicated by the fact that Moscow was not notified of the planned outbreak of hostilities until US Secretary of State James Baker contacted the Soviet government only one hour prior to the start of the war on the night of 17 January 1991.[51] At the end of January 1991, the new Soviet foreign minister, Alexander Bessmertnykh, 'cautioned the Americans against destroying Iraq rather than concentrating on the withdrawal of Iraq from Kuwait',[52] and the Central Committee of the Soviet Communist Party called on Gorbachev to 'take the necessary steps' to bring about an end to the bloodshed.[53] On 12 February 1991 Primakov left for Baghdad as a special presidential envoy and as a result of his negotiations a Soviet plan for a ceasefire and an Iraqi withdrawal from Kuwait was submitted.[54] The plan was further elaborated in talks with Tariq Aziz when he visited Moscow on 21–22 February 1991 where, in addition to the agreed withdrawal of Iraqi forces from Kuwait, the agreement called for the lifting of UN economic sanctions once the majority of Iraqi troops had left Kuwait and once international supervision over the ceasefire's implementation had been established.[55] However, the Soviet diplomatic effort caused an extremely negative American reaction 'on a scope unprecedented since Gorbachev's coming to power',[56] and President Bush stated that the Soviet proposal 'falls well short of what would be required'.[57] With Gorbachev's approval, Primakov submitted a revised proposal taking into account the American objections. The Iraqi government accepted the revised proposal on 23 February 1991 in a statement by Saddam Hussein.[58] However, as he did not accept an American ultimatum from 22 February 1991, the US-led land attack then began. According to a Russian scholar: 'A last minute agreement reached between Mikhail Gorbachev and Saddam Hussein on Iraqi troop withdrawal from Kuwait was turned down by the US, which reciprocated with an ultimatum unacceptable to Iraq.'[59]

Facing the *fait accompli*, the disappointed Gorbachev had to accept the logic of the emerging unipolar world and the collapsing Soviet Union was both too weak and too internally divided to react forcefully.[60] In fact, it co-operated fully with the US in the subsequent dramatic events and its representative joined with the members of the victorious coalition at the Security Council in dictating harsh terms of surrender on Baghdad, particularly in Resolution 687 of 3 April 1991.[61] The sanctions committee, which had been established in order to supervise the resolution's implementation, saw the USSR and later Russia, represented. However, its real role was quite negligible and Gorbachev's relations with the Hussein regime deteriorated further when Iraq officially supported the unsuccessful coup in Moscow in August 1991.[62] Although the USSR became co-chairman of the Madrid Peace Conference in November 1991, its role was negligible and the well-known Russian journalist Stanislav Kondrashev described it as 'the last tango'. Kondrashev also predicted: 'Our next dance will be something else. We are no longer partners as we have been recently and no longer rivals as we were for a long period before. To call a spade a spade, the US has become our protector.'[63] Two months after the Madrid Conference, the Soviet Union finally disintegrated and its successor state, the Russian Federation, inherited both its close links with the region and most of its political and economic assets, which were in a greatly diminished capacity.

POST-SOVIET RUSSIA AND IRAQ

I. The Kozyrev Period, 1991–95

Since its inception in December 1991, up to the first months of 2003, post-Soviet Russian foreign policy, including its relations with Iraq, has undergone substantial transformations. Following a period of immense change, the contours of its goals and directions can now be discerned and analysed. Compared with the Soviet era, Russia's first and most striking feature is its weakness. At present the country has no material basis to support its international stature and aspirations. Its population is less than 50 per cent of the Soviet population and as early as 1995, its GNP was already less than 10 per cent of the US.[64] From the point of view of its foreign policy, at least equally important is the virtual collapse of its military might. Both unsuccessful operations in Chechnya and the submarine *Kursk* catastrophe bear witness to the very serious shortcomings of the Russian military. According to reliable American research, employing virtually every standard used to measure military capabilities, Russia's military is in a state of crisis and decline caused primarily by a sharp decline in defence expenditure, which is down 80 per cent from Soviet-era levels.[65] A second factor informing the 1992–95 period was that the people surrounding Russian President Boris Yeltsin were predominantly of a neo-liberal and Western orientation. They wanted to reject the Soviet heritage as much as possible, and as the first Russian Foreign Minister, Andrei Kozyrev, put it, to join the 'civilised world'.[66] The avoidance of past links with the compromised Iraqi regime was seen by the Yeltsin administration almost as a test of political correctness. The Iraqi ambassador to Moscow complained to a group of Russian parliamentarians that, when he wanted to initiate talks with the Russian government about outstanding Iraqi debt, which amounted to US$7 billion, none of the Russian leaders would receive him.[67] As a result of Russia's participation in the sanctions, its economic relations with Iraq were severely curtailed and, because a number of previous obligations had not been fulfilled, it lost approximately US$9 billion dollars.[68]

However, in response to a number of international and domestic factors, the situation quickly started to change again from the end of 1993 and the beginning of 1994.[69] First, the Russian political elite was deeply disappointed by the lack of promised economic aid from the US and its allies, and their recognition of Russian interests in the former Soviet bloc area. Feeling rejected by the West – especially after the unsuccessful effort to block NATO expansion into East-Central Europe – Russian leaders began to look for alternatives to their previous pro-American foreign policy.[70] Second, the 'new' Russia did not receive any substantial financial help from the wealthy and pro-Western Arab oil-producing countries – particularly Saudi Arabia and Kuwait – and the return to the 'radical' states such as Iraq and Libya and, in the 1990s, also Iran, in fact became an economic necessity.[71] Third,

Iraq's strategic location at the Persian Gulf and its proximity to the former Soviet borders made it too important to be ignored by any government in Moscow – especially in view of its influence on the new Islamic states in the Russian 'near abroad' and the substantial Muslim population in Russia itself.[72] Finally, since the end of 1992, domestic opposition to the pro-Atlantist foreign policy, which was symbolised by Andrei Kozyrev, started to be increasingly voiced by the supporters of a Eurasian orientation, nationalists, and communists in the Russian parliament, the Duma, and public opinion in general. After the elections won by them in December 1992, even President Yeltsin demanded that a more 'patriotic' foreign policy be conducted.[73]

When, on 27 June 1993, the US Air Force attacked Baghdad, despite the Russian government's official approval, the Russian media was unanimous in its condemnation of the operation. 'The most deplorable thing is that American piracy was justified by Russian leaders', wrote the communist *Pravda*.[74] The liberal *Izvestia* described it as 'an act of retribution which looked more like muscle-flexing' and expressed the opinion that 'our multi-polar and interdependent world' should not give any state 'the unlimited right to act as supreme judge and bearer of the ultimate truth'.[75] In a similar vein, *Komsomalskaya Pravda* suggested that 'the White House needs an enemy' and indicated that 'had Saddam Hussein been killed the US would have had to find a new villain'.[76] Also, a June 1993 meeting in Prague brought together the deputy foreign ministers of Russia and Iraq for the first time.[77] The practical outcome of this meeting was an August 1993 agreement on the continuation by Russia of all work contracts signed during the Soviet period and on further economic co-operation between the two states.[78] The next year brought a flurry of visits and high-level contacts between the two countries. Iraq's Deputy Foreign Minister, R. Quesi, had been in Moscow on 21 February 1994 and twice in August 1994 (9–10 and 29).[79] Following in his footsteps, between August and December of the same year Iraq's deputy Prime Minister, Tariq Aziz, a man who had been for many years in charge of Iraqi foreign policy and who was a personal confidante of Saddam Hussein, visited Russia on three separate occasions.[80] His December visit was conspicuously timed to coincide with a sharp deterioration in Russian-Western relations. As a Russian journalist noted: 'It was no accident that the arrival of the Iraqi Deputy Prime Minister took place at a time when there was a cooling down of Russian-US relations (which in this case took the form of open clashes of Russian and American positions at the C.S.C.E. summit in Budapest).'[81]

At this time the official Russian position on the UN sanctions regime against Iraq was also publicly altered. In June and July 1994 the Russian representative at the Security Council, Sergey Lavrov, argued that the Security Council should respond to the positive steps which had been undertaken by Iraq and to weaken, if not completely abolish, the sanctions regime.[82] Replying to the other member's opposition to his motion, the Russian Ambassador expressed the opinion that the UN resolutions should be complied with not only by the countries which were originally addressed, but also by the members of the Security Council, including the US and the UK.[83] During the July 1994 UN Security Council session Russia stressed the necessity for parallel and balanced fulfilment of legal obligations by all parties to the Iraqi-Kuwaiti conflict.[84] The Russian government began persuading the Iraqis to recognise the independence and the territorial integrity of Kuwait, which official Iraqi statements had previously referred to as the 19th province of Iraq. In order to achieve Iraqi acceptance and to regain influence in the region, the Russian Foreign Minister, Andrej Kozyrev, who just a year earlier had called Saddam Hussein an 'international ruffian', visited Baghdad twice in the fall of 1994 (October–November).[85] As a result of his talks with the Iraqi leadership, Iraq, for the first time, officially recognised Kuwait as a sovereign nation.[86] However, Kozyrev's diplomatic success was not well received by the US, which saw it as harmful to their interests in the region. They were particularly displeased both because of the possible damage to their propaganda war against Iraq and because of the successful re-entry of Russian diplomacy into the region.[87] As Russian Deputy Foreign Minister Victor Posuvalyuk stated in his briefing on 1 August 1995, Russia did more for the normalisation of Iraqi-Kuwaiti relations than any other state and did not want to play one country against the other.[88]

In May 1995 the Russian Duma (Parliament) adopted a resolution calling for the removal of the oil embargo against Iraq.[89] However, the resolution was not binding for the Russian authorities, but rather had symbolic importance. The Russian leaders, generally, wanted to preserve a kind of balance in their links with both Iraq and Kuwait as well as the West and, while demanding from Baghdad compliance with the relevant UN resolutions, including releasing all Kuwaiti prisoners of war and compensation for lost or stolen property,[90] nevertheless preserved and further developed co-operation with Iraq through the advocacy to end the sanctions. Particularly promising for the Russian side, co-operation in the field of oil production increased. In April 1995 an intergovernmental agreement was concluded which provided for Russian drilling in the oilfields of West Qurna and North Rumaili for a total amount of US$15 billion.[91] In March 1997 another major contract between the Iraqi company SKOP and a group of Russian companies was signed. It provided for the development of the second stage of the West Qurna oilfields, with extractive deposits of oil amounting to 1 billion tons.[92] According to the estimations of the Iraqi experts, the future profits of the Russian companies might have been as high as US$70 billion.[93] However, it is necessary to remember that, at least from a legal point of view, all such projects would start only after the end of the UN-imposed sanctions on Iraq[94] and that the end of sanctions appeared to be quite uncertain. For Iraq the provision of lucrative contracts to Russian petroleum companies represented a method of stimulating Russia to make further efforts towards the lifting of sanctions.[95]

Moreover, Russian corporations and the Russian government were also keenly interested in the repayment by Iraq of its debts, which amount to an estimated US$8.5 billion.[96] For neo-capitalist Russia, which for over a decade has been in a dire economic situation, all this foreign currency is obviously very important. However, Minister Posuvalyuk stressed that economic considerations were not the sole reasons for Russian involvement.[97] Iraq, he said, is 'very geographically close to the former Soviet borders and even Russia itself. It is not a far away country where one can play political games. The developments there have an impact on the political life in Russia, including its domestic problems.'[98] It was, therefore, to be expected that in June 1995 Minister Kozyrev stated that Moscow and Baghdad had 'co-ordinated a course aimed at ending Iraq's international isolation', still contingent on its compliance with the UN resolutions.[99] However, in spite of his efforts in the 1994–95 period, Kozyrev was still widely blamed for neglecting Russian goals and interests in the Middle East.[100] According to many Russian scholars and political commentators, his policy had caused a noticeable decline in Russia's prestige and political influence and a loss of significant economic relations in the region.[101] Kozyrev's ousting in December 1995 came as little surprise. His replacement by Eugenii Primakov, a noted Middle Eastern scholar and a man with a first-hand knowledge of the Arab world, including Iraq, was thus welcomed by many Russians as a positive turning point and an opportunity for an improvement in Russian policy in the region.[102]

II. The Primakov Period, 1996–99

Primakov, first as Foreign Minister (January 1996 to September 1998) and then as Prime Minister (September 1998 to May 1999), has been credited by Russian scholars and commentators with both a clear formulation of Russian foreign policy and the introduction of new ideas and directions.[103] According to a Russian scholar:

> the geostrategic principles which were established by him [have essentially] continued after his departure from the Prime Minister's office. In fact there is no alternative to them and they correspond to Russia's geopolitical aspirations and its new political class which became more pragmatic and less pro-western.[104]

Expressing a wide consensus among the Russian political elite and following trends which were already noticeable during the last two years before he came to power, Primakov wanted to stress both the greatness and global interest of Russia. As he stated during his first press conference as Russian Foreign Minister: 'Russian foreign policy should correspond to its great power status and be active in all azimuths.'[105] This obviously needs to include the Middle East where, as in October 1997 one senior Israeli official said, after his meeting with Primakov, 'he made [it] clear that he wants Russia to demonstrate its sense of being a power in the region'.[106] For a number of geopolitical and economic reasons, Iraq had to become one of his priorities and in addition, he had long established personal links with that country. Between 1968 and 1970 he had worked as a Soviet press correspondent in Baghdad and since that time had had friendly relations with Saddam Hussein.[107] As he admitted himself, he even mediated between Saddam Hussein and the Kurdish nationalists.[108] Primakov's role as Gorbachev's envoy during the second Gulf War was allegedly remembered positively in Iraq and, in any case, when he assumed the post of Russian Foreign Minister, it was welcomed with great satisfaction.[109]

The first major test of his relations with Iraq came in the fall of 1996 when on 4 September 1996 American cruise missiles were launched against Iraqi territory. The US government claimed that the attack was in retaliation for Iraqi military incursions into the specially protected zone in its northern region. According to Russian sources, however, Russian Deputy Foreign Minister Victor Posuvalyuk had already received guarantees from Tariq Aziz on 2 September 1996 that the Iraqi troops that had entered Kurdish territory had been immediately ordered to withdraw on 3–4 September.[110] When, on 2 September 1996, the Americans indicated to the Russians that 'a US strike was inevitable', Moscow disagreed, arguing that because of their diplomatic efforts, the 'situation was basically moving towards a denouement'.[111] However, that was followed by unilateral US and UK aerial bombardments that brought about a predictably strong Russian reaction. Not only did the Ministry of Foreign Affairs protest, but the government as a whole issued a special statement calling the action both 'inadequate and unacceptable'.[112] Moreover, Russian and Iraqi political and economic co-operation was expanded, and in order to stay in touch with Primakov, Tariq Aziz repeatedly visited Moscow: on 11 November 1996, 4–6 March 1997 and 9 May 1997.[113] From that time, Russia, together with other states, especially France and China, created an informal 'pro-Iraqi lobby' in the UN Security Council in order to weaken the sanctions and to constrain US action.[114]

Nevertheless, these efforts were frustrated by US diplomacy and unilateral actions. The diplomatic battle in the UN Security Council on the report by the UN Special Commission and the resolution on Iraq focused on the request by Russia, France and some other states to include in it a clear statement on the many positive steps taken by Iraq and its co-operation with the disarmament programme, and on their opposition to the additional sanctions against that country.[115] The final text of Resolution 1134, which was adopted by the majority of Security Council members on 23 October 1997, did not introduce additional sanctions directly, but also did not mention Iraqi positive co-operation.[116] Consequently, Russia had considered it to be both 'unbalanced and not objective' and together with France, China, Kenya and Egypt, abstained on the motion.[117] The situation was further aggravated when, on 29 October 1997, Iraq ordered all American inspectors of the UN Special Commission (UNSCOM) to leave Iraq within one week while also demanding the cessation of US air surveillance flights over Iraqi territory. Russia, together with France, then issued a statement on 1 November 1997, which condemned Iraqi actions but stressed that all new steps concerning Iraq should be undertaken only with the authorisation of the Security Council.[118] The statement also made it clear that the outcome of Iraqi co-operation with the UNSCOM should be 'lifting of the oil embargo and full reintegration of Iraq into the international community'.[119]

The same goals were reiterated in a joint Russian-Iraqi statement on 19 November 1997. The statement, which was formulated by Primakov and Tariq Aziz, promised that:

> On the basis of Iraq's fulfilment of the relevant UN Security Council resolutions, Russia...will energetically work for the earliest possible lifting of the sanctions against Iraq and, above all, for putting into effect point 22 of Resolution No. 687....To this end, active steps will be taken to increase the effectiveness of the special Commission's work while showing respect for the sovereignty and security of Iraq.[120]

With that statement in hand, Primakov called to Geneva on 20 November 1997 those representatives of the five countries that are permanent members of the UN Security Council, and persuaded them to accept the arrangement.[121] After the talks ended, he concluded with understandable satisfaction: 'this is a great success for Russian diplomacy, one that is recognised by absolutely everyone....It was achieved without the use of force and without a show of force; it was achieved through diplomatic means.'[122] His satisfaction was shared by virtually all Russian scholars and commentators, who indicated that this success was 'the first of its kind in recent years', and that 'this time Moscow...played the role of a world power that averted what at first had seemed to be an inevitable war in the Persian Gulf'.[123]

Thanks to Russian mediation in November 1997, a new outbreak of violence was avoided, but the underlying conflict was not resolved. In fact it soon reignited, focusing this time both on the dispute over the UNSCOM's inspectors' access to presidential palace sites and the widely held allegations that the Americans and the Israelis used UNSCOM as a shield for their own intelligence penetration.[124] On 11 January 1998 Baghdad blocked inspections by UNSCOM teams led by Scott Ritter, who indeed later admitted his co-operation with the Israeli agencies.[125] Iraq argued that UNSCOM had too many members from the US and did not work in a manner that promoted a 'respect for the sovereignty and security of Iraq', as had been agreed upon in previous negotiations. When the US and their UK allies wanted to use their military might, Russia once again argued that a diplomatic solution in the framework of the UN system should be found. The Russian position was by and large in line with the opinions of the Arab world, France, China and the great majority of the other UN members. In February 1998 the Russian Minister of Defence, Igor

Sergeyev, indicated to his US counterpart, William Cohen, during the latter's visit to Russia, that Moscow believed that the Iraqi crisis represented a threat to vital Russian national interests and it could not be approached only in the context of US-Iraqi relations.[126] With the very few exceptions of 'radical democrats' who have always been pro-American,[127] Russian public opinion thought that in a war against Iraq the US 'would be pursuing purely hegemonistic aims' and that although 'one can condemn Hussein's totalitarian regime, and demands that Iraq destroy its weapons of mass destruction...one cannot hold hostage to American interests the entire long suffering Iraqi people...who will be the first casualties of American bombing'.[128]

On 3 February 1998 Primakov approved the draft of a resolution on the Iraqi crisis that was adopted the next day by the Duma. The resolution condemned the trend towards the use of force against Iraq and emphasised the need to resolve the crisis by peaceful means. It also stressed particularly that it was not permissible to use tactical nuclear weapons, which the Americans were then preparing to use in their planned operation.[129] The same day President Yeltsin warned US President Clinton that by his threats of military action against Iraq he 'might run right into a new world war'.[130] Russia had again been actively mediating in the new round of crises and Deputy Foreign Minister Posuvalyuk was shuttling between Moscow and Baghdad. However, in view of the very serious situation which was dangerous for regional peace, on 13 February 1998 Primakov concluded that 'the time has come for a visit to Baghdad by the UN Secretary-General Kofi Annan'. As he then asserted, 'one cannot talk about failed diplomatic efforts or reach a verdict before Annan goes to Baghdad'.[131]

Annan's mission, which took place in February 1998, was strongly supported by Russian diplomacy. It was none other than Primakov who, at Kofi Annan's request, had persuaded Saddam Hussein to back down from insisting on a time limit for the inspection of his presidential sites.[132] The Memorandum on Mutual Understanding between the UN and Iraq, which was signed by Kofi Annan with the Iraqi authorities on 23 February 1998, provided for unhindered work by the UNSCOM inspectors in exchange for recognition of Iraqi sovereignty and a comprehensive review of sanctions. The Memorandum was hailed by the Russian government and was unanimously approved by UN Security Council Resolution 1154 on 2 March 1998.[133] However, the resolution also included a clause threatening the 'severest consequences' if Iraq reneged on the agreement.[134] Nevertheless, according to its Russian interpretation, it did not authorise use of force without the previous approval of the Security Council.[135]

The problem of interpretation of this clause became very controversial when on 5 August 1998 Iraq suspended its co-operation with UNSCOM. Baghdad argued that the inspectors were intentionally delaying the completion of their task in order to prolong the sanctions regime, and that the Security Council could not have obtained an adequate picture of the situation from them.[136] In response to this new round of crises, Russia reiterated its position, according to which Iraq should fulfil all the obligations that had been imposed by the Security Council and co-operate in a constructive manner with the UNSCOM inspectors. As a result, the Iraqi disarmament file would be closed and, according to point 22, Resolution 687, the Security Council would be able to remove the oil embargo.[137] It was recognised that, at that particular time, the most important factor was the preservation of restraint by all parties in order to avoid any further deterioration.[138] The crisis was then temporarily solved and UNSCOM returned to Iraq in September. After this short conflict, Baghdad provided its solemn promise no longer to obstruct UNSCOM's work.[139] The Russian position and Russian-Iraqi co-operation were confirmed again by Primakov, who was by then Russian Prime Minister, when Tariq Aziz visited Moscow on 7 December 1998.[140]

Both Russian intentions and Iraqi expectations, however, became frustrated when on 17 December 1998 the US and the UK began bombing Iraqi territory. According to Russian sources, the attack was not provoked by any Iraqi actions and took place exactly at the time when an emergency session of the UN Security Council, which had been convened at Russia's request, met to discuss the tensions between Baghdad and UNSCOM.[141] The attack was preceded by the provocative actions of the UNSCOM head, Richard Butler, who during the week prior to the attack deliberately became confrontational with the Iraqi authorities. On 15 December 1998 he submitted a biased report to the UN Security Council and immediately ordered his staff to leave Baghdad. As the Russian press indicated, 'only about 24 hours passed between Butler's report and the first strike'.[142]

Russian politicians of all orientations reacted to the events with strong condemnation and protests. According to President Yeltsin's statement, the UN Security Council resolutions did not provide authorisation for such actions.[143] Yeltsin considered it to be 'a gross violation of the UN Charter and universally accepted principles of international law' and called for an immediate end to the attacks.[144] Primakov stressed that Iraq did not provoke the bombardment and that the sole responsibility rested on the US administration, which had acted against Russia's warnings and advice. He characterised Richard Butler's behaviour as scandalous and announced that Russia would call an urgent meeting of the UN Security Council.[145] On 18 December 1998 the Russian Duma asked President Yeltsin to:

1. Get Russia out of participation in the sanctions against Iraq imposed by the UN Security Council Resolutions as all of them 'have been trampled upon by the recent aggression'.
2. Take all necessary means in order to fully re-establish normal economic and military-technological relations with Iraq.[146]

Russian politicians were particularly concerned that, as President Yeltsin indicated, they were 'essentially dealing with an action that undermines the entire international security system', and that the voice of Russia was apparently being neglected.[147] Expressing those fears, powerful Russian businessman and then CIS Executive Secretary Boris Berezovsky openly admitted that 'a new page was opened in a world order in which the dominant role of the US is absolute',[148] and that 'Russia joined a number of countries that don't have to be reckoned with.'[149]

In addition to concerns about the new structure of the international system and the place of their country in it, Russian politicians also defended Iraq in pursuit of more directly economic interests. According to some Russian diplomats: 'Iraq is virtually the only place on earth where the interests of Russia and the US are not simply at cross purposes, but essentially in rigid opposition to each other.'[150] A struggle was going on between Russian and American oil companies over the exploitation of Iraq's natural resources and for investment in that country.[151] Because of hostility between the US and the Baghdad regime, American companies had found themselves at a disadvantage and Russian companies, strongly supported by Russian diplomacy, had won many lucrative contracts.[152] Since the passage of UN Security Council Resolution 986 of 14 April 1995, that allowed Iraq to sell $2 billion worth of oil over a period of six months in order to pay for essential humanitarian imports (the oil-for-food programme) Russian companies received highly favourable treatment by the Iraqi authorities.[153] Their share in exporting Iraqi oil during the first six stages of the oil-for-food programme, amounted to approximately 40 per cent of the total volume of Iraqi oil exports.[154] Between 1998 and 1999 Russian companies also procured the highest volume of non-military goods delivered to Iraq (approximately US$500 million) and in 2000 all of Iraq's orders to Russia exceeded US$20 billion.[155] Consequently, since the mid-1990s the Russians have believed that it is precisely because of Russian economic success and even better prospects for the future profit that 'Washington will now do everything in its power to prevent an easing of the embargo.'[156] Because of the Iraqi government's guarantees to pay the debt it owed to Russia as its first priority, Moscow was additionally interested in the prevention of war and further destruction and, in the end, of the sanctions.[157]

When the American and British bombardment ended on 20 December 1998, President Yeltsin hailed an end to the 'senseless, unlawful action' and called for 'extensive aid in the form of food, medicine and all the other things which are needed to lead a peaceful existence' for the 'Iraqi people, the victims of the bombing'.[158] However, on all these occasions there were some clear limits to the level of Russia's independent action and to its resistance to US pressure. Despite all its efforts towards the lifting of sanctions against Iraq, the Russian government did not accede to the demand from the Russian Duma to abolish these unilaterally and, while continuing in its attempts to protect Iraq against new US military interventions, Russia at the same time stressed that Iraq should comply fully with all relevant UN resolutions and submit to further UNSCOM disarmament inspections.[159] In spite of all the harsh protests against the US and UK air strikes against Iraq, an informed source in Russian diplomatic circles told the press, on 19 December 1998 that 'a return to confrontation [with the US] is not worth it for the very reason that it is not in our interests'.[160] Even earlier, on 18 December 1998, President Yeltsin's spokesman, Dimitry Yakushkin, stated to the media that: 'There can be no talk of a rift between Russia and the US and the UK...we mustn't slip into the rhetoric of confrontation',[161] and Boris Berezovski called for 'a separation of our emotions from a rational assessment of events'.[162]

On 12 May 1999 Primakov was forced to quit the office of Prime Minister, but even after his dismissal Russian policy toward Iraq, although now without his direct personal involvement and expertise, had remained basically unchanged. On 1 June 1999 the Director of the Russian Ministry of Foreign Affairs' Press Office, V.O. Rahmanin, again reiterated 'the persistent and continuous efforts of Russian diplomacy to achieve a political solution to the Iraqi problem on the basis of lifting sanctions from Iraq'.[163] Towards that end, in April

1999 Russia, China and France submitted a draft of the Security Council's resolution which proposed replacing 'Butler's Special Commission which compromised itself' by a new system of international monitoring of Iraqi military potential with simultaneous lifting of most of the economic sanctions.[164] Under this proposal the oil embargo and the ban on civil imports into the country would come to an end, although the ban on all kinds of military co-operation and strict control over the delivery of dual-purpose goods would be maintained.[165] The proposals were opposed by the US, which instead supported a draft resolution that was submitted at the same time by the UK and the Netherlands, which preserved UNSCOM and the sanctions regime.[166] According to Russian sources, despite the differences between the two positions, Russian diplomacy aimed to avoid an open clash between the permanent members and looked for a compromise.[167] After a prolonged stalemate, on 17 December 1999 the Security Council adopted Resolution 1284 which provided for some improvement of humanitarian conditions in Iraq but, according to Moscow, still contained 'ambiguous wording' which allowed for the postponement of the lifting of sanctions.[168] As a result, Russia, China, France and Malaysia, the latter then being a non-permanent Security Council member, abstained from voting,[169] and the Russian representative indicated that the effectiveness of the resolution would be shown when it was put into practice.[170] Earlier, on 28 September 1999, Russian Deputy Foreign Minister Vasilii O. Sredin reiterated the Russian position on Iraq, calling for a rapid lifting of the sanctions on the basis of Iraqi fulfilment of the UN Security Council resolutions.[171] He characterised the American and British bombardment of Iraq in December 1998 as 'absolutely illegal' and made them responsible for the 'destruction of the unique mechanism of international control' over Iraqi military development. In October 1999 the Russian Minister of Trade and Energy, Victor Kaluzhnyi, went to Baghdad and passed a personal letter to Saddam Hussein from Yeltsin, in which he declared himself to be in favour of ending the embargo.[172] Yeltsin resigned in December 1999, and in early 2000 Vladimir Putin, who inaugurated a new period in post-Soviet Russian history, took his place following the Russian presidential elections.

III. The Putin Period 1999–2002

Primakov's Iraqi politics, like his foreign policy in general, was characterised by an effort toward Russian self-assertiveness, a continuity of the country's old traditions, and considerable self-restraint caused by its present weakness and general economic and social crises. Under somewhat different circumstances, Putin and his Foreign Minister, Igor Ivanov's policy toward Iraq for some time largely followed the same path, although perhaps in an even more cautious and circumspect way. In addition to the still increasing general weakness of the country and the fact that neither Putin nor his Foreign Minister Ivanov had any personal knowledge of, or links with the Middle East as a whole, or Iraq specifically, there were two critical political factors which were now to impact on Russian policy toward Iraq.

First, in marked contrast to the Soviet era and to a certain point even the post-Soviet Primakov period, Israel has emerged as a desirable strategic ally in the Middle East for the Russian ruling elite.[173] According to A. Malygin, who teaches at the Moscow State Institute of International Relations of the Russian Ministry of Foreign Affairs, Russia does not have any conflicting interests with that country, and their co-operation will be further promoted by the Russian-language diaspora in Israel and the common threat of Islamic extremism.[174] In addition, co-operation with Israel seems more profitable to the Russians than co-operation with any other country in the Middle East. Israel can provide access to modern Western technology and both the Israeli and the world Jewish diaspora's international influence is incomparably stronger than those of any other single state in the region.[175]

A second important factor was the new and improved Russian relations with Iraq's neighbours, Iran and Turkey. On 1 December 2000, under Putin's leadership, Moscow repudiated the Gore–Chernomyrdin Agreement of 30 June 1995 and decided to resume arms sales to Iran.[176] This was not only repudiation of the agreement itself, but also signalled Russia's intention to reconsider the basic tenets of Russian foreign policy as it had been formulated in the mid-1990s when that policy was led by Yeltsin, Chernomyrdin and Kozyrev.[177] The Russian media commented: 'within Moscow political circles, both Indian and Iranian experiences have helped shape the conviction that never again should relations with any of Moscow's partners serve as a bargaining chip for trade with the US or any other country'.[178] The geopolitical goal in the case of success is 'an informal Indian-Iranian-Russian alliance, one that will make the vulnerable "soft underbelly" of the CIS into a firm foundation for the post-Soviet space'.[179] Although there were still a number of outstanding political problems between Russia and Turkey,[180] from an economic viewpoint

Turkey now became the most important Russian partner in the region and both countries already had advanced co-operation in the fields of security and the struggle against 'terrorism'.[181] In view of all these developments, Iraq's strategic value for Russia, which was so important for it in the past, had now apparently declined.[182]

However, this does not necessarily mean that Iraq had now become unimportant to Russia and that Putin's administration had not paid particular attention to its relationship with Iraq. Speaking to the media on the tenth anniversary of the Second Gulf War, Sergei Zhiravlev, the head of the Russian Society for Friendship with Iraq, expressed the opinion that, while Mikhail Gorbachev had failed to defend Russia's national interests at the time of the Second Gulf War, the Putin government appeared to be taking a different stand.[183] Although obviously optimistic, his view was nevertheless not inaccurate. For a number of political and economic reasons, the Iraqi case probably represented one of the few issues on which Russian leaders were still willing to openly and persistently disagree with the US and its allies.[184] During his first visit to Moscow since Putin came to power in June 2000, Tariq Aziz was told by the Russian Security Council Secretary, Sergei V. Ivanov, that: 'Russia continues to apply maximum pressure for the quickest end, and then the permanent lifting of international sanctions against Iraq.'[185] The Russian side also stressed the importance of the reinstallation of international monitoring of Iraqi military programmes which were forbidden after the Second Gulf War and the need for its full co-operation with the new organ of supervision, the United Nations Monitoring, Verification and Inspection Commission (UNMOVIC).[186] However, in the view of the Russian government, the Security Council should have strictly controlled UNMOVIC in order to avoid the fate of its discredited predecessor, UNSCOM.[187]

During his next visit to Moscow in November 2000, Tariq Aziz had long and reportedly difficult talks with Russian leaders, but Russian-Iraqi friendship was not in question.[188] Before his departure, he stated on Russian national television:

> For the last 10 years, some people have held jobs in the Russian government without knowing the country's history of relations with its Soviet-era friends....But...now Russian authorities can feel the traditions extending over the centuries of good relations with the East, with Iraq, the Arab world, India and China.[189]

In February 2001, when US and UK forces attacked Iraq yet again, President Putin stated that such 'unprovoked actions do not help settle the situation regarding Iraq'[190] and immediately called the French President, Jacques Chirac, regarding the 'impermissibility' of the actions.[191] The Russian Foreign Ministry issued an official statement criticising the military intervention[192] and Dimitrii Rogozin, the Chairman of the Duma's Foreign Affairs Committee, went as far as to announce that he would ask the Duma to pass a resolution calling on President Putin to lift the sanctions on Iraq unilaterally in response to the bombardment.[193] In the final outcome, however, the Duma on 22 February 2001 approved by a vote of 359 to 2 a resolution calling on President Putin simply to seek a UN decision to lift the sanctions regime against Iraq, thus rejecting Rogozin's original proposal.[194] Two days earlier, Foreign Ministry spokesman Aleksandr Yakovenko admitted that it was '"virtually impossible" for Russia...to raise the issue of US and British air strikes in the UN Security Council'.[195] Russia's post-Soviet weakened position was once again noted, even more so than during the previous US and UK attacks in 1996 and 1998.

The unsuccessful Russian efforts to have the sanctions lifted or even temporarily suspended caused dissatisfaction in Iraq, which started to threaten a cancellation of a contract with the Russian company, Lukoil, for the development of Iraqi oil fields.[196] The Russian government answered these criticisms with increased diplomatic and political activity at the UN, which was, however, only of symbolic value. Members of the Duma began to form a Russian-Iraqi interparliamentary commission on bilateral co-operation,[197] and there continued a lively exchange of delegations between the two countries.[198]

In addition to these geopolitical and economic factors, the Russian political elite also turned its attention to Iraq in response to strong Russian public opinion supporting the lifting of the sanctions. A poll conducted by the All Russian Centre for the Study of Public Opinion, published on 2 March 2001, found that 58 per cent of Russians were upset and angry about the February 2001 American and British attack on Iraq. Only 2 per cent of those polled approved of the attack.[199] Bearing in mind today's very low level of interest in, and even less sympathy for, the Arabs among Eastern Europeans, Russian popular support for Iraq was a fairly puzzling phenomenon and could probably be partly explained by their feeling of solidarity with their former ally of the Soviet era and a dislike of American arrogance. However, it is also necessary to remember that: 'Moscow was now far from speaking "with one voice on Iraq"'[200] and that there were also some influential circles there which were ready to sacrifice Iraq on the altar of better relations with the West – particularly with the US.[201] Since the mid-1990s these had just been a minority, but because of the dramatic world events and Putin's political pragmatism, their influence would again increase in the future.

During the spring and summer of 2002, the situation in the Middle East, both in Palestine/Israel and in the Gulf region, deteriorated still further. In spite of the Saudi proposal to put an end to the protracted Arab-Israeli conflict, George W. Bush's administration decided to fully support Israeli policy and to prepare for a military invasion of Iraq. Bush himself had spoken to such an extent about 'destroying Saddam' that he could hardly be re-elected in 2004 without some show of US military power.[202] American leaders repeatedly spoke about their fears of Iraq's development and acquisition of chemical, biological and even nuclear weapons and the threat they would represent to Iraq's neighbours and to US interests in the region. It was now becoming apparent that many US leaders wanted to win control over Iraq's immense oil resources, which would enhance US energy security and dramatically decrease Saudi Arabia's leverage on US policy.[203] However, according to an American analyst, the main problem was still the fact that 'the European Union, Russia and China are none too keen on Washington's plan'.[204] Thanks to its geographic proximity, its well-established economic co-operation with Baghdad, and a new-found subservience to the United States, Russia still played an important strategic role in the post-September 11 international system as a gateway to Central Asia and an indispensable provider of intelligence information to the US 'war on terror'.

Nevertheless, Russia's official position towards the Iraqi question for a long time had remained unchanged. On 17 July 2002 Russian Foreign Minister Igor Ivanov stated that his country 'does not share the US position on the need to remove Iraqi leader Saddam Hussein from power'.[205] As he then warned, 'if military plans in relation to Iraq are put into practice, this will further complicate the situation [in the area of] the Palestine–Israeli [conflict], in the Gulf area, and in the Middle East as a whole'.[206] One day earlier, Russian Defence Minister Sergei Ivanov had made a similar point stating that: 'Russia is against any unilateral force action against Iraq...taken without sanction by the UN Security Council.'[207] He admitted that apart from purely geopolitical interests, Moscow also has economic interests and that as 'Iraq is our longstanding partner and debtor...we cannot be indifferent to events happening there.'[208] Russia's position was then highly appreciated by the Arab leaders.

In April 2001 Jasim al Khurafi, Speaker of the Kuwaiti National Assembly, was received in Moscow at the time of the Iraqi Vice President's visit. After his return, he told the London-based Arab daily *Al Sharq al-Awsad* that, according to him:

> Russia's position is a principled and moral one...Russia demonstrated this position at the time of the [Iraqi] invasion of Kuwait [in 1990–91]. Russia had clear, firm stands on all measures pertaining to the invasion of Kuwait.[209]

He also recalled that Kuwait's ties with Russia have a long tradition behind them and that Kuwait was one of the first Gulf states to establish diplomatic relations with Moscow. He believed that 'the special relationship between Russia and Kuwait is no less important than Russia's relationship with Iraq'.[210]

Continuing its previous support of Baghdad, Moscow wanted to strengthen its links with the other Gulf countries and as far as possible, to avoid confrontation with the Americans. However, in spite of all its caution and restraint, Russia had then remained Iraq's closest ally among the UN Security Council Permanent Members, including France and China. In so doing, it was obviously acting in defence of its own vested interests. In addition to strategic and geopolitical considerations such as Iraqi support in Chechyna, Russia had enormous economic and financial stakes in Iraq. According to Russian Deputy Foreign Minister A. Saltanov, in the first ten months of 2001 Russia and Iraq signed contracts worth more than its US$1.85 billion and under the sanctions programme the trade links between both countries exceeded US$25 billion. He stated that 'In 2001, Iraq secured its position as Russia's leading partner in the Arab world, with a turnover of goods with that country accounting for 60 per cent of that with all Arab countries.'[211]

However, the international sanctions against Iraq had a very negative impact on the Russian economy. According to Russian Foreign Minister Igor Ivanov's detailed report which he sent to UN Secretary-General Kofi Annan in the spring of 2001, all Moscow's losses over the previous ten years amounted to about US$30 billion.[212] In August 2001 Yury Shafranik, a former Russian fuel and energy minister, who then worked as liaison between Russian companies, the government and Iraq, admitted that because of Russia's opposition to 'smart sanctions' against Iraq proposed by the US and the UK, it had acquired a kind of 'favoured nation status' with Baghdad. He told journalists that 'Russia will be given priorities on all tenders, UN approved and otherwise.'[213] Also in August 2001, Iraqi Oil Minister Amir Muhammed Rasheed confirmed that his country would favour Russia, Syria, Jordan and Turkey in concluding oil contracts because of their support for Iraq at the UN. However, he stressed that 'Russia is in the first place, then neighbouring countries, and co-operation with these states will be reflected in all economic and political spheres.'[214]

Even earlier, Russian diplomats signed a document with Baghdad called 'Directions on the Priority of Russian Companies', under which contracts of more than US$1.2 billion were made during the year 2000 alone,[215] and in January 2002 Russia had risen to first place on the list of Iraq's main trading partners, leaving behind Egypt and France.[216] It was no wonder that the Russian-Iraqi economic forum which was held in November 2001 called on President Putin and the Russian government to take every possible measure to block the draft of the British-American resolution concerning 'smart sanctions' against Iraq in the UN Security Council and even to use the veto power, if necessary.[217] Russian political and business leaders genuinely believed that new, tighter restrictions against Baghdad could cost them billions of dollars.

The major debate on the new regime of sanctions, which was proposed by Britain and supported by the US, comprised two stages. The first lasted from the submission of the British proposal on 22 May 2001 until 3 July 2001, when the Security Council finally approved a five-month extension of the UN oil-for-food programme, without any reference to a new system of sanctions.[218] On 22 May 2001 Britain attached its plan to a resolution extending the oil-for-food programme, which would expire by the end of the month. Both US and British diplomats tried to push through the proposal in just eight working days, but ran against opposition from the other three permanent UN Security Council members: China, France and Russia. The three powers argued that they needed more time to study the proposal, which included long lists of allegedly military and/or 'dual-use' goods that should not be made available to Iraq,[219] and Russian Foreign Minister I. Ivanov openly threatened to use the veto if the resolution was still submitted to a vote.[220] As a temporary measure, the Security Council then agreed on 1 June 2001 to extend the oil-for-food programme for one month instead of the usual six, in order to allow more time for further talks. Resolution 1352, which was adopted however, then indicated the intention of the Council to 'agree on new rules for the supply of goods to Iraq within a month'.[221] While the Russians interpreted that as 'the possibility of lifting sanctions', in the Iraqi view it was rather a tacit acceptance of the 'smart sanctions' which Iraq had categorically rejected.[222]

By the end of June, despite all diplomatic efforts, the differences of opinions remained unsolved. France and China agreed to the Anglo-American proposals, but Russia did not. Moscow argued that any overhaul of sanctions must address the lifting of sanctions that were widely blamed for human suffering in Iraq and submitted its own rival resolution that would suspend sanctions on civilian goods once UN inspectors certified that a long-term weapons monitoring programme for Iraq was installed.[223] In the Russian view, Resolution 1360, which was finally adopted on 3 July 2001 and which extended the oil-for-food programme for 150 days, reflected a possible consensus among Security Council members and could open the way for a solution to the UN-Iraqi problem.[224] Nevertheless, some other parties considered it to be 'a victory for Baghdad',[225] and Saddam Hussein expressed his gratitude for 'Russia's approach'. He stated to a Putin envoy:

> We are pleased with your position, not because it aborted a Security Council Resolution...we were pleased because you knew the right way...while bearing in mind the historical relations between Baghdad and Moscow and the geographical factor that makes you the closest big power to the Arab world and not to Iraq alone.[226]

After the 11 September 2001 terrorist attacks on American soil, and in view of the subsequent hardening of US policy and Putin's new rapprochement with Washington DC, the Iraqi situation deteriorated markedly. In November 2001, during the next stage of the sanctions debate, Russia had originally opposed the Anglo-American proposals. On 1 November 2001, after his talks with Russian Foreign Minister Ivanov, British Foreign Secretary Jack Straw admitted that 'there is not yet agreement with Russia',[227] and even after US Secretary of State Colin Powell's talks with Ivanov on 26 November, it was widely assumed that the US and Russia were still at odds over the future of sanctions.[228] Two days later, however, Russia had apparently compromised and as Vladimir Safrankov, a political counsellor at the Russian Mission to the UN, admitted, Moscow 'accepted the philosophy' of the British-American proposals.[229] On 28 November 2001 the five permanent members of the UN Security Council agreed to extend the oil-for-food programme for six months to 31 May 2002, and to adopt a review of goods by then in order to ban the dual-use items entering Iraq.[230] The Security Council approved Resolution 1382 containing the compromise on 29 November, thus setting the stage for an overhaul of UN sanctions against Baghdad in the coming months.[231] Iraq's reactions were sharp and there was open disappointment there about the Russian position. On 1 December 2001, Iraqi Foreign Minister Naji Sabri al Hadith stated that: 'those who concocted this resolution sought to ignore Iraq's right to obtain a lifting of the embargo, and skirt the provisions of the [1996] Memorandum of Understanding, which established the oil-for-food programme, clamping new restrictions on Iraqi imports'.[232] The editorial in the paper *Babil*, which is owned by Odai Hussein, the son of President Saddam Hussein, expressed the opinion that

> The US pushes the Security Council to approve a six-month extension of the Oil for Food Programme in order to have enough time to finish its work in Afghanistan and also to fabricate pretexts acceptable to the allies to attack Iraq.[233]

The paper added that those countries that oppose a US attack on Iraq are 'motivated by mere trade interests, rather than any ethical or humanitarian considerations'.[234] Although it did not mention states by name, it was nevertheless widely assumed that it was referring to Russia and France.[235]

At the time Resolution 1382 was being approved, a more serious threat to Baghdad was already raising its head. On 26 November 2001 President G.W. Bush warned Saddam Hussein that he must allow the weapons inspectors back into the country or face the consequences.[236] It was perceived as a veiled threat that Iraq could be next on America's hit-list once the then ongoing operation in Afghanistan was over. Russia immediately opposed possible US military strikes against Iraq, stressing that diplomacy was the only way to solve the arms inspections impasse between the UN and Baghdad.[237] At the same time, however, Russia also called for Iraq's unconditional compliance with the respective resolutions of the UN Security Council, and on 9 December 2001 Vladimir Titorenko, Deputy Director of the Russian

Foreign Ministry's Department for the Near East and Africa, emphasised that Moscow linked the lifting of sanctions against Iraq with a resumption of the work of UN disarmament inspectors in that country.[238]

On the eve of Iraqi Deputy Prime Minister Tariq Aziz's arrival in Moscow on 23 January 2002, Russian Foreign Ministry sources told French journalists that Russia would use his visit to press Baghdad to resume co-operation with the inspectors in return for the suspension of sanctions.[239]

The Russian Foreign Ministry's ambassador at large, Nikolai Kartuzov, in a comment on media reports of the US intention to bomb Iraq in an extension of the anti-terrorist operations in Afghanistan, nevertheless stressed that there were 'no reasons for American retaliatory action against Iraq'.[240] He stated that

There is no evidence of Baghdad's complicity in the events of September 11, nor is there proof that Iraqi supports terrorists....If the Americans decide to deliver a blow to Iraq, it will be the worst case scenario that would lead to catastrophic consequences for the region....The Iraqi problem warrants a political settlement.[241]

The talks that Prime Minister Tariq Aziz had during his two visits to Moscow in the last ten days of January 2002 were described by the Iraqi ambassador to Russia, Dr Maujir Al-Dauri, as 'extremely constructive and useful'.[242] He stated the exchange of 'visits by Russian and Iraqi political leaders will be continued'.[243] According to the well-informed Russian daily, *Nezavisimaya Gazeta*, however, Russian Foreign Minister Ivanov tried to persuade Tariq Aziz to let the UN inspectors back into Iraq as soon as possible. Moscow wanted Iraq to compromise, since it did not want to provoke the US and believed that sanctions could be suspended only after international monitoring was in place.[244] In contrast to the issue of UN observers, Moscow and Baghdad had no differences regarding possible American aggression against Iraq, and Russia saw no grounds for US retaliatory action against that country.[245]

Although in his State of the Union Address before the US Congress on 29 January 2002, President G.W. Bush was 'extremely aggressive with regard to Iraq',[246] and reinforced his previous threats and intimidation regarding that country, and implicitly to its supporters,[247] Moscow had not then changed its mind.[248] Russia was engaged in consultations with the US on the sanctions, and according to 'a well connected' diplomatic source in Moscow, 'a certain headway [had] been achieved in the course of these negotiations'.[249] The US Ambassador to the UN Security Council, John Negroponte, was even more optimistic. In his speech on 27 February 2002 at Georgetown University he expressed his confidence that Washington and Moscow would work out an agreement by the 1 June 2002 deadline on a list of goods for Iraq.[250] According to him, differences in positions of the sides mostly concerned the volume of the list of goods imported into Iraq under the so-called 'accelerated' scheme, that is, without the approval of the UN sanctions committee, which was in practice very difficult to get.[251] Russia also supported all UN resolutions on Iraq and continued to put pressure on Saddam Hussein to let international inspectors back into the country.[252]

Security Council Resolution 1409, which was adopted on 14 May 2002, again extended the oil-for-food programme for a six-month period but also included the goods review list (GRL), which contained items that allegedly may have dual military and civilian uses. Availability of materials on the GRL to be imported into Iraq would still require submission to the strictly elaborated UN supervision and control mechanism. The GRL was an outcome of long negotiations, item by item, by diplomats from Russia, France, China, the United Kingdom and the United States. Moscow, which a year earlier had staunchly opposed the implementation of 'smart sanctions', now approved the GRL, arguing that it was not 'prohibitive in character' but only 'corrected the malfunctioning "oil for food" system'.[253] However, Resolution 1409 was also only a partial US success. Under intense protests from Iraq's neighbours, most of the US-UK proposals related to 'smart sanctions', such as closer monitoring of Iraq's borders to prevent oil smuggling, were abandoned.[254] According to the head of the Russian Foreign Ministry's International Organisation Department, Yuri Fedotov, the main goal of the Russian approval of the resolution was to prevent further US military strikes at targets in Iraq. In his view, Washington would find it 'much more difficult to justify its actions against Iraq before the international community' after the approval of Resolution 1409.[255] The Russian Foreign Ministry at the same time stressed that 'corrections of the UN humanitarian programme', introduced by the resolution, did 'not change the essence of our perception of the mechanism' which Moscow viewed as 'temporary' and not meant to become a 'full-scale alternative to Iraqi social and economic development which will only be possible after the existing sanctions against [Iraq] are lifted on the conditions envisaged by the respective resolutions on the UN Security Council'.[256] Russia sharply criticised the practice of a retroactive pricing policy on Iraqi oil that had been initiated by the US and Britain in October 2001.[257] According to the Russian Foreign Ministry, such a pricing policy had made it difficult for Iraq to negotiate oil contracts, 'since no one will buy oil without knowing the price'.[258] Russia also complained that the interests of oil companies, including its own, were suffering as a result of the action by the US and Britain.[259] On the other hand, Russian Foreign Minister Igor Ivanov pointed out that 'if the process of political settlement of the situation surrounding Iraq is dragged out, this will naturally produce grounds for talks to those who favour other solutions, presumably a military intervention'.[260] According to the Russian leaders, it was in order to avoid this outcome that their country was 'taking all necessary efforts to find a political solution to the problem of Iraq',[261] and for that purpose international observers should be sent there 'but not for good'.[262] The results of their inspections should be linked directly to the possibility of lifting sanctions from Iraq and 'if international inspectors say there are no weapons of mass destruction in Iraq, the sanctions must be lifted'.[263]

In the extremely tense and uncertain atmosphere following September 11, the Israeli incursions and reoccupation of the West Bank, and the spiralling escalation of the 'war on terror', there was no lack of rumours pointing to an alleged Russian acceptance of the prospective American military strike against Iraq which Washington 'succeeded in buying with promises to maintain its commercial, oil, and economic interests in Iraq after [the fall of] Saddam'.[264] The analysis of the known facts and data suggests that Moscow had, for a long time, genuinely opposed a prospective third Gulf war near its borders and traditional zones of influence. In the existing balance of power, however, it had neither the means nor sufficient interest to stop a unilateral United States invasion of Iraq.[265] In July 2002 Russian Foreign Minister Igor Ivanov admitted: 'if the bombing of Iraq became inevitable, we will proceed from the situation arising',[266] and 'the task of Russian diplomacy now is to avoid the complication of Russia's relations with the West over Iraq'.[267] There is no doubt that the clash of interests and priorities involved in the Iraqi crisis represented a major challenge to the Putin administration as Moscow tried to protect its interests under the existing conditions of US hegemony along with its own determination to preserve its traditional great power status. On 16 July 2002 Russia condemned US and British air strikes against Iraq, and on the same day, President Vladimir Putin sent a cable to Iraqi President Saddam Hussein on the occasion of an Iraqi national holiday, pledging to help prevent US military intervention and to work in order to reach 'a comprehensive solution to the Iraqi issue through diplomatic and political means only'.[268] At that time, in Moscow's view, such a solution still needed to take into account both 'inspectors resuming work in Iraq...and...working out models for taking this country out of the sanctions regime'.[269]

Between September and November 2002 the Bush administration used all sorts of pressure and promises in order to persuade Russia and other great powers to follow its lead on Iraq. As former CIA director R. James Woolsey, who has also been one of the leading proponents of the invasion of Iraq, openly indicated:

> France and Russia have oil companies and interests in Iraq. They should be told that if they are in need of assistance in moving Iraq toward a decent government, we'll do the best we can to ensure that the new government and American companies work closely with them...[but] if they throw in their lot with Saddam, it will be difficult to the point of impossibility to persuade the new Iraqi government to work with them.[270]

A thinly veiled threat was made more explicit in a project submitted by Ariel Cohen of the Heritage Foundation, a right-wing American lobby group that has close links with the current US administration. In his paper, 'The Future of a Post-Saddam Iraq: A Blueprint for American Involvement', Cohen suggested that the Iraqi oil industry should be privatised, split up into three large companies following the lines of ethno-religious divisions, with French, Russian and Chinese companies' oil contracts dishonoured.[271]

These sort of pressures, as well as the influence of Putin's generally pro-American orientation, contributed to Russia's final approval of the UN Security Council Resolution 1441 on 8 November 2002. This resolution, which was unanimously accepted by the UN Security Council, represented undoubted proof of US power and influence. However, it was also the outcome of long and difficult negotiations, during which Moscow forced several changes to be made in the original American draft.[272] After the resolution was adopted, Russia's UN Ambassador, Sergey Lavrov, stated: 'What is most important is that the resolution deflects the direct threat of war' and opens the road to 'a political diplomatic settlement'.[273] Although the Israeli daily *Ha'aretz* then expressed the view that the 'international community foiled the US plot to wage war' against Iraq,[274] this was, nevertheless, far too optimistic an opinion. In spite of a lack of world support, American military threats and preparations in the Gulf continued and the situation up to the moment of military action remained quite uncertain.

Moscow warmly welcomed the start of the UNMOVIC operation in Iraq and Iraqi government co-operation with the UN inspectors, which it recognised as a promising beginning. On 3 December 2002 Russian Deputy Foreign Minister Yuri Fedotov stressed that they 'are acting in keeping with the UN Security Council Resolution 1441'. According to him, although 'major complex work is ahead...it is extremely important that it is going in a positive key'.[275] On the same day, the Speaker of the Russian Duma, Gennady Seleznyov, appealed to the US government to 'adhere to international legal norms, and not to undertake anything bypassing the UN Security Council'.[276] Expressing his concern that 'the [American] public is being prepared for the idea that Iraq must be bombed regardless of the outcomes of the inspections',[277] Seleznyov commented that 'this attitude is absolutely incorrect' and that Russia did not share the American position.[278] Earlier, on 24 November 2002, during President Bush's visit to St Petersburg, Putin himself urged Bush not to go to war without the consent of the UN Security Council. He stated that: 'Diplomats have carried out very difficult and very complex work, and we believe that we have to stay within the framework of the work being carried out by the UN.'[279]

The Russians were apparently concerned about their vested interests in Iraq, and probably even more about the likelihood of a sharp drop in oil prices after the US invasion of Iraq. Seleznyov admitted 'it would mean the collapse of our budget, and a lot of other problems for Russia'.[280] Despite Moscow's own economic interests, it was strongly against the US invasion of Iraq and was concerned for the future of Saudi Arabia. Moscow also opposed the threat of a US invasion for very critical political reasons. According to the Director of the Institute for the US and Canada Affairs, Sergei Rogov: 'The position of Russia, which stands for peaceful settlement of the Iraqi problem with the use of UN mechanisms, deters the American policy on Iraq and thus prevents a war of civilisations.' Also: 'If the US attacks Iraq without an apparent reason and authorisation of the Security Council, the international anti-terrorist coalition will crack.'[281] However, he had little doubt that, if the US administration decided to start a new Gulf war, there was little Moscow could do about it, and it would not be willing to endanger its relations with mighty Washington. Further, he predicted: 'Russia will not become involved in the American military campaign.'[282]

On 28 January 2003 Putin, speaking in Kiev, went one step further, warning that if Iraq started hampering the inspectors' work, he would not exclude the possibility that 'Russia could change its position. We are ready to work towards different solutions. I am not saying which, but they could be tougher than before.'[283] However, this statement, which subsequently caused a great deal of speculation in the media, did not necessarily mean any real change in the previous Russian position. On the same occasion, Putin said that 'as of today, [the inspectors] are not saying that they had any difficulties or problems. We should give them an opportunity to work.'[284] According to a number of official statements, Russia still wanted 'a political resolution to the Iraqi situation' based on the UN Security Council resolutions, and it opposed any unilateral, especially military, actions against Iraq.[285] Moscow also supported the continuation of further international inspections in Iraq, especially in view of the fact that they 'have yielded the first positive results'.[286] The Russian Minister of Foreign Affairs, Igor Ivanov, called for the international community to deal with the problem of Iraq only 'through the UN Security Council', reiterating that 'Naturally we will be unable to support unilateral moves.'[287] He also stressed that all issues related to the future regime of Iraq and the personal fate of President Saddam Hussein were unrelated to the UN Security Council resolutions, and that 'Russia is not discussing these questions and will not [do so]'.[288]

Speaking at the World Economic Forum in Davos, Switzerland in January 2003, Putin's economic advisor, Andrei Illarionov, commented that '[the Russian leaders] don't take such a militant position as the US, which relies on force. On the other hand, we are not copying the position of France and Germany, which are on a collision course with the US on the Iraqi issue.'[289] Ivanov himself did not reply to the question of whether Moscow would be ready to veto a resolution at the UN Security Council in the case of a war with Iraq.[290] As Putin openly admitted: 'We are not in accordance with and oppose certain American decisions, but the nature of our relations [with the US] does not allow us to descend to a point of confrontation.'[291]

Although it is quite likely that Moscow tacitly accepted US domination of Iraq and had negotiated with Washington on the future of its oil interests there, it was still unwilling to approve the

American invasion of the country. On 4 February 2003 Putin again stressed that 'he and most Russians' continue to believe that military force should be used only 'in the most extreme case'.[292] Additionally, Moscow did not seem to be impressed by Colin Powell's arguments against Iraq, which were presented to the UN Security Council on 5 February 2003. Both President Vladimir Putin and Minister Igor Ivanov replied to Powell's speech by saying that Russia's position had not changed, and both spoke in favour of a diplomatic solution.[293] Ivanov even told the reporters that 'a first analysis indicates that there is no new evidence to prove that Iraq has weapons of mass destruction'.[294] During the UN Security Council meeting, he joined his French, Chinese and German counterparts, stating that Powell's presentation 'indicates that activities of the international inspectors in Iraq should be continued', and argued that 'the UN Security Council Resolution 1441 is based on practical results rather than on time limits'.[295]

In their initial response to US President George W. Bush's 7 February 2003 call for a new resolution authorising the military invasion of Iraq, Russian leaders unanimously spoke out against any new resolution at such a point.[296] According to Ivanov, 'there was currently no grounds for a military operation against Iraq'.[297] His colleague, the Russian Defence Minister, Sergei Ivanov, added that 'Even if the inspectors in Iraq find weapons of mass destruction, we believe it is essential to achieve Iraq's disarmament without use of military force.'[298] In 2002, Russia signed humanitarian assistance agreements with Iraq worth a total of $1.5 billion, and in the first two months of 2003 more contracts worth approximately $200 million were to be finalised,[299] partly as a reward for its opposition to the outbreak of a new war in Iraq.

All of the diplomatic and economic activities notwithstanding, the mood of the Russian public was full of foreboding. At this time, according to the popular NTV station, Moscow would not resist the seemingly inevitable US military action against Iraq, but still continue its efforts to delay it.[300] In response to unrelenting American pressure and arm-twisting, Moscow, just like many other countries such as Turkey, had no other choice but to try to save face and look after its own direct interests.

The relatively quick and easy American victory in Iraq, the ensuing collapse of Saddam Hussein's regime, and the US military occupation of the country represented an unexpected and heavy blow for the

Russian leaders, who had believed that the war would last longer and would cause the Americans more problems.

From the middle of April 2003 or even earlier, following the apparently decisive American victory, and in view of the overwhelming American military superiority, Moscow made moves to accommodate itself to the winner and, if possible, to preserve at least some of its own economic interests in Iraq. As early as 7 April 2003, after the meeting between President Putin and the US President's National Security Advisor, Condoleezza Rice, both Russian and American officials 'decided to co-ordinate their efforts for post-conflict settlement in Iraq'.[301] A 'subtle' shift in Moscow's Iraqi position had been noticed even earlier when President Putin, on the evening of 2 April 2003, stressed that Russia 'does not want the US to suffer defeat in Iraq'.[302] One day later, on 3 April, Russian Foreign Minister Igor Ivanov after his meeting with the US Secretary of State, Colin Powell, admitted that 'There is no question that the war is about to end and the sooner it does, the better it is. This would be beneficial to all concerned, including the United States.'[303] Although, on 7 April 2003, Russia, together with France and Germany, called for the halting of hostilities in Iraq, and a central role for the UN in the country from this point on,[304] according to some observers the Russian contribution to the end of the Iraqi war went much further. The Putin administration staunchly condemned the Russian Central Religious Islamic Board (TsDUM) led by Mufti Talgat Tajuddin, for declaring a jihad against the US because of the invasion of Iraq.[305] Some analysts also noticed the coincidence that when US forces drew close to Baghdad, US National Security Advisor Condoleezza Rice made a quick trip to Moscow and met with President Putin. Immediately after the meeting, the world witnessed the fall of Baghdad, almost without any resistance from the allegedly well-trained Special Republican Guards, an easy triumph for the US-led coalition forces.[306] The quick fall of the Iraqi regime certainly had a number of causes, but Moscow's early secret acceptance of the events, and a likely secret deal with Washington about the mutual co-operation during the developments, cannot be completely excluded. It is true, nevertheless, that after the end of the war, President Putin invited the other leaders of the anti-war axis, France and Germany, to a summit in St Petersburg on 11 April 2003 in order to demonstrate their unity and to discuss the post-war arrangements and reconstruction in Iraq. The leaders of the three countries displayed their apparent unity, calling for a 'leading UN role' in post-war Iraqi affairs; however, the Americans virtually ignored them. Putin now had to intensify his efforts to restore the 'partnership with the US and to defend Russia's own economic interests in Iraq'.

The outcome of the 2003 Iraqi war, and the US occupation of the country, took a heavy toll on Russia's economy. According to the Russian Security Council First Deputy Secretary, Oleg Chernov, Russian losses as a result of the Iraqi crisis were estimated at about $12 billion.[307]

Russian officials have also been deeply concerned about the potential impact of the new US-controlled Iraqi oil industry on the future of their own economy. At present, oil exports account for one-third of Russia's GDP, and a drop of $1 per barrel in oil prices means a loss of $1 billion in the government budget.[308] In geopolitical terms, the damage to Russian interests was obvious, although the Putin administration tried to play down the issue, stressing instead that the disagreements over the Iraqi crisis should not affect the activity of the international anti-terrorist coalition.[309] The Russian leaders went on to claim that 'Russia had succeeded in exiting the hot phase of the Iraqi crisis with minimal losses in its relations with the US and partners, both in the West and the East.'[310] The last claim, even though exaggerated, was, nevertheless, not completely unfounded. As early as 16 April the US Ambassador to Russia, Alexander Vershbov, stated that although the 'damage done to Russian-American relations by their differences of opinions over Iraq is difficult to estimate...both countries should stop their ideological disputes and get down to practical work instead of fighting old battles again'.[311] According to various leaks, and in the opinion of many analysts, US President George W. Bush has adopted a straightforward approach 'to punish France, ignore Germany and forgive Russia'.[312] On 28 April 2003 Ambassador Vershbov stated in Moscow that 'Both Russia and the new Iraqi government need good relations, and that it is in the United States' interests that Russia take part in the post-war reconstruction of Iraq.'[313]

During the six weeks following the defeat of the Iraqi military, before the adoption by the UN Security Council Resolution 1483 of 22 May 2003, the diplomatic hassle between the US and the former anti-war coalition, including Russia, focused around two basic issues:

1. The role of the UN in the administration and the rehabilitation of Iraq which, by necessity, involved the crucial issue of lifting sanctions from the country.

2. The economic future of Iraq and the division of its rich natural resources, especially oil.

The draft resolution submitted by the US, Britain and Spain on the Iraqi crisis, which, in practice, secured all political and economic domination of the country by the Americans and their allies, was originally opposed quite vocally by many states including Russia. On 12 May 2003 Dymitry Rogozin, Chairman of the Duma's International Affairs Committee, went as far as to say that Russia would be prepared to support the lifting of sanctions immediately 'if the Americans show us the reasons the sanctions were introduced'.[314] In his view, they should have to show either that there had been weapons of mass destruction in Iraq, or confess that there had been none. In the latter case, the strikes against Iraq were unjustified and a crude violation of international law, and that as soon as the Americans made either statement, Russia would be prepared to support the lifting of sanctions.[315] The tough original demands notwithstanding, in the following weeks both Moscow and Paris went a long way in order to satisfy the American superpower, and to preserve for themselves at least some minimal political and/or economic benefits. As an outcome of that, on 22 May 2003 the UN Security Council, in the absence of Syria, unanimously voted for Resolution 1483 concerning Iraq.

Although Russia's Ambassador to the UN, Sergei Lavrov, praised the resolution, saying that it 'has laid down an international legal framework for the world communities' joint efforts to overcome the crisis, and outlined clear targets and principles of these efforts',[316] and Russian Foreign Minister Igor Ivanov called the resolution 'the result of compromise' and stressed that 'unity has been restored to the UN Security Council',[317] the reactions of Duma members and political analysts in the country were far more critical. One of Moscow's leading dailies, *Nezavisimaya Gazeta,* admitted in headlines that: 'Russia did not receive any substantial concessions.'[318]

The influential political analyst and Duma member Alexei Arbatov sharply criticised the Russian diplomatic moves, writing that the resolution of 22 May 2003 'amounted to the retrospective legitimisation of the occupation regime of the US and Britain, and consequently, of the military action in Iraq itself'.[319] He indicated that the role of the UN representative in Iraq had not been clearly determined, and that real control of the country and its financial resources would stay in US hands. According to him, the lifting of the UN sanctions without the return of its international inspectors on which Moscow had insisted, was in no way compensated by the scheduled mission to Iraq by IAEA representatives, or the 'incomprehensible mention of the importance of confirmation of Iraq's disarmament sometime in the future'.[320] Arbatov also argued that as far as the economic aspect was concerned, the extension for two extra months of the oil-for-food programme in which Russian business had, for a long time, been deeply involved, and vague promises to settle the Iraqi foreign debt against the Soviet debt in the Paris Club in order to compensate Russian companies for the loss of the contract for the Qurnah-2 field 'can hardly be considered a serious victory for Russian diplomacy'.[321]

Moscow's acceptance of UN Security Council Resolution 1483 opened the way for the further improvement in US-Russian relations, which were demonstrated by the participation of President G.W. Bush in the celebration of the 300th Anniversary of St Petersburg and the 'warm' Bush–Putin relations during the following G8 meeting in Evian. Victor Kremenyuk, Deputy Director of the Russian Academy of Sciences Institute of the US and Canada, commented that

> One got the impression that Moscow apologised to Washington for its behaviour. The fact that Bush had the warmest relations with Putin of all persons, attests that the White House wants to prevent the forming and strengthening of an anti-US coalition. Russia is currently the weakest link in the chain it forms jointly with Germany and France.[322]

There are three possible reasons for the Putin administration's recent political shift on the Iraqi issue.

First of all, Putin wants, at almost any price, to preserve and to uphold his administration's links with Washington and his personal relations with Bush. On 3 June 2003, addressing a briefing in Evian, he stressed that the 'US is Russia's major partner, and in some areas such as the strengthening of international security and strategic stability, the role of the US is absolutely unique for Russia'.[323] There are, in fact, a number of Russian and Western European analysts who believe that Russian-American relations and mutual co-operation are much stronger and more future-oriented than the relations between the EU countries and the US.[324] As many observers noticed during their meetings, Bush spent more than one hour with Putin, but had just 30 minutes for the French President, Jacques Chirac. Some Russian politicians and analysts, while opposed to the excessively pro-

American line, have, nevertheless, become seriously concerned about the future of Russia itself.

At this time a large number of Russian experts started to believe that reinforcement of the US domination of other countries, the so-called Pax Americana, had become a key feature of the contemporary world. On 19 April 2003, the President of the Institute of Israeli and Middle Eastern Studies in Moscow, Yevegeny Satanovsky, a man with close links to the Kremlin, expressed his opinion that 'the Fourth Rome is doing what the First Rome failed to accomplish, but it not forever, maybe not for a long time'.[325] He suggested that, in the wake of the Iraqi war, Russia should behave 'calmly, steadily and reasonably. It must not rush from one side to another or to try to catch a passing train.'[326] In his view, the US 'is a main competitor and senior partner, but it is not Russia's enemy'.[327] On 17 April 2003, during the experts' discussion of the implications of the Iraqi war for Russian foreign policy, the gathering focused especially on the issue of Russia's sovereignty in the wake of the Iraqi events. According to the press report, in the opinion of the majority present at this meeting, there was no immediate risk, 'but in the future, we must be on our guard and...not put our finger in Bush's mouth'.[328]

As an outcome of that, it seems that in the present consensus of Russian political elite, there is 'no sense in sacrificing its relationship with the US for the sake of "active disagreement", if, of course American actions do not touch the questions of one's own surviv-ability, territorial integrity, security of the perimeter of the border, and other vital questions'.[329]

Second, Russia, just like India[330] and the European countries,[331] has been deeply concerned about the threat of a radicalisation of the Islamic world 'resulting from the recent war in the Persian Gulf'. According to some Western European analysts, the common fear of the 'Green threat' of radical Islam, which Moscow is claiming to face in Chechnya and among its own Muslim population, is the most important basis for the Russian-American rapprochement.[332]

Last but not least, Moscow and its business circles still hope that, by co-operating with the Americans, they will be able to preserve at least some of their economic positions in Iraq. On 29 April 2003, Russian Senator Yevgeny Bushmin, chairman of the Upper House Budget Committee, expressed his conviction that in exchange for political co-operation, the US would prove to be economically generous to Russia. He stated: 'By responding to this kind of co-operation, we will simply forget about this [Iraqi] debt.'[333] He hoped that 'the US may give preference to our enterprises and lift quotas, or facilitate our admission to the World Trade Organisation'.[334] Following this, in May 2003, Sergey Shishkarev, Deputy Chairman of the State Duma Committee for International Affairs, argued that, because of the enormous Iraqi indebtedness to Arab countries (more than $60 billion), the relatively modest debt to Russia was quietly 'forgotten by the former Iraqi regime, and that the chances of redeeming or servicing this debt while Saddam remained in power were close to zero'. According to Shishkarev, things have now changed. The inevitable restructuring of Iraq's foreign debt, for example, in the framework of the Paris Club, gives Russia a definite chance of recovering, or offsetting, a certain proportion of Iraq's debt.[335]

The majority of Russian business people also believed that 'Russia let itself be led along by France, and took a position of "unwarranted toughness", fighting for someone else's interests.'[336] Russian business representatives have now put a lot of trust in 'colossal personal links' between the Russian and Iraqi elites.[337] They argue that 'In Iraq, practically everyone, including those who are going to stay there out of a sense of professionalism to their work, under any regime, know our oligarchies.'[338] Consequently, business representatives have been prone to believe that, if American political interests have not been antagonised, the US will throw its money into the development of new oilfields rather than into the reconstruction of the old ones, where Soviet machinery is still operating, and that these will be left to Russia.[339] Chairman of the Russian Chamber of Commerce and Industry, former Russian Prime Minister and well-known expert on the Arab world, Yevgeny Primakov, went as far as to express the hope that in the post-Saddam Hussein Iraq, Russia will be able to even increase its profits from Iraq, if 'it banks on its personal contacts with Iraq's private business sector, which is beginning to be active again following Saddam Hussein's collapse'.[340]

It is too early to assess whether the hopes and expectations of the Russian elites concerning post-Saddam Iraq and Washington's policy prove to be realistic, and for them, beneficial. Putin's policy on the political turnabout concerning Iraq has, nevertheless, been implemented.[341] On 26 June 2003, while on his state visit in Britain, President Putin stated that the 'so called Iraq "disarmament dossier" should be closed' and that 'Moscow is ready to do what it can in this issue.'[342] He noted with satisfaction 'an improvement in relations between our [Russian and British] secret services', and said that 'we can and should work together...I believe we have a good example in joint work in Afghanistan of an action which we can follow in Iraq. If we act together, we will surely act more effectively.'[343] On the same day *Nezavisimaya Gazeta* in Moscow published an article comparing Iraqi resistance against the American and British occupation forces with the Chechnya uprising against Russian rule in the country.[344]

However, Putin's political adjustments to the Iraqi developments mean neither a carte blanche acceptance of the present American actions there nor an abandonment of Russian interests in Iraq. In London Putin drew attention to the need to go beyond security and basic services and find a 'political solution' to the long-festering Iraqi problem.[345] His analogy with the developments in Afghanistan was very revealing. During the joint press conference with the British Prime Minister, Tony Blair, Putin reminded the audience 'that the new authority in Afghanistan was organised and legitimate'.[346] At the end of the Afghan war the UN held a round-table conference of all Afghan factions which, within less than a month, led to an interim Afghani government.

Current developments in Iraq are strikingly different. After almost two months of occupation, the US is still quite reluctant to open up the political process and build the formation of a new Iraqi government (with the exception of the Kurdish sector which already has a relatively stable government) and continues to minimalise the UN involvement. Moscow is still holding to its previous view that the UN should play a key role in Iraq's reconstruction. According to Putin, 'whatever Iraqi leadership is created in the future, it will be legitimate, and it will be able to count on support, only if the process goes through the UN'.[347] The growing Iraqi Arab resistance against foreign occupation seems to provide additional validity to his argument. Concerning Russian economic interests in Iraq, Russian officials still insist that Russian contracts concluded with the regime of former Iraqi President Saddam Hussein should be fully honoured by any successor government.[348] On 26 June 2003, Russian Energy Minister Igor Yusuofov said that all contracts concluded by Russia in Iraq 'have an impeccable international legal basis, and we expect these contracts to be carried out by all sides'.[349] Although it is probably no more than a tough starting posture before further negotiations, at least at this point the original position of Russia has not been subjected to any changes.

CONCLUSION

During the whole Iraqi crisis, both before the recent US invasion of Iraq in March 2003, and since the military operations began, Moscow's diplomatic policies seem to have been guided by three main principles:

1. For a number of rather obvious reasons, both geopolitical and economic, Moscow truly did not want a US occupation of Iraq, and tried to prevent the outbreak of a new large-scale military conflict in its close neighbourhood.
2. At the same time, however, Moscow did not want to endanger its new 'partnership' with Washington and tried to keep a relatively low profile in its condemnations of the American war preparations. Indeed, a number of Russian politicians and journalists argued that Russia's position vis-à-vis the possible conflict was different from that of France. In their view, Russia as a fallen superpower and former rival of the US needed to be much more cautious and prudent in its dealings with an overwhelming American might.
3. Last but not least, as time went by, Moscow focused more and more on the defence of its own economic interests in Iraq, such as the future repayment of the Iraqi loans, and even more, on the uncertain future of the Russian oil companies' concessions in post-Saddam Iraq.

There is no doubt that Russian-Iraqi relations after a long and complex history are now at a very critical juncture. Their future is by no means certain, but as a well-known Iraqi politician has recently indicated, 'a country as big as Russia cannot keep aloof from the processes taking place in Iraq',[350] and there were going to be 'major prospects' of bilateral co-operation in the future,[351] and still further, because of their geopolitical proximity and previous connections, both countries sooner or later would need to re-establish their relations and start a new chapter in this history. In this relationship however, Iraq will not be able to use Russia as a counterbalance in its political dealings with the United States, although the Russian economic and cultural presence in Iraq will continue. In addition, a joint operation against Islamic fundamentalism will continue, and almost certainly be expanded with American support.

As evidenced by a recent visit to Moscow by Yalal Talabani, leader of the Patriotic Union of Kurdistan, Russia continues to preserve and cultivate its historic links with the country.[352]

Notes

PREFACE

1. Barbara W. Tuchman. *March of Folly* (New York: The Folio Society, 1997), p. 2.
2. Ibid.

CHAPTER 1

1. Zbigniew Brzezinski. *The Grand Chessboard: American Primacy and its Geo-strategic Imperatives* (New York: Basic Books, 1997), pp. xiii–xiv.
2. Ibid. The book is an elaborate justification of the need for American global domination.
3. Gore Vidal. 'The Enemy Within', *Observer* (27 October 2002).
4. Maurice Lemoine. 'Uncle Sam's Manifest Destiny' www.mondediplo. com/2003/05/03lemoine.
5. Annie Lacroix-Riz. 'When the US Wanted to Take Over France' www.mondediplo.com/2003/05/05lacroix.
6. Gore Vidal, 'The Enemy Within'.
7. Ibid.
8. David Hoffman. 'About US and Iraq: Why Were We Lied To', *Pravda* (17 June 2003).
9. Noam Chomsky. 'Iraq: Invasion that will Live in Infamy', *Z-magazine* (11 August 2003).
10. Ibid.
11. Ibid.
12. Michael Meacher, 'This War on Terrorism is Bogus', *Guardian* (London, 6 September 2003).

CHAPTER 2

1. The sanctions maintained against Iraq violate a number of international laws, treaties and declarations. These include: the Geneva Convention (1977), Protocol 1 Additional to the Geneva Conventions, which states that

    (1) Starvation of civilians as a method of warfare is prohibited. (2) It is prohibited to attack, destroy, remove, or render useless objects indispensable to the agricultural areas for the production of foodstuffs, crops, livestock, drinking water installations and supplies, and irrigation works, for the specific purpose of denying them for their sustenance value to the civilian population or to the adverse Party,

whatever the motive, whether in order to starve out civilians, to cause them to move away, or for any other motive;

the UN General Assembly Resolution 44/215 (22 December 1989) which calls on developed countries to refrain from unilaterally using politically coercive economic instruments to achieve political or social goals; the Universal Declaration of Human Rights Article 25 (1948), which states that

> Everyone has the right to a standard of living adequate for the health and well-being of himself and of his family, including food, clothing, housing and medical care and necessary social services, and the right to security in the event of unemployment, sickness, disability, widowhood, old age or other lack of livelihood in circumstances beyond his control...You have the right to basic human needs of food, shelter, clothing, household requirements and community services in respect to water, sanitation, health, and education;

the Charter of Economic Rights and Duties of States, adopted by the UN General Assembly (1974), stating that '[N]o state may use or encourage the use of economic, political or any other type of measures to coerce another State in order to obtain from it the subordination of the exercise of its sovereign rights or to secure from it advantages of any kind', as well as the World Declaration on Nutrition, FAO/WHO (1992) and the Constitution of the World Health Organisation (1946).

2. The United Nations Security Council (UNSC) has passed over 120 resolutions dealing with the Palestinian-Israeli conflict, and since 1967 the vast majority of them have dealt with the security of the Palestinian population. Most notable of the UNSC Resolutions are: 1435 (2002) Mideast situation/Palestine question – Demand for cessation of violence reiterated/Israel to withdraw from Palestinian cities/PA to meet its expressed commitment – SecCo resolution; 1405 (2002), Humanitarian situation in the OPT – Urgency of access of humanitarian organisations emphasised/SecGen's fact-finding team on Jenin – SecCo resolution; 1403 (2002) Mideast situation/Palestine question/'Quartet' efforts – SecCo resolution; 1402 (2002) Mideast situation/Palestine question – Cease-fire, withdrawal of Israeli troops from Palestinian cities called for – SecCo resolution; 1397 (2002) Mideast situation/Palestine question – Two-States, Israel and Palestine, vision affirmed – SecCo resolution; 1353 (2001) Mideast situation/Peacekeeping operations – SecCo resolution; 1325 (2000), SecCo resolution; 1322 (2000) Palestine question – Excessive use of force against Palestinians condemned/Israel to abide by Fourth Geneva Convention/Inquiry efforts welcomed – SecCo resolution; 1296 (2000) SecCo resolution; 1265 (1999) Protection of civilians/Preventive military and civilian deployments – SecCo resolution; 1073 (1996) Situation in the OPT/Jerusalem tunnel – Calls for the protection of Palestinian civilians, resumption of peace negotiations – SecCo resolution; 904 (1994) Hebron – Measures to guarantee protection/Efforts to invigorate peace process – SecCo

resolution; 799 (1992) Deportations – Occupying Power's deportation of hundreds of Palestinian civilians condemned – SecCo resolution; 726 (1992) Deportations of Palestinians – Occupying Power's decision condemned – SecCo resolution; 694 (1991) Deportations of Palestinians – Israel in violation of the Fourth Geneva Convention – SecCo resolution; 681 (1990) Situation in the OPT/Deportations/ Protection efforts/ Fourth Geneva Convention meeting, measures/UN monitoring – SecCo resolution; 673 (1990) Situation in the OPT – Israel to comply fully with S/RES/672 (1990) – SecCo resolution; 672 (1990) Jerusalem/Al-Haram al-Shareef incidents – SecGen to send mission – SecCo resolution; 641 (1989) Deportations – Continuing deportation by the occupying Power of Palestinian civilians deplored – SecCo resolution; 636 (1989) Deportations – Israel to desist from deporting other Palestinian civilians – SecCo resolution; 611 (1988) Mideast situation/Assassination of Khalil El-Wazir in Tunisia by Israel – SecCo resolution; 608 (1988) Deportations – Israel to rescind the order to deport Palestinian civilians – SecCo resolution; 607 (1988) Deportations – Israel to refrain from deporting any Palestinian civilians – SecCo resolution; 605 (1987) Situation in the OPT, OATs/Occupying Power's human rights violations strongly deplored/ SecGen's recommendations on protection requested – SecCo resolution; 592 (1986) Situation in the OPT, OATs – Israel to abide by Fourth Geneva Convention – SecCo resolution; 573 (1985) Attack on PLO HQ – Armed aggression perpetrated by Israel condemned – SecCo resolution; 521 (1982) Situation in Lebanon/Sabra and Shatila – SecCo resolution; 484 (1980) Situation in the OPT/Expulsions – Mayors to return – SecCo resolution; 478 (1980) Jerusalem – Israel's 'basic law', refusal censured/ Measures null and void/ Obstruction to peace/ Diplomatic missions to be withdrawn – SecCo resolution; 476 (1980) Jerusalem/Concern over Knesset steps/Necessity to end occupation/Israel to abide by SecCo resns – SecCo resolution; 471 (1980) Situation in the OPT/Settlements – States not to provide settlements with assistance, need to end the prolonged occupation – SecCo resolution; 469 (1980) Expulsions of Palestinian officials – Israel to rescind these illegal measures – SecCo resolution; 468 (1980) Expulsions of Palestinian officials – Israel to rescind these illegal measures – SecCo resolution; 465 (1980) Israeli settlements/Fourth Geneva Convention – Establishment of settlements to cease, no legal validity – SecCo resolution; 452 (1979) Israeli settlements/Fourth Geneva Convention – Establishment of settlements to cease, no legal validity – SecCo resolution; 446 (1979) Israeli settlements – Israel to abide by SecCo resns, not to transfer own population/Commission to be appointed – SecCo resolution; 298 (1971) Jerusalem/Israel to rescind measures which may change the status of the City – SecCo resolution; 286 (1970) Mideast situation/Aircraft hijacking – SecCo resolution; 271 (1969) Holy places/Al-Aqsa arson damage – Condemns Israel's failure to comply/Israel scrupulously to observe the Geneva Conventions, military occupation law – SecCo resolution; 267 (1969) Jerusalem – Israel to rescind all measures taken which may tend to change the status of the City/Security Council to reconvene – SecCo resolution; 259 (1968) Situation in the OATs/Safety, welfare and security of the inhabitants/Requests to dispatch a Special Representative – SecCo resolution; 258 (1968) Mideast situation/Cease-fire ordered/Peaceful settlement/Special Representative – SecCo resolution; 256 (1968) Mideast situation/Condemns Israel's further military attacks – SecCo resolution; 252 (1968) Jerusalem – Israel's legislative and administrative measures invalid/Israel to rescind all such measures – SecCo resolution; 251 (1968) Jerusalem/Military parade – SecCo resolution; 250 (1968) Jerusalem/ Military parade – SecCo resolution; 248 (1968) Mideast situation – SecCo condemns Israel's military action in Jordan – SecCo resolution; 242 (1967) Mideast situation – Acquisition of territory by war/ Withdrawal of Israel/Refugee problem/ Special Representative – SecCo resolution; 240 (1967) Mideast situation/Recent military activities – SecCo resolution; 237 (1967) Mideast situation/Displaced persons/Return of inhabitants/Respect for inalienable human rights/Humanitarian questions – SecCo resolution.

3. There has been a substantial amount of material published with regard to the humanitarian crisis in Iraq resulting in part from the sanctions imposed upon the country. Among the organisations that performed extensive studies are the World Health Organisation (WHO), the Food and Agriculture Organisation (FAO) of the United Nations, the United Nations Children's Fund (UNICEF), Save the Children UK: Global Policy Forum, New Internationalism Project, Center for Economic and Social Rights, Institute for Policy Studies, Mennonite Central Committee, Anglican Observer Office at the UN, Arab Commission for Human Rights, Center for Development of International Law, Fellowship of Reconciliation, Middle East and Europe Office of Global Ministries of the United Church of Christ, United Church of Christ UN Office, World Economy, Ecology and Development Association (WEED) and the Quaker UN Office.

4. Samuel P. Huntington. 'The Clash of Civilisations', *Foreign Affairs*, **72**, no. 3 (Summer 1993), pp. 22–8.

5. For further examples of human rights violations see the Annual Reports of Human Rights Watch: www.hrw.org.

6.

Area	GNI per capita[a] $US 2000	Under-5 mortality rate Per 1000 live births 2000	Life expectancy at birth, total years 2000	School enrolment secondary (% net) 1999	Percentage of female enrolment secondary education 1998
Gulf Co-operation Council States					
Bahrain	9,370 (1999)	11	73	82	51
Kuwait	18,030	13	77	50 (1998)	50
Oman	..	22	74	59	49
Qatar	..	19	75	78 (1998)	56
Saudi Arabia	7,230	23	73	..	46
UAE	18,060 (1998)	10	75	67	50

	Non-Gulf Co-operation Council Arab Areas				
Algeria	1,580	39	71	59	50
Egypt	1,490	52	67	79	47
Iraq	..	121	61	33	35
Jordan	1,720	30	72	76	49
Lebanon	4,010	30	70	70 (1998)	52
Libya	..	32	71	..	52
Syria	950	29	70	38 (1998)	46
West Bank & Gaza	1,650	26	72	..	..
Yemen	420	95	56	37	26

Notes: Figures in italics are for years other than specified.

a. Atlas method; see WDI *Statistical methods*.

Source: *2002 World Development Indicators* database, World Bank, 20 April 2002.

7. 'Peace Must Guarantee Refugees the Right of Return Says the Jordanian Prime Minister to the 103rd IPU Conference', press release of the Inter-Parliamentary Union No. 6 (Amman, Jordan: 4 May 2000) as found at: www.ipu.org/press-e/amman6.htm.

8. 'Continued Sanctions on Iraq, Unacceptable, Void of Logic for Arabs, Minister of Foreign Affairs Amr Moussa Reiterated' (Cairo: 28 July 2000), as found at: www.mfa.gov.eg/getdoc.asp?id=1017&cat=0404.

9. Statement of the Sultanate of Oman, H.E. Yousef Bin Alawi Bin Abdullah, Minister Responsible for Foreign Affairs at the 55th Session of the United Nations General Assembly, (16 September 2000) as found at: www.un.org/ga/webcast/statements/omanE.htm; see also Statement of the Sultanate of Oman at the 54th Session of the United Nations General Assembly (24 September 1999).

10. 'Morocco defends Kuwait's unity and security, calls to end Iraqi sanctions', Arabic News.com (28 September 2000) as found at: www.arabicnews.com/ansub/Daily/Day/000928/2000092834.html.

11. Saad G. Hattar, 'Rawabdeh Calls for End to Sanctions on Iraq', *Jordan Times* (Friday–Saturday, 5–6 May 2000) as found at: www.jordanembassyus.org/05052000002.htm.

12. With the announcement of a US $1 billion trade deal between Iraq and Syria, including the resumption of diplomatic relations and regular rail service from Damascus to Baghdad, Syrian Foreign Minister Farouq al-Sharaa stated: 'We believe the preservation of sanctions is not justified because the people of Iraq are those who are mainly suffering as a result.' See 'Syria and Iraq Forge Closer Ties', BBC World News (27 September 2000). As found at: news.bbc.co.uk/hi/english/world/middle_east/newsid_943000/943472.stm.

13. On 11 November 2000, while attending the 9th Organisation of the Islamic Conference (OIC) ministerial meetings in Doha, Qatar Iranian Foreign Minister Kamal Kharrazi called for 'lifting the UN sanctions against Iraq', saying 'the sanctions have caused many sufferings to the Iraqi people.' See 'Dr. Kharrazi Calls for Lifting of UN Sanctions on

Iraq', press release, Islamic Republic of Iran Ministry of Foreign Affairs (11 November 2000). See http://mfa.gov.ir/.

14. Kuwait's staunch support for the sanctions has been moderated through statements by its Foreign Minister, Sheikh Sabah al-Ahmad al-Sabah, who was reported by Reuters on 20 March 2001 to have stated: 'I say that Kuwait has no objection to the launching of a call to lift the economic sanctions from Iraq', prior to his attendance at the Arab League summit. See: Reuters, 'Kuwait to Welcome Arab Call to End Iraq Sanctions', CNN News Online (22 January 2001). As found at: www.casi.org.uk/discuss/2001/msg00070.html.

15. See James Der Derian and Paul Virilio. *Desert Screen: War at the Speed of Light*, trans. Michael Degener (London: Athlone, 2001); Karim H. Karim. *Islamic Peril: Media and Global Violence* (Montreal/New York/London: Black Rose Books, 2000); Philip M Taylor. *War and the Media: Propaganda and Persuasion in the Gulf War*, 2nd edn (Manchester: Manchester University Press, 1998); Edward Said. *Covering Islam: How the Media and the Experts Determine How We See the Rest of the World*, 2nd edn (New York: Vintage Books, 1997); Richard Keeble. *Secret State, Silent Press: New Militarism, the Gulf and the Modern Image of Warfare* (Luton, Bedfordshire, UK: University of Luton Press, 1997); Yahya R. Kamalipour. *The US Media and the Middle East: Image and Perception* (Westport, Conn.: Praeger, 1997); Paul Leslie. *The Gulf War as Popular Entertainment: An Analysis of the Military-Industrial Media Complex* (Lewiston, NY: E. Mellen Press, 1997); Mark McKenzie. 'In Quest of Presence: Virtuality, Aurality, and Television's Gulf War', in Simon Penny (ed.) *Critical Issues in Electronic Media* (Albany: State University of New York Press, 1995); Susan Jeffords and Lauren Rabinovitz. *Seeing Through the Media: The Persian Gulf War* (New Brunswick, N.J. : Rutgers University Press, 1994); W. Lance Bennett and David L. Paletz (eds) *Taken by Storm: The Media, Public Opinion, and US Foreign Policy in the Gulf War* (Chicago: University of Chicago Press, 1994); Zuhair Kashmeri. *The Gulf Within: Canadian Arabs, Racism and the Gulf War* (Toronto: James Lorimer & Company, 1991).

16. See Tareq Y. and Jacqueline S. Ismael. 'Arab Politics and the Gulf War: Political Opinion and Political Culture', *Arab Studies Quarterly*, **15**, no. 1 (Winter 1993), pp. 1–11.

17. Ibid.

18. The state system, inequality and dependency have been consistently identified in the scholarly literature on Middle East politics as characteristics of the Arab political system causally related to the region's most serious social and political problems. See Nazih N.M. Ayubi. *Over-stating the Arab State: Politics and Society in the Middle East* (London; New York: I.B. Tauris, 1999); Dan Tschirgi and Bassam Tibi. *Perspectives on the Gulf Crisis*, **14**, no. 1 (Cairo: Cairo Papers in Social Science, Spring 1991).

19. See: Shireen Hunter (ed.). *The Politics of Islamic Revivalism: Diversity and Unity* (Bloomington: Indiana University Press, 1987); Tareq Y. Ismael. *The Arab Left* (Syracuse: Syracuse University Press, 1976).

20. See: Tareq Y. Ismael (ed.). *The International Relations of the Middle East in the 21st Century: Patterns of Continuity and Change* (Aldershot: Ashgate,

2000); Tareq Y. Ismael. *The International Relations of the Contemporary Middle East* (Syracuse: Syracuse University Press, 1986).

21. Shortly following the Gulf War Arab intellectuals held a number of conferences on the future of the Arab world reflecting concern over the fundamental changes in Arab politics. Central themes included the breakdown of inter-Arab conflict management, political legitimacy, inequality and dependency. Among the major meetings were: the Symposium on the Gulf War: Historic Roots and Future Expectations, 2–3 March 1991, Tunis; The Gulf Crisis and its Ramifications for the Arab world, Beirut Center for Arab Unity Studies, Cairo, 21–22 April 1991; Symposium on the Gulf Crisis and the Future of the Arab world, Ibn Khaldun Center for Development Studies, Cairo, 28–30 April 1991; and Second Pan-Arab National Conference, 27–29 May 1991, Amman.

22. For the role of Islam in the emergence of contemporary Arab political thought, see Hastings Donnan. *Interpreting Islam* (London: Sage Publications, 2002); Aziz Al-Azmeh. *Islams and Modernities*, 2nd edn (New York: Verso, 1993); and Malcolm H. Kerr *Islamic Reform: The Political and Legal Theories of Muhammad Abduh and Rashid Rida* (Berkeley: University of California Press, 1966). The debate generated in contemporary Arabic literature on culture and politics is succinctly summarised in Issa J. Boullata. *Trends and Issues in Contemporary Arab Thought* (Albany: SUNY Press, 1990).

23. See: Ramsey Clark. *The Fire This Time: US Crimes in the Gulf* (St. Paul, MN: Pub Group West, 1994); *War Crimes: A Report on United States War Crimes Against Iraq* (University Park, MD: Maisonneuve Press, 1992).

24. See: Sarah Graham Brown. *Sanctioning Saddam: The Politics of Intervention in Iraq* (London: Palgrave, 2002); Geoff Simons. *Imposing Economic Sanctions: Legal Remedy or Genocidal Tool?* (London: Pluto Press, 1999); Geoff Simons. *The Scourging of Iraq: Sanctions, Law and Natural Justice*, 2nd edn (New York: St. Martin's Press, 1998).

25. Mubarak's interview to CNN (November 20th, 1997). As found at: www.sis.gov.eg/egyptinf/politics/preside/intview/html/int2011.htm.

26. Tareq Y. Ismael. 'Arafat's Palestine National Authority', *Durham Middle East Papers No. 71* (University of Durham, Institute for Middle Eastern & Islamic Studies, June 2002).

27. Edward W. Said. *The End of the Peace Process: Oslo and After* (New York: Vintage, 2001); Avi Shlaim. *The Iron Wall: Israel and the Arab world* (New York: W. W. Norton & Company, 2001).

28. Brian Whitaker. 'Saddam's Trump Card: The world needs Iraq's oil as never before – and the Iraqi president seems certain to exact whatever concessions he can for it', *Guardian* (September 26, 2000). As found at: www.guardian.co.uk/analysis/story/0,3604,373249,00.html.

29. Scott Ritter. *Endgame: Solving the Iraq Problem Once and for All* (New York: Simon & Schuster, 1999).

30. Richard Butler, chief UN weapons inspector, waffled on whether UNSCOM had been compromised by US, UK and Israeli intelligence organisations, and was prohibited from participating in the debate over UNSCOM's future role (it was disbanded) by Sergey Lavrov, the Russian representative on the Security Council. In spite of what can only be

identified as either dereliction of duty to his post as an impartial representative of the United Nations, or outright complicity with the intelligence agencies of Western states, Mr Butler has denied all involvement and knowledge of the spying operation. Following publication of his book *The Greatest Threat: Iraq, Weapons of Mass Destruction, and the Growing Crisis of Global Security* (New York: BBS/Public Affairs, 2000), he has become a public champion of the pro-war cause while serving with the Council on Foreign Relations in New York. His oft-repeated claim that UNSCOM was 'kicked out' of Iraq by the Iraqi regime is both factually erroneous and in contradiction to his own characterisation of events at the time.

31. On 27 September 1998 Turkey restored full diplomatic ties with Iraq ahead of many of Iraq's fellow Arab states.

32. 'Syria Calls for End to Sanctions on Iraq', *China Daily* (25 January 1999).

33. General Assembly press release GA/9607 (24 September 1999).

34. Statement by H.E. Mr Rashid Abdullah Al-Noaimi. Minister of Foreign Affairs of The United Arab Emirates In the General Debate of the 54th Session of the General Assembly of the UN (New York, 21 September 1999).

35. UNICEF. *Child and Maternal Mortality Survey 1999: Preliminary Report* (July August 1999).

36. 'Security Council Considers Humanitarian Situation in Iraq', *United Nations Daily Highlights* (24 March 2000).

37. 'Peace Must Guarantee the Right of Return Says the Jordanian Prime Minister to the 103rd IPU Conference', Press Release of the Inter-Parliamentary Union (Amman: 4 May 2000). As found at: www. ipu.org/press-e/amman6.htm; see also Saad G. Hattar. 'Rawabdeh calls for End to Sanctions on Iraq', *Jordan Times* (Friday–Saturday, 5–6 May 2000). As found at: http://www.jordanembassyus.org/05052000002. htm.

38. 'Continued Sanctions on Iraq, Unacceptable, Void of Logic for Arabs, Minister of Foreign Affairs Amr Moussa Reiterated. Cairo: July 28, 2000', Public and Press Statements. Egyptian Ministry of Foreign Affairs (30 July 2000). As found at: www.mfa.gov.eg/getdoc.asp?id=1017&cat=0404.

39. 'Iranian Foreign Minister's Answers to 3 Questions Raised by Daily Al-Hayat', Foreign Ministry of Iran, *Viewpoints* (1 August 2000). As found at: www.MFA.gov.ir/English/Html-Files/Viewpoints/Regional/Arab-African/Persian-Gulf/Iraq/Minister/Iraq-5.htm.

40. 'Iraq Greets Defiant Chavez', BBC World News (10 August 2000).

41. CNN. 'Coalition crumbling? The Gulf War coalition of nations disagrees on future policy toward Iraq', CNN.com, *The Unfinished War: A Decade Since Desert Storm* (2001).

42. Reuters. 'Qatar Renews Initiative to Lift Iraq Sanctions: Qatari official said the initiative was aimed at opening a "channel for dialogue" with the Iraqi people' (5 September 2000).

43. Statement of the Sultanate of Oman H.E. Yousef Bin Alawi Bin Abdullah Minister Responsible for Foreign Affairs at the 55th Session of the United Nations General Assembly (16 September 2000). As found at: www.un.org/ga/webcast/statements/omanE.htm.

44. AP. 'Iraq Says U.N. Sanctions "Fizzling" as Saddam Riding High', CNN.com News (10 November 2000). As found at: www.cnn.com/2000/US/11/10/us.iraq.sanctions.ap/.

45. AFP. 'Russia Says it Complied with UN Requirements on Iraq Flights', Agence France-Presse (26 September 2000).

46. 'Egypt Intensifies Contacts on the Peace Process and Pursues Diligent Efforts on the Iraqi Issue to Get Sanctions Lifted', Cairo: 21 September 2000. Public and Press Statements. Egyptian Ministry of Foreign Affairs (23 September 2000). As found at: www.mfa.gov.eg/getdoc.asp?id=1070.

47. 'Morocco Defends Kuwait's Unity and Security, Calls to End Iraqi Sanctions', Arabic News.com (9/28/2000). As found at: www.arabicnews.com/ansub/Daily/Day/000928/2000092834.html; 'Morocco Renews Call to Lift Embargo on Iraq', speech by King Mohammed VI reported by Maghreb Arabe Presse (27 April 2000).

48. As quoted in 'Flights Affect Arab Attitudes Toward Embargo', BBC News (25 September 2000).

49. Abdul Jalil Mustafa. 'Baghdad Notifies Trade Partners of Shift to Euro', *BridgeNews* (27 September 2000). Iraq had wanted to make the switch a year previously, but needed to wait to notify the UN and study the feasibility of such a move. Libya had also made the switch while under sanctions, demanding its oil proceeds be paid in Deutsche marks and Swiss francs.

50. AFP. 'Iraq's Aziz Leaves Syria after Brief Visit', Agence France-Presse (27 September 2000); AP. 'Jordan to Become Third Nation in Week to Send Passenger Flight to Iraq' (28 September 2000).

51. 'Sanctions on Iraq Going to the Outer Limits Should Come to an End', Cairo: 30 September 2000 (1 October 2000), Public and Press Statements. Egyptian Ministry of Foreign Affairs. As found at: www.mfa.gov.eg/getdoc.asp?id=986.

52. 'Syria Seeks End to Iraq sanctions', BBC World News Online (2 October 2000). As found at: http://news.bbc.co.uk/2/hi/world/middle_east/952930.stm.

53. AFP. 'Icelandic, Russian Planes Set to Fly to Iraq in Defiance of Embargo', Agence France-Presse (27 September 2000); 'Tunisia, Turkey Join Solidarity Flights to Iraq', *DAWN: The Internet Edition* (5 October 2000).

54. Anton La Guardia. 'MP to Defy Sanctions with Flight to Iraq', *Daily Telegraph* (26 September 2000).

55. Michael White and Richard Norton-Taylor. 'Doubts over Iraq Air Strikes: MPs Express Anger at Raids as Legality is Questioned', *Guardian* (19 February 2001); Richard Norton-Taylor. 'US Shows Impact of Air Strikes: Damage Camp, Missile Site Razed, Airfield Hit', *Guardian* (10 October 2001). As found at: www.guardian.co.uk/waronterror/story/0,1361,566620,00.html; see also: Frederic L. Kirgis. 'US-British Air Strikes on Targets in Iraq', *American Society of International Law: Insights* (February 2001): www.guardian.co.uk/Iraq/Story/0,2763,439958,00.html.

56. 'DOD Press Conference on Iraq Air Strikes: US Military Says Strikes Needed for Self-Defense' (16 February 2001): www.usembassy-israel.org.il/publish/peace/archives/2001/february/me0216e.html.

57. 'Air Strikes against Iraq Unjustified – Important Talks during the Fourth Session of Egyptian-Algerian Committee', Cairo: 19 February 2001 (26 February 2001). Public and Press Statements. Egyptian Ministry of Foreign Affairs. As found at: www.mfa.gov.eg/getdoc.asp?id=1329&cat= 0404; Minister of Foreign Affairs 'Amr Moussa and US Secretary of State Colin Powell, Cairo: 24 February 2001 (26 February 2001). Public and Press Statements. Egyptian Ministry of Foreign Affairs. As found at: http://www.mfa.gov.eg/getdoc.asp?id=1319; 'Egypt Deplores Air Strikes against Iraq: Foreign Minister Moussa Underlines They are Unjustified, Defying Legitimacy', Rome: 18 February 2001. Public and Press Statements. Egyptian Ministry of Foreign Affairs (20 February 2001). As found at: www.mfa.gov.eg/getdoc.asp?id=1308; 'Air Strikes against Iraq Unjustified – Important Talks during the Fourth Session of Egyptian-Algerian Committee', Cairo: 19 February 2001 (26 February 2001). Public and Press Statements. Egyptian Ministry of Foreign Affairs. As found at: www.mfa.gov.eg/getdoc.asp?id=1329&cat=0404; 'Foreign Minister Moussa: Air Raids against Iraq Serious Negative Step', Algiers: 17 February 2001 (20 February 2001). Public and Press Statements. Egyptian Ministry of Foreign Affairs. As found at: www.mfa.gov.eg/getdoc.asp?id=1310; 'The Situation in the Gulf: Foreign Minister Amr Moussa Calls for Reassessment', Davos: 27 January 2001 (4 February 2001). Public and Press Statements. Egyptian Ministry of Foreign Affairs. As found at: www.mfa.gov.eg/getdoc.asp?id=1283.
58. 'The Text of Dr. Kamal Kharrazi's Interview in Egypt', Iranian Ministry of Foreign Affairs (24 February 2001). As found at: www.MFA.gov.ir/English/Html-Files/Viewpoints/Regional/Arab-African/Persian-Gulf/Iraq/Minister/Iraq-18.htm.
59. His Majesty King Abdullah II. 'Address to the Arab Summit', Amman, Jordan (27 March 2001). As found at: www.jordanembassyus.org/03282001005.htm.
60. Nissar Hoath, 'UAE says UN must overhaul its approach to global developments', Gulf News Online Edition (29 March 2001). As found at: www.gulf-news.com/Articles/news.asp?ArticleID=13217.
61. Mubarak in an interview with Newsweek's Lally Weymouth in Cairo (1 April 2001). As found at: www.sis.gov.eg/online/html4/o0104.htm#
62. Robin Wright. 'Jordan's Leader Worries Violence in Middle East Could Ignite Region', Los Angeles Times (8 April 2001). As found at: www.jordanembassyus.org/robinwright.htm.
63. Ibid.
64. 'At meeting with Bush, King stresses commitment to working for peace', Jordan Times (11 April 2001). As found at: www.jordanembassyus.org/04112001001.htm; see also: 'King Abdullah Reiterates Call for Lifting Sanctions on Iraq', Jordan Times (12 April 2001). As found at: www.jordanembassyus.org/04122001001.htm; His Majesty King Abdullah II. 'Question & Answer Session', The National Press Club, Washington, DC (11 April 2001). As found at: www.jordanembassyus.org/hmkanpc0401q&a.htm.

65. 'Jordan's Opposition to Impose Smart Sanctions on Iraq', *Arabic News.com* (13 June 2001). As found at: www.arabicnews.com/ansub/Daily/Day/010613/2001061310.html.

66. United Nations Security Council 4336th meeting S/PV.4336 26 (June 2001). As found at: www.cam.ac.uk/societies/casi/info/undocs/sc010626open.pdf.

67. 'The Statement of Mr. Shobokshi, Representative of Saudi Arabia at the UN, at the Security Council', Security Council 4336th meeting S/PV.4336 (New York: 26 June 2001), pp. 29–30. As found at: www.cam.ac.uk/societies/casi/info/undocs/sc010626open.pdf.

68. 'Interview with Prince Sultan ibn Abdul Aziz', *Asharq Al Awsat* (24 August 2001). As found at: www.ain-al-yaqeen.com/issues/20010824/feat4en.htm.

69. 'The Line in the Sand: Tony Blair Must Oppose Attacks on Iraq', *Guardian* (10 October 2001).

70. 'Support Grows for Middle East Peace Plan', *Guardian* (26 February 2002); see also Graham Usher. 'The Saudi Initiative: Everyone Welcomes It. No One Agrees on What it Means', *Al-Ahram Weekly Online*, Issue No. 575 (28 February–6 March 2002).

71. 'Friends Again', *Khaleej Times* (15 April 2002). As found at: www.khaleejtimes.co.ae/ktarchive/150402/editor.htm.

72. Associated Press, 27 February 2003 and ABCNEWS.com. 27 February 2003.

73. Reuters, 27 February 2003. (www.alertnet.org) and BBC News. (http://newsvote.bbc.co.uk), 27 February 2003.

74. BBC News (http://newsvote.bbc.co.uk), 27 February 2003.

75. Abdullatif al-Mannawi. 'Drama at the Arab League.' *Asharq Alawsat* (Cairo), 2 March 2003. (www.arabnews.com 6 March 2003). Also see Sarah Deeb, 'Arab Summit Shows Sharp Divisions on Iraq', (www.newsday.com) 6 March 2003.

CHAPTER 3

1. Joseph S. Nye Jr. *The Paradox of American Power* (Oxford: Oxford University Press, 2002), p. 39.

2. William Clark. 'The Real Reasons for the Upcoming War with Iraq': www.ecapc.org/eurodollariraq.asps.

3. Joseph S. Nye, *The Paradox of American Power*, p. 39

4. Jim Lobe. 'Pentagon Steps Closer to GloboCop Role', *Asia Times* (14 June 2003).

5. Air University. 'Strategic Environment: USCENTCOM' (15 January 2002): www.au.af.mil/au/database/projects/ay1995/acsc/95-002/chap1/strategic.htm.

6. Edward Said. 'The Other America', *Counter Punch* (21 March 2003).

7. Ian S. Lustick. 'The Absence of Middle Eastern Great Powers: Political Backwardness in Historical Perspective', *International Organisation* (51)4, (Autumn 1997); pp. 662–3.

8. For details of Israeli influence in the American administration, see *New Trend Magazine* (April 2002).

9. Laurence Toenjes. 'US Policy Towards Iraq: Unravelling the Web of People, Think Tanks, etc' (19 July 2003): www.opednews.com/toenjes-summary.htm.

10. Ibid.

11. Michael Lind. 'Distorting the US Foreign Policy: The Israeli Lobby and American Power', *Third World Traveller* (May 2002): www.thirdworld-traveler.com/Israel/Israel_lobby_US.html.

12. Centre for Security Policy. 'What To Do Now About Iraq' (28 November 2001): www.centerforsecuritypolicy.otg/index.jsp?section=papers&code= 01-D_76.

13. 'US Think Tanks Give Lessons in Foreign Policy', *Guardian* (19 August 2002): www.guardian.co.uk/elsewhere/journalist/story.

14. Michael Dolny. 'Spectrum Narrows Further in 2002', *FAIR* (July/August 2003): www.fair.org/extra/0307/thinktanks2002.html.

15. Ibid.

16. 'US Think Tanks Give Lessons in Foreign Policy'.

17. Edward Said. *Orientalism* (New York: Vintage Books, 1979), p. 317.

18. Edward Said. 'The Academy of Lagado', *London Review of Books*, **25**, no. 8 (17 April 2003). See also: www.lrb.co.uk/v25/n08/print/said01_.html.

19. Ibid.

20. Ibid.

21. *US News & World Report* (23 December 2002).

22. For more information, see discussion at: www.itszone.co.uk/zone0/viewtopic.php?t=1709 (19 December 2002).

23. For further information on Pipes activities see: www.danielpipes.org/bios/?PHPSESSID=1f9fe687ef9032f04b0e9c64e0c74cc0.

24. Ian Williams. 'Of Pipes and Sources', *Middle East International* (8 August 2003), p. 9.

25. Michael Scherer. 'Daniel Pipes, Peacemaker?' (26 May 2003): www.motherjones.com/news/update/2003/22/we_420_01.html.

26. Edward Said. 'American Zionism: The Real Problem', *Media Monitors Network* (14 March 2001): www.mediamonitors.net/edward13.html.

27. Michael Lind. 'Distorting U.S Foreign Policy: The Israel Lobby and American Power', *Third World Traveller* (May 2002): www.third world-traveler.com/Israel?israel_lobby_us.html.

28. Ibid.

29. Ibid.

30. Edward Said. 'Israel, Iraq and the United States', *Al-Ahram Weekly*, Issue # 607 (10–16 October 2002).

31. Edward Said. 'A Monument to Hypocrisy', *Al-Ahram Weekly*, Issue # 625 (February 2003).

32. Edward Said. 'Israel, Iraq and the United States'.

33. Jane's Foreign Report. 'The Israeli General's Plan' (10 July 2001): www.janes.com

34. Christian Salmon. 'Palestine Near and Far: The Bulldozer War', *Le Monde Diplomatique* (17 May 2002).

35. Edward Said. 'Israel, Iraq and the United States'.

36. As quoted from Public Papers of the Presidents, Dwight D. Eisenhower (1960), pp. 1035–1040 at: http://coursesa.matrix.msu.edu/~hst306/documents/indust.html.

37. Ken Silverstein. *Private Warriors* (New York: Verso Books, 2000), p. 5.

38. Ibid., p. 6.

39. Seymour Hersh. 'Lunch With the Chairman: Why was Richard Perle Meeting with Adnan Khashoggi?' *The New Yorker* (17 March 2003): www.newyorker.com/printable/?fact/030317fa_fact.

40. Stephen Labaton. 'Pentagon Advisor is also Advising Global Crossing', *New York Times* (21 March 2003).

41. These are the company's objectives as cited in a letter sent by one of the representatives of Trireme Partners L.P. to Adnan Khashoggi in November 2002. Seymour Hersh. 'Lunch With the Chairman'.

42. In an article in the *New York Times* (21 March 2003) Stephen Labaton asserted that Perle's dealings with Global Crossing (in which he was contracted to ease the process of selling the company's assets, including a global fibre optics network, despite Pentagon resistance) were potentially a conflict of interest. Perle had been offered $125,000 with a $600,000 bonus if the deal went through. It could be inferred that the intent of Global Crossing's choice of Perle, especially given the nature of the bonus, was an attempt to obtain his influence to pressure the Committee on Foreign Investment in the US to approve the sale. This inference is reinforced by the fact that he resigned from the Defence Policy Board and rejected the Global Crossing offer only after it became a public scandal.

    See Stephen Labaton. 'Pentagon Advisor is also Advising Global Crossing'. Also see Jack Shafer. 'Richard Perle Libel Watch, Week 9: What Happened to Richard Perle's Big, Bad, Libel Stick?' *The Slate* (7 May 2003), found online at: http://slate. msn.com/toolbar.aspx?action=print&id=2082676.

43. Seymour Hersh. 'Lunch With the Chairman'.

44. In an interview with Wolf Blitzer on CNN, when questioned about the accusations levelled by Hersh that Perle would be profiting from war, Perle responded by saying, 'I don't believe that a company would gain from a war. On the contrary, I believe that the successful removal of Saddam Hussein, and I've said this over and over again, will diminish the threat of terrorism. And what he's talking about is investments in homeland defence, which I think are vital and are necessary. Look, Sy Hersh is the closest thing American journalism has to a terrorist, frankly': www.cnn.com/TRANSCRIPTS/0303/09/le.00.html.

45. According to Herman and Chomsky: 'Flak from the powerful can be either direct or indirect. The direct would include letters or phone calls from the White House to Dan Rather or William Paley, or from the FCC to the television networks asking for documents used in putting together a programme, or from irate officials of ad agencies or corporate sponsors to media officials asking for reply time or threatening retaliation.' Although the authors specifically mention 'retaliation' from corporate sponsors, reason tells us that this would also apply to irate government officials who may have been caught with their hand in the proverbial

cookie jar. Edward S. Herman and Noam Chomsky. *Manufacturing Consent* (New York: Pantheon Books, 1988) p. 26.

46. Jack Shafer asserted that the lawsuit was unlikely and even offered to pay for it himself just to see it happen. Jack Shafer. 'Richard Perle, Libel Watch, Week 20: Only 32 More Weeks Before the Statute of Limitations Runs Out', *Slate* (5 August 2003): http://politics.slate.msn.com/id/2086650/.

47. Berman claimed that Perle had abused his post for his own personal gain and was in violation of 'Regulations Code 5 CFR 2635.702'. See Ari Berman. 'Payments for Perle', *The Nation* (18 August 2003): www.thenation.com/docprint.mhtml?i=20030818&s=berman.

48. Ken Silverstein. *Private Warriors* (New York: Verso Books, 2000), p. 5.

49. For further information see Research Unit for political Economy. *Behind the Invasion of Iraq* (New York: Monthly Review Press, 2003).

50. Henry C.K Liu. 'US Dollar Hegemony Must Go', *Asia Times* (11 April 2002).

51. William Clark. 'The Real Reasons'.

52. For details, see Henry C.K. Liu and Javad Yarjani. 'The Choice of Currency for the Denomination of the Oil Bill' (14 April 2002). www.opec.org/newsInfo/Speeches/sp2002/spAraqueSpainAp14.htm.

53. Michael Hodges. 'Grandfather Economic Report Series' http://home.att.net/~mhodges/debt.htm. See also Mary Deibel. 'Tax Shortfall Feeds Seas of Red Ink' (11 May 2003). www.gomemphis.com/mca/business/article/0,1426,MCA_440_1950272,00.htm.

54. William Clark. 'The Real Reasons'.

55. Michael Moore. *Stupid White Men* (New York: Regan Books, 2001), p. xviii.

56. Ibid., pp. 8, 14.

57. Robert Dreyfuss. 'The Misinformers', *Mother Jones*: www.motherjones.com/news.qa/2003/15/we_352_01.html.

58. Jean-Charles Brisard and Guillaume Dasquie. *The Forbidden Truth* (trans. Lucy Rounds) (New York: Thunder's Mouth Press/Nation Books, 2002), pp. 37–8, 43–4.

59. Philip S. Golub. 'Background to Washington's War on Terror: American Caesar', *Le Monde Diplomatique* in English (16 January 2002).

60. Clark Kissinger. 'The New Domestic Order' (25 July 2003): www.zmag.org/content/print_article.cfm?itemID=3955&sectionID=43.

61. Naomi Klein. 'Bush to NGO's: Watch Your Mouths' (24 June 2003): www.zmag.org/content/showarticle.cfm?SectionID=43&ItemID=3826.

62. Robert Cox and Michael G. Schechter. *The Political Economy of a Plural World: Critical Reflections on Power, Morals and Civilisation* (London: Routledge, 2002).

63. The text of the speech may be found at the White House official website (www.whitehouse.gov/); see also 'US Strikes at Afghan Targets', BBC News (7 October 2001); by 6 November Bush had shortened the charge to 'You're either with us or against us in the fight against terror.' See 'Bush Says it is Time for Action', CNN.com/US (6 November 2001).

64. Bernard Lewis. 'Did You Say "American Imperialism"?' *National Review* (17 December 2001).

65. Maxime Rodinson. *Europe and the Mystique of Islam* (trans. Roger Veinus) (Seattle: University of Washington Press, 1987). Translation of *La Fascination de l'Islam*. For an excellent examination of theologocentrism and its adaptation in the American response to September 11 see As'ad Abu Khalil. *Bin Laden, Islam and America's New 'War on Terrorism'* (New York: Seven Stories Press, 2002).

66. See Edward W. Said. *Covering Islam: How the Media and the Experts Determine How we See the Rest of the World* (New York: Vintage Books, 1997); and Norman G. Finkelstein. *Image and Reality of the Israel–Palestine Conflict* (New York: Verso, 1995).

67. Gail Russell Chaddock. 'A Revival of Public Religion – on Capitol Hill', *Christian Science Monitor* (7 January 2002): www.csmonitor.com/ 2002/0107/p1s4-usgn.html.

68. Kim Lawton report for the PBS show, *Religion and Ethics Newsweekly* (7 February 2003). Found at: www.pbs.org/wnet/religionandethics/ week623/news.html.

69. From Kim Lawton's interview of Princeton religion professor Elaine Pagels for the PBS show *Religion and Ethics Newsweekly* (7 February 2003). The interview can be found on the website at: www.pbs.org/ wnet/religionandethics/week623/pagels.html.

70. Accounts in the US media for the 48 hours between the bombing and the arrest of Timothy McVeigh were filled with accusations of Arab involvement. Former United States Representative Dave McCurdy of Oklahoma (former Chairman of the House Intelligence Committee) told CBS News that there was 'very clear evidence of the involvement of fundamentalist Islamic terrorist groups'. Speaking on CNN, ATF director John Magaw said: 'I think any time you have this kind of damage, this kind of explosion, you have to look there (Middle East terrorists) first.' Steven Emerson, a self-described 'terrorism expert', employed first by CBS News and then NBC as well as the *Wall Street Journal*, made claims on CBS News (29 April 1995) in the wake of the 1995 Oklahoma City bombing that the terrorist act quickly found to be conducted by Timothy McVeigh showed 'a Middle Eastern trait' because it 'was done with the intent to inflict as many casualties as possible'.

71. For an excellent synopsis of the reportage of the morning see: Jill Geisler. 'Minute by Minute with the Broadcast News', Poynter Institute, www.poynter.org (11 September 2001).

72. CNN (11 September 2001) as quoted in FAIR. 'Media Advisory: Media March to War', Fairness & Accuracy in Reporting (17 September 2001): www.fair.org/press-releases/wtc-war-punditry.html.

73. *New York Times* (13 September 2001).

74. Statement by the President in his Address to the Nation on 11 September 2001: www.whitehouse.gov/news/releases/2001/09/20010911-16.html.

75. *Washington Post* (13 September 2001) as quoted in FAIR. 'Media Advisory: Media March to War', Fairness & Accuracy in Reporting (17 September 2001). www.fair.org/press-releases/wtc-war-punditry.html.

76. Statement by the President in his Address to the Nation on 11 September 2001. www.whitehouse.gov/news/releases/2001/09/20010911-16.html.

77. Andy Rooney. 'Why Islam Has a Hold on Muslims' (17 December 2001). www.cbsnews.com/stories/2001/12/14/60minutes/rooney/main321447. shtml.

78. T.Y. Ismael and J.S. Ismael (1999). 'Cowboy Warfare, Biological Diplomacy: Disarming Metaphors as Weapons of Mass Destruction', *Politics and the Life Sciences*, pp. 16–24 (March).

79. See White House official website, www.whitehouse.gov.

80. Ingrid Mattson. 'Saving Islam From the Terrorists: American Muslims Have a "Special Obligation"' www.beliefnet.com/frameset.asp?pageLoc=/ story/89/story_8987_1.html&boardID=26483.

81. Robert Dreyfuss. 'Devising Bad Intelligence to Promote Bad Policy', (December 2002): www.truthout.org/docs_02/12.06E.pentagon.cia.htm.

82. Geoffrey Aronson. 'Palestine Near and Far: A Sideshow to the Conquest of Iraq', *Le Monde Diplomatique* (17 May 2002).

83. Ibid.

84. Patrick Cockburn. 'CIA Survey of Iraq Airfields Heralds Attack', *Independent* (18 March 2002): http://news.independent.co.uk/world/ middle_east/story.jsp?story=275699.

85. These reports were widespread in the media but dismissed by the Prime Minister's Office.

86. Kamal Ahmed, Jason Burke and Peter Beaumont. 'Bush Wants 25,000 UK Iraq Force: Britain Considers Joint Invasion Plan', *Observer* (10 March 2002): www.observer.co.uk/international/story/0,6903,665083,00.html.

87. Javad Yarjani. 'The Choice of Currency for the Denomination of the Oil Bill'. Speech to the EU on the International Role of the Euro (14 April 2002): www.opec.org/newsInfo/Speeches/sp2002/spAraqueSpain Apr14.htm.

88. Amir Butler. 'The Euro and the War with Iraq' (29 March 2003): www.atrueword.com/index.php/article/articleview/49/1/2.

89. William Clark. 'The Real Reasons'.

90. During Cheney's visit, he declared that Washington 'should not strike Iraq because such an attack would only raise animosity in the region against the United States'. See Julian Borger. 'US Paves Way for War on Iraq: Attack Base to be Moved into Qatar to Bypass Saudi Objections', *Guardian* (27 March 2002).

91. Ibid.

92. See Howard Schneider. 'Mideast Allies Warn US Not to Attack Iraq: Leaders of Jordan, Turkey Say Move Against Hussein Could Destabilize Region', *Washington Post* (11 March 2002), p. A14: www.washington-post.com/wp-dyn/articles/A5422-2002Mar10.html; Alan Sipress. 'Jordan Advises US Against a Military Campaign in Iraq', *Washington Post* (13 March 2002), p. A24: www.washingtonpost.com/wp-dyn/articles/ A16757-2002Mar12.html. For the Israeli perspective see Yossi Verter and Aluf Benn. 'Israel to US: Don't Wait for Calm Here Before Hitting Iraq', *Ha'aretz* (3 May 2002). www.haaretz.co.il/hasen/pages/ShArt. jhtml?itemNo=151228&contrassID=2&subContrassID=1&sbSubContras sID=0.

93. Alan Sipress. 'Cheney Plays Down Arab Criticism Over Iraq', *Washington Post* (18 March 2002), p. A10: www.washingtonpost.com/wp-dyn/articles/A42203-2002Mar17.html.

94. Dana Milbank and Mike Allen. 'US Will Take Action Against Iraq, Bush Says: "All Options Are on the Table" Against States That Pose Threat', *Washington Post* (14 March 2002), p. A01: www.washingtonpost.com/wp-dyn/articles/A22091-2002Mar13.html.

95. Geoffrey Aronson. 'A Sideshow to the Conquest of Iraq', *Le Monde Diplomatique* (17 May 2002).

96. Denis Staunton. 'EU Refuses to Adopt French Middle East Plan', *The Irish Times* (11 February 2002): www.ireland.com/newspaper/world/2002/0211/3780008927FR11EUDENIS.html. See also 12th GCC-EU Joint Council/Ministerial Meeting – Joint Communiqué (27–28 February 2002): http://europa.eu.int/comm/external_relations/gulf_cooperation/intro/12thgcc_eu.htm.

97. As quoted by Peter Schwarz. 'European Foreign Ministers Attack Bush's Policy', *World Socialist Web Site News* (15 February 2002): www.wsws.org/articles/2002/feb2002/euro-f15.shtml.

98. Jonathan Freedland. 'Patten Lays into Bush's America: Fury at President's "Axis of Evil" Speech', *Guardian* (9 February 2002): www.guardian.co.uk/bush/story/0,7369,647554,00.html.

99. Steven Everts. 'Why Should Bush Take Europe Seriously?' *Observer* (17 February 2002): www.observer.co.uk/Print/0,3858,4357611,00.html. See also 'Peremptory Tendencies: France Fires a Warning Shot at the US', *Guardian* (7 February 2002): www.guardian.co.uk/leaders/story/0,3604,646014,00.html.

100. 'Germany Warns US Against Unilateralism', BBC News (12 February 2002): http://news.bbc.co.uk/hi/english/world/europe/newsid_1816000/1816395.stm.

101. Speech by US President, George W. Bush to the German Bundestag, Berlin (23 May 2002): http://usinfo.state.gov/cgi-bin/washfile/ display.pl?p=/products/washfile/geog/eu&f=02052321.wwe&t=/products/washfile/newsitem.shtml.

102. US Department of State. 'Bush, Schroeder Say No Concrete Plans to Attack Iraq', (23 May 2002): http://usinfo.state.gov/cgi-bin/washfile/display.pl?p=/products/washfile/geog/eu&f=02052320.wwe&t=/products/washfile/newsitem.shtml.

103. Ian Traynor. 'Georgia: US Opens New Front in War on Terror', *Guardian* (20 March 2002): www.guardian.co.uk/international/story/0,3604,670542,00.html.

104. Anayat Durrani. 'Trooping Across the World', *Al-Ahram Weekly* Online (7–13 March 2002, Issue No.576): www.ahram.org.eg/weekly/2002/576/re74.htm See also Agence France-Presse. 'Yemen Downplays US "Experts" Role on Anti-Terror Mission' (2 March 2002): www.inq7.net/brk/2002/mar/02/brkafp_3-1.htm.

105. 'US Troops Begin Philippine Exercises', BBC News (17 February 2002): http://news.bbc.co.uk/hi/english/world/asia-pacific/newsid_1825000/1825688.stm. See also 'Focus on the Philippines: American

Advisers have Raised Stakes in Troubled Area', *Pittsburgh Post-gazette* (26 April 2002): www.post-gazette.com/forum/20020426edphil26p2.asp.

106. Peter Baker. 'For US Forces, a Secret and Futile Hunt: Local Guides Describe Furtive Trip into Pakistan in Search of Fugitives', *Washington Post* (5 May 2002): www.washingtonpost.com/ac2/wp-dyn?pagename=article&node=&contentId=A33591-2002May4&notFound=true.

107. Derk Kinnane Roelofsma. 'US, Islam, and Central Asia', United Press International/*The Washington Times* (7 March 2002): www.washtimes.com/upi-breaking/07032002-110409-5870r.htm.

108. President George W. Bush. 'President Thanks World Coalition for Anti-Terrorism Efforts' (11 March 2002): www.whitehouse.gov/news/releases/2002/03/20020311-1.html.

109. US Department of State. 'Patterns of Global Terrorism 2001', May 2002: www.state.gov/documents/organization/10319.pdf. The US Department of State found that Iran 'remained the most active state sponsor of terrorism in 2001'. The seven designated state sponsors of terrorism are Cuba, Iran, Iraq, Libya, North Korea, Syria and Sudan.

110. Geoffrey Aronson. 'A Sideshow to the Conquest of Iraq', *Le Monde Diplomatique* (17 May 2002).

111. United Press International. 'US May Grant $50mn to Iran Dissidents', *Middle East Times*: www.metimes.com/2k3/issue2003-15/reg/us_may_grant.html.

112. Rober Dreyfuss. 'The Thirty Year Itch', *Mother Jones* (March/April 2003): www.redrat.net/BUSH_WAR/dreyfuss.htm.

113. *Guardian*. 'Wolfowitz: Iraq War was About Oil' (4 June 2003).

114. Jim Lobe. 'Pentagon Steps Closer to "GloboCop" Role', *Asia Times* (14 June 2003).

115. Michel Chossudovsky. 'The Anglo-American Military Axis', *Global Research* (10 March 2003): http://globalresearch.ca/articles/CHO303B.html.

116. Zbigniew Brzezinski. *The Grand Chessboard: American Primacy and its Geo-strategic Imperatives* (New York: Basic Books, 1997), pp. 198–9.

117. www.counterpunch.org/said06/42003.html.

118. Edward Said. 'Archeology of the Road Map', *Al-Ahram Weekly* (12–18 June 2003).

119. Khilafah (27 May 2003): www.khilafah.com/home/category.php?DocumentID=7234&TagID=2.

120. *Al-Ahram* (24 May 2003): www.ahram.org.eg/Index.asp?CurFN=FILE9.HTM&DID=7765.

121. Ibid.

122. Patrick Martin. 'How and Why the US Encouraged Looting in Iraq': www.wsws.org/articles//2003/apr2003/iraq-a15_prn.html. See also Robert Fisk. 'Books, Priceless Documents Burn in Sacking of Baghdad', *Independent* (14 April 2003).

123. Robert Fisk. 'For the People on the Streets, This is Not Liberation but a New Colonial Oppression', *Independent* (17 April 2003): http://argument.independent.co.uk/commentators/story.jsp?story=397925.

124. Patrick Tyler. 'After the War: The Political Scene; Iraqi's Frustrated by Shift Favouring US-British Rule', *New York Times* (26 May 2003), p. A1.

125. Sheldon Rampton and John Stauber. 'How to Sell a War', *In These Times* (4 August 2003): http://inthesetimes.com/print.php?id=299_0_1_0.
126. E.A. Khammas. 'A Closed Circle of Collaborators', *Occupation Watch Centre* (28 July 2003): www.occupationwatch.org/print_article.php?id=340&print=1.
127. *Financial Times* (8 June 2003).
128. George Wright. 'Amnesty Accuses the US-led Forces of Abuses', *Guardian* (23 July 2003). See also: www.guardian.co.uk/international/story/0,3604,1004537,00.html.
129. Ibid.
130. Robert Fisk. 'Censorship of the Press', *Independent* (11 June 2003).
131. Jim Lobe. 'US Fails Post-War Iraq Examination', *Asia Times* (June 27, 2003).
132. Dick Cheney on *Meet the Press* (16 March 2003): www.msnbc.com/news/966470.asp.
133. Quoting a US official in *Financial Times* (4 August 2003).
134. Reuters. 'Perle Cites Errors in Iraq, Urges Power Transfer' (27 August 2003).
135. Eric Hobsbawm. 'America's Imperial Delusion', *Guardian* (14 June 2003).
136. Media reports (22 May 2003). Printed Media (23 May 2003).

CHAPTER 4

1. Geoff Simons. *Targeting Iraq* (London: Saqi Books, 2002), pp. 108–9.
2. Ibid., p. 120.
3. Ibid., p. 233.
4. Enid Hill. 'The New World Order and the Gulf War: Rhetoric, Policy, and Politics in the United States', pp. 184–223, in Tareq Y. Ismael and Jacqueline S. Ismael (eds) *The Gulf War and the New World Order* (Gainesville: University of Florida Press, 1994), pp. 184–7.
5. Paragraph six contains the mechanism implementing the 661 Committee. It should be noted that paragraphs three and four are copied from UNSCR 253 (29 May 1968) which was one of the resolutions imposing economic sanctions on Rhodesia (now Zimbabwe) beginning in 1966.
6. Soon after its adoption France and the United States detailed divergent opinions, articulating an early disagreement of legal interpretation, over whether UNSCR 670 required Resolution 661's approval for flights without cargo. This disagreement would resurface again by 2000 when a number of commercial and relief flights into Iraq occurred in August of 2000 with the reopening of Baghdad's international airport. To avoid a confrontation with US forces in the region and their maintenance of the blockade through US interpretations of 670, the flights were labelled as humanitarian missions. A series of international and regional flights, many organised by countries and organisations in the campaign to bring an end to the sanctions, became physical manifestations of the crumbling support for sanctions in the international community.

7. See Raymond Baker. 'Imagining Egypt in the New Age: Civil Society and the Leftist Critique', pp. 399–434 in Tareq Y. Ismael and Jacqueline S. Ismael (eds) *The Gulf War and the New World Order* (Gainesville: University Press of Florida, 1994). Also see the introduction to this edited volume, pp. 1–21 for an overview of the various actors and implications of the so-called 'new world order'.

8. Enid Hill. 'The New World Order'.

9. Ibid., p. 110.

10. Noam Chomsky. *A New Generation Draws the Line: Kosovo, East Timor and the Standards of the West* (New York: Verso Books, 2000), p. 25.

11. The coalition consisted of: Afghanistan, Argentina, Australia, Bahrain, Bangladesh, Belgium, Canada, Czechoslovakia, Denmark, Egypt, France, Germany, Greece, Hungary, Honduras, Italy, Kuwait, Morocco, the Netherlands, New Zealand, Niger, Norway, Oman, Pakistan, Poland, Portugal, Qatar, Saudi Arabia, Senegal, South Korea, Spain, Syria Turkey, the United Arab Emirates, the United Kingdom, and the United States.

12. For a summary of the diplomatic and political machinations during this period see Bob Woodward. *The Commanders* (New York: Simon & Schuster, 2002).

13. Frontline. 'The Gulf War'. PBS and WGBH website, 1998: www.pbs.org/wgh/pages/frontline/gulf/appendix/.

14. See Steven R. Ratner (1995). 'Image and Reality in the UN's Peaceful Settlement of Disputes', *European Journal of International Law*, 6, no. 3, pp. 426–44. For the Charter itself see: www.un.org/Overview/Charter/chapter7.html.

15. Ibid., pp. 110–11.

16. Graham S. Pearson. *The UNSCOM Saga: Chemical and Biological Weapons Non-Proliferation*. (New York: St. Martin's Press, 1999).

17. On the imposition of the no-fly zones and their legality see Christine Gray. 'From Unity to Polarization: International Law and the Use of Force against Iraq', *European Journal of International Law*, 13, no. 1 (2002), pp. 1–20.

18. Ibid., p. 112.

19. Initially pilots were reported to be responding to attacks from Iraqi military forces, then they would retaliate against the threat of attack – as identified as the use of radar to lock missile batteries onto allied aircraft, to then retaliating against Iraqi transgressions days later (removing the urgency of any Iraqi representing a true threat to allied air crews) and finally to attacking targets in the central portion of Iraq not covered by the 'no-fly zones'. That these attacks and punitive raids have been ongoing for over a decade without response from the international community again undermines the impartiality of international law required to develop a sustainable global order.

20. UNIKOM's website is: www.un.org/Depts/DPKO/Missions/unikom/unikom_body.htm.

21. The Commission and the most up-to-date figures may be accessed through their website at: www.unog.ch/uncc/start.htm.

22. Ibid., p. 113.

23. Following the passage of UNSCR 986 and months of negotiation between Iraq and the UN Secretariat, a Memorandum of Understanding was signed, setting out arrangements for the implementation of 986. The Office of the Iraq Programme (OIP) was established in March 1997 to implement the oil-for-food programme. The first oil under this programme was exported in December 1996, and the first shipments of food arrived in March 1997. Office of the Iraq Programme, *Oil-for-Food* (www.unorg/Depts/oip/index.htm).

24. For an alternative analysis to the mainstream media portrayal of the confrontation between the government of Iraq and the government of the United States that led to the bombings of December 1998 see K.M. Fierke. 'Logics of Force and Dialogue: The Iraq/UNSCOM Crisis as Social Interaction', *European Journal of International Relations*, **06**, no. 03 (15 September 1998).

25. 'UN Inspectors Withdraw to Bahrain from Iraq', *Reuters* (11 November 1998).

26. William S. Cohen. DoD News Briefing (19 December 1998). Available at: www.defenselink.mil/news/Dec1998/t12201998_t1219coh.html.

27. Colum Lynch. 'US Spying Goals in Iraq Called Difficult', *Boston Globe* (7 January 1999); Stephen J. Hedges. 'Ex-Inspector: Butler OK'd Spying Device: US Purported to Have Sole Control of Eavesdropping Equipment in Baghdad Office', *Chicago Tribune* (10 January 1999) 'Iraq: UNSCOM Spying Confirmed', *Guardian*, 27 January; Mohamed Sid-Ahmed. 'Spying in the Name of the UN', *Al-Ahram Weekly* Online (21–28 January 1999); J.J. Richardson. 'Clinton's Other War', *Mother Jones* (6 April 1999).

28. See UNSCR 1284.

29. See the UNMOVIC website: www.un.org/Depts/unmovic/ for details about its organisational framework.

30. The President of the Security Council had established two panels in 1999 to report on Iraqi disarmament and humanitarian issues inside Iraq, and Kuwaiti claims (see S/1999/100, 30 January 1999).

31. Campaign Against the Sanctions on Iraq, Cambridge, England, Briefing 2:24 December 1999.

32. 'Iraq's Oil Industry and it's Oil Revenue Prospects For 2000'; this brief discusses the state of Iraq's oil sector which is responsible for generating the revenues under which the humanitarian programme in Iraq operates: http://leb.net/~erik/congresswatch/oilsectorbrief.html; see also: 'Iraq Welcomes Security Council Decision to Increase Oil Equipment Purchases', CNN.com (31 March 2000): www.cnn.com/2000/WORLD/meast/03/31/iraq.un.02/index.html.

33. Geoff Simons. *Targeting Iraq*, pp. 221, 224.

34. Ibid., p. 229.

35. Ibid., p. 230.

36. The Bush administration had adopted an aggressive unilateralist policy of attacking or removing unwelcome heads of international bodies – working on human rights, climate change or chemical weapons – with which the US had disagreements. This, combined with the US rejection of the Comprehensive Test Ban Treaty (CTBT), has undermined US protestations to be supportive of anti-proliferation goals. The successful

ousting of José Bustani, head of the Organisation for the Prohibition of Chemical Weapons, came about after the United States threatened to withhold funding (see Reuters, 'UN Chemical Arms Chief Ousted in US – Led Vote', *New York Times* (22 April 2002) and Richard Norton-Taylor. 'US Ousts Director of Chemical Arms Body', *Guardian* (23 April 2002)) and attacks on the arms control record of Hans Blix, formerly head of the IAEA and now of UNMOVIC, emerged in *The Times* and *Washington Post*. The Central Intelligence Agency had been asked to investigate Blix by Under Secretary of Defense Paul Wolfowitz, an advocate of regime change in Iraq. The CIA found that Blix had conscientiously conducted inspections while with IAEA and 'performed as well as he could within the rules governing inspections of Iraqi nuclear facilities'. Blix, for his part, has presented UNMOVIC's position as quite firm, stating that Iraq would need to give the inspectors hard proof that its WMD had been destroyed. (See James Bone 'UN's Chief Weapons Inspector Turns Hawkish', *The Times* (15 April 2002).) At the same time he held out the possibility that if Iraq co-operated fully, sanctions could be lifted within a year. (See Walter Pincus and Colum Lynch. 'Crisscrosses Hamper Arms Inspection in Iraq', *Washington Post* (15 April 2002) and Julian Borger. 'US Hawk "Tried to Sully Iraq Arms Inspector". Pentagon No 2 Ordered CIA to Investigate Record of UN Agency Chief', *Guardian* (16 April 2002).)

37. 21 November 2002: http://jurist.law.pitt.edu/forum/forumnew74.php.
38. See the sensationalistic account by John F. Burns of the first UN inspection of Iraqi Presidential Palaces, 'Inspectors in Iraq Shift to Nuclear Plant and Former Factory', *New York Times* (4 December 2002). As an interesting aside, the *Guardian*'s (UK) coverage of the event was entitled 'First Palace Visit is a Propaganda Coup for Saddam', and *Globe and Mail*'s (Canada) coverage was entitled 'US Skeptical Despite Iraq's Co-operation with UN Team'. Although all three articles have a decidedly spun headline, the *New York Times*, despite the fact that the majority of the article deals with the visit to al-Sajoud, makes no mention or inference to a higher level of Iraqi co-operation. Rather, the words 'Iraq' and 'Nuclear' appear together in the headline of an American publication once again.
39. 'The Status of Nuclear Inspections in Iraq'. Mohammed El-Baradei, Director-General of the International Atomic Energy Agency. Statement to the United Nations Security Council. New York (27 January 2003).
40. For the full text and video of Powell's presentation, see: www.state.gov/secretary/rm/2003/17300.htm.
41. Colum Lynch. 'Powell Accuses Iraq of Undermining Inspectors: At. U.N., Secretary of State Says Iraqis Dispersing Rockets', *Washington Post* (5 February 2003).
42. 'The Status of Nuclear Inspections in Iraq'. Mohammed El-Baradei, Director-General of the International Atomic Energy Agency. Statement to the United Nations Security Council. New York (7 March 2003).
43. Dr Hans Blix, 'Oral Introduction of the 12th Quarterly Report of UNMOVIC', UN News service (7 March 2003).

44. Tony Blair was threatened by members of his own party that he would be challenged and perhaps recalled if the UK was to go to war without UN backing. See Alan Freeman. 'Blair's MPs Threaten Revolt', *Globe and Mail* (12 March 2003).

45. 'America is Referred to as a "Rogue State" in Europe Now as Often as Iraq'. See the editorial by Thomas L. Friedman, 'Foreign Affairs; Noblesse Oblige', *New York Times* (31 July 2001).

46. H. O'Connor, *World Crisis in Oil* (New York, 1962), p. 79.

47. See David R. Sands. 'Petroleum Fuels Debate on Iraq War', *Washington Times* (7 October 2002): www.washtimes.com/world/20021007-8413366.htm.

48. Deborah Lamb, *Venture*, CBC Television (1 December 2002), 'Iraqi Oil'.

49. See comments made by former CIA director R. James Woolsey in the *Washington Post* article by Dan Morgan and David B. Ottaway (15 September 2002), 'In Iraqi War Scenario, Oil is Key Issue: US Drillers Eye Huge Petroleum Pool'.

50. 'Blueprint Gives Coalition Control of Oil': www.guardian.co.uk/iraq/story/0,2763,952935,00.html.

51. www.globepolicy.org/security/sanction/iraq/lift/2003/0528occupation.htm.

CHAPTER 5

1. Jacqueline S. Ismael and Shereen T. Ismael. 'Gender and State in Iraq', in S. Joseph (ed.) *Citizenship and Gender in the Middle East* (Syracuse: Syracuse University Press, 2000), pp. 185–211.

2. R.L. Sivard. *World Military and Social Expenditures*, 11th edition (plus the 12th, 14th, and 15th editions) (Leesburg, VA: World Priorities, 1980).

3. Ibid.

4. K.G. Fenelon, V. Manjiakin and W. Rasaputram. *National Income in Iraq: Selected Studies* (Republic of Iraq: Ministry of Planning, Central Statistical Office, 1970), p. 6.

5. Ibid., p. 7.

6. Ibid.

7. Oil exports were also rapidly increasing, from 6 million long tons in 1950 to 110.6 million in 1976. (See Fenelon *et al.*, *National Income in Iraq*, p. 7, and Central Statistics Organisation, *Annual Abstract of Statistics, 1976* (Republic of Iraq: Ministry of Planning, 1976), p. 170.) In addition, with the formation of OPEC in 1960, Iraq, along with other oil-exporting countries, had achieved better royalty terms.

8. In addition, there were 6515 beds in specialised hospitals. Central Statistical Organisation. *Annual Abstract of Statistics, 1976*, pp. 370–1.

9. Ibid, p. 342.

10. For an examination of this, see Abbas Alnaswari. *The Economy of Iraq: Wars, Destruction of Development and Prospects, 1950–2010* (Greenwood Press, 1994) and Stephen Heydemann (ed.) *War, Institutions, and Social Change in the Middle East* (Berkeley: University of California Press, 2000).

11. Ismael and Ismael. 'Gender and State in Iraq', pp. 195–201.

12. Samir al-Khalil. *Republic of Fear* (Berkeley: University of California Press, 1989).
13. M. Phythian. *Arming Iraq: How the US and Britain Built Saddam's War Machine* (Boston: Northeastern University Press).
14. R.L. Sivard. (1991) *World Military and Social Expenditures.*
15. Ibid.
16. Ibid.
17. Jacqueline S. Ismael. 'Social Policy and Social Change: The Case of Iraq', *Arab Studies Quarterly*, 2 (3), (1980), p. 248.
18. Geoff Simons. *Targeting Iraq* (London: Saqi Books, 2002), p. 64.
19. United Nations. 'Report of the Second Panel Established Pursuant to the Note by the President of the Security Council of 30 January 1999 (S/1999/100), Concerning the Current Humanitarian Situation in Iraq', 30 March 1999: www.un.org/Depts/oip/panelrep.html.
20. Ibid.
21. Ibid.
22. United Nations Development Programme (UNDP). 'S/2001/566. Report of the Team of Experts Established Pursuant to Paragraph 15 of Security Council Resolution 1330' (6 June 2001): www.un.org/Depts/oip/reports/2001.
23. United Nations Development Programme (UNDP). '1999–2000 Report', Iraq Country Office: www.iq.undp.org.
24. Office of the Iraq Programme. 'Oil-for-Food, Basic Figures', United Nations (18 May 2002): www.un.org/Depts/oip/background.
25. Office of the Iraq Programme. 'Oil-for-Food', United Nations (18 May 2002): www.un.org/Depts/oip/cpmd/roleofoip.
26. Ibid., pp. 69–71, 74–5.
27. UNICEF. Press release located at www.unicef.org/newsline/99pr29.htm and the report itself at: www.unicef.org/reseval/iraqr.html.
28. Ibid., p. 75.
29. In the three northern governates of Erbil, Dohuk and Sulaimaniyah, the UNDP manages a similar rehabilitation programme. Costing US $570 million, it is the largest programme the UNDP has ever been involved in.
30. United Nations Development Programme (UNDP/UNDESA). 'Analysis of Contracts On Hold, (As of 31/10/10/2000) Electricity Sector (Centre/South)' (November 2000): http://mirror.undop.org/iraq/; United Nations Development Programme (UNDP). '1999–2000 Report: as of June 2000', *Iraq Country Office* (July 2000): http://mirror.undop/iraq/REPORT.pdf.
31. United Nations Development Programme (UNDP/UNDESA). 'Analysis of Contracts On Hold'.
32. UNICEF. Press release located at: www.unicef.org/newsline/99pr29.htm and the report itself on: www.unicef.org/reseval/iraqr.html.
33. UN, FAO. 'Assessment of the Food and Nutrition Situation: Iraq', *Technical Report Prepared for the Government of Iraq by the Food and Agriculture Organisation of the United Nations* (2000) FAO Technical Co-operation Programme. [ES:TCP/IRQ/8924] www.reliefweb.int/library/documents/iraqnutrition.pdf.

34. United Nations. 'Report of the Second Panel Established Pursuant to the Note by the President of the Security Council of 30 January 1999.

35. Ibid., pp. 80–1.

36. UNSC Resolutions 700, 705, 706, 712, 778, 986, 1111, 1129, 1143, 1153, 1158, 1175, 1210, 1242, 1266, 1275, 1280, 1281, 1292, 1302, 1330, 1352, 1360, 1382 and 1409.

37. James Orbinski. 'New Frontiers in Health in a Changing Global Context', in J.S. Ismael (ed.) *Social Welfare in a Changing World* (Calgary: Detselig Enterprises, 1996), p. 145.

38. Hans von Sponek. public address at 'A Day and Night for the People of Iraq' 6 May 2000; as quoted in Colin Rowat. 'UN Agency Reports on the Humanitarian Situation in Iraq', *Campaign Against Sanctions on Iraq* (12 August 2000).

39. Ibid., p. 82.

40. Martti Ahtisaari, who was then serving as Under-Secretary-General for Administration and Management, was elected president of Finland in February 1994, a post in which he served until February 2000.

41. United Nations. 'Report on Humanitarian Needs in Iraq in the Immediate Post-Crisis Environment by a Mission to the Area Led by the Under-Secretary General for Administration and Management, 10–17 March 1991 S/22366' (20 March 1991).

42. When briefing the international media, with the jubilant declaration that the coalition had achieved air superiority over Iraq, US Commander General Norman Schwarzkopf intoned 'We never had any intention of destroying 100 per cent of all the Iraqi electrical power,...Because of our interest in making sure that civilians did not suffer unduly, we felt we had to leave some of the electrical power in effect, and we've done that', as quoted in George Lopez. 'The Gulf War: Not So Clean', *Bulletin of the Atomic Scientists*, **47**, no. 7 (September 1991).

43. Harvard Study Team. 'The Effect of the Gulf Crisis on the Children of Iraq', *New England Journal of Medicine*, **325** (1991), pp. 977–80.

44. United Nations. 'Report to the Secretary-General dated 15 July 1991 on Humanitarian Needs in Iraq Prepared by a Mission Led By the Executive Delegate of the Secretary-General for Humanitarian Assistance in Iraq'. S/22799, Geneva (17 July 1991).

45. International Study Team (1991). *Health and Welfare in Iraq After the Gulf Crisis: An In-Depth Assessment from August, 1991*; portions dealing with the medical findings were published as A.R. Asherio and T. Chase *et al.* (1992). 'Effect of the Gulf War on Infant and Child Mortality in Iraq', *New England Journal of Medicine*, **327**, pp. 931–6.

46. Food and Agriculture Organisation – Technical Co-operation Programme. 'Evaluation of Food and Nutrition Situation in Iraq: Terminal Statement', FAO Prepared for the Government of Iraq (1995).

47. S. Zaidi and M.C. Smith-Fawzi. 'Health of Baghdad's Children', *Lancet*, **346**, no. 1485 (December 1995).

48. WHO/23, 1998.

49. Ibid., p. 67.

50. Ibid., pp. 65–6.

51. UNICEF. 'Situation Analysis of Children and Women in Iraq – 1997', United Nations (April 1998).

52. Ibid., p. 14.

53. UN Agencies. 'Special Topics on Social Conditions in Iraq. An Overview Submitted by the UN System to the Security Council Panel on Humanitarian Issues', *United Nations* (24 March 1999).

54. United Nations. 'Report of the Second Panel Established Pursuant to the Note by the President of the Security Council of 30 January 1999 (s/1999/100), Concerning the Humanitarian Situation in Iraq. S/1999/356 Annex II', United Nations (30 March 1999).

55. UNICEF. 'Child and Maternal Mortality Survey 1999: Preliminary Report', United Nations (July–August 1999).

56. UNICEF. 'UNICEF: Questions and Answers for the Iraq Child Mortality Surveys', Baghdad (16 September 1999).

57. M.M. Ali and I.H. Shah. 'Sanctions and Childhood Mortality in Iraq', *Lancet*, **355**, (27 May 2000) pp. 1851–7.

58. See Richard Garfield (2000). 'Changes in Health and Well-being in Iraq during the 1990s: What Do We Know and How Do We Know It?' as found in CASI. *SANCTIONS ON IRAQ: Background, Consequences, Strategies.* (Cambridge, UK: Campaign Against Sanctions on Iraq), pp. 32–51; B.O. Daponte and R.M. Garfield. 'Do Sanctions Harm Children? A Case Study in Estimating the Impact of Sanctions on Child Survival in Iraq', *American Journal of Public Health* (2000). **90**, No. 4, pp. 546–52; 'The Impact of Economic Sanctions on Health and Well-being' *Relief and Rehabilitation Network (RRN) Paper 31* (London: Relief and Rehabilitation Network, 1999); (1999) *Morbidity and Mortality Among Iraqi Children from 1990 Through 1998: Assessing the Impact of the Gulf War and Economic Sanctions.* A report commissioned by the Fourth Freedom Forum and the Joan B. Kroc Institute for International Peace Studies at the University of Notre Dame.

59. Colin Rowat. 'UN Agency Reports on the Humanitarian Situation in Iraq', *Campaign Against Sanctions on Iraq* (12 August 2000), p. 16.

60. FAO. 'Assessment of the Food & Nutrition Situation, Iraq – FAO Technical Co-operation Programme' (Rome, 2000), p. 7.

61. Ibid., p. 9.

62. Ibid., p. 15.

63. Ibid., p. 31.

64. Ibid., p. 33.

65. Federation of American Scientists (FAS). See the depleted uranium ammunition page: www.fas.org/man/dod-101/sys/land/du.htm; see also the Military Toxics Project: www.miltoxproj.org, a campaign against depleted uranium weapons.

66. Federation of American Scientists (FAS) Military Toxics Project. 'Depleted Uranium; Agent Orange of the 90's: Another Pentagon Cover-up' (June 1999): www.miltoxproj.org/DU/DU_Faqs/Du_Faqs.htm.

67. M. Simons. 'Gulf War Studies Link Cancer to Depleted Uranium', *New York Times* (29 January 2001).

68. K. Birchard. 'Does Iraq's Depleted Uranium Pose a Health Risk?' *Lancet*, **351** (9103) (28 February 1998), p. 657.

69. K. Sikora. 'Cancer Services are Suffering in Iraq', *British Medical Journal* (16 January 1999), pp. 318, 203

70. H. N. Harley, E. C. Foulkes, L. H. Hilbourne, A. Hudson and C. R. Anthony. 'A Review of the Scientific Literature as it Pertains to Gulf War Illness', *Depleted Uranium, Volume 7* (RAND: National Defense Research Institute, 1999).

71. J. J. Richardson. 'Depleted Uranium: The Invisible Threat' *Mother Jones* Online (23 June 1999): www.motherjones.com/total_coverage/kosovo/reality_check/du.html; see also, 'DU Dangers "Known" before Gulf War', BBC News Online' (15 January 2001): http://news.bbc.co.uk/hi/english/world/europe/newsid_1118000/1118590.stm.

72. D. Fahey. 'DoD Analysis; The Good, the Bad and The Ugly' (June 1999): www.globaldialog.com/~kornkven/DOD_Analysis_II_Fahey.pdf.

73. World Health Organisation. 'Depleted Uranium: Sources, Exposure and Health Effects' (2001).

74. S. Fetter and F.N. von Hippel. 'The Hazard Posed by Depleted Uranium Munitions', *Science & Global Security*, **8** (2) (1999), pp. 125–61.

75. Ibid., pp. 15–16.

76. Jean-Marie Le Pen, a French right-wing politician, commenting on the Holocaust.

77. 'Press Briefing on Humanitarian Preparations for Iraq' (13 February 2003): www.un.org/News/briefings/docs/2003/ Oshimabreifing.doc.htm.

78. UN News Service. 'Transcript of the UN Humanitarian Briefing in Amman, Jordan' (20 March 2003): www.un.org/apps/news/printfocus news.asp?nid=40.

79. 'Press Briefing on Humanitarian Preparations for Iraq' (13 February 2003): www.un.org/News/briefings/docs/2003/ OshimaBriefing.doc.htm.

80. 'NGO Press Conference on Humanitarian Situation in Iraq' (13 February 2003): www.un.org/News/briefings/docs/2003/ OshimaBriefing.doc.htm.

81. UN News Service. 'Transcript of the UN Humanitarian Briefing in Amman, Jordan' (20 March 2003): www.un.org/apps/news/printfocus news.asp?nid=40

82. Ibid.

83. UN News Service. 'Transcript of the UN Humanitarian Briefing in Amman, Jordan' (24 March 2003): www.un.org/apps/news/printfocus news.asp?nid=449.

84. Campaign Against Sanctions on Iraq. 'Confidential UN Document Predicts Humanitarian Emergency in Event of War on Iraq', Press Release (7 January 2003).

85. Roger Normand. 'Special Report: Water Under Siege In Iraq. US/UK Military Forces Risk Committing War Crimes by Depriving Civilians of Safe Water', Centre for Economic and Social Rights (April 2003).

86. Ibid.

87. Amnesty International. 'Iraq: Civilians Under Fire – April 2003', AI Index: MDE14/071/2003.

88. UNICEF. 'Iraq Briefing Note' (20 April 2003).

89. 'Iraq at Risk of Cholera Epidemic', AFP (7 April 2003).

90. 'US Troops Fire on Ambulance, Two Killed', AFP (10 April 2003); A resident of Najaf is also quoted in an 29 April AFP report saying that

'Why did the Americans target civilians? They even hit ambulances trying to rescue those injured and killed five medics', in 'US Cluster Bombing Leaves Iraqi City Angry Over Dead, Maimed', AFP (29 April 2003).

91. ICRC. 'Red Crescent Maternity Hospital Damaged in Attack' (3 April 2003).
92. Simon Jeffery. 'Baghdad Hospital Bombed', *Guardian* (2 April 2003).
93. UNICEF. 'Iraq Briefing Note' (20 Apr 2003).
94. ICRC. 'The Medical System in Baghdad has Virtually Collapsed' (11 April 2003): www.icrc.org.
95. ICRC. 'Baghdad Yarmouk hospital: One Hundred Patients an Hour' (6 April 2003): www.icrc.org.
96. ICRC 'Yarmouk hospital: Corpses were Piled in the Entrance Hall before being Buried in the Hospital Grounds' (13 April 2003): www.icrc.org.
97. ICRC. 'ICRC: Dire Situation in Hospitals' (17 April 2003): www.icrc.org.
98. Mark Baker. 'Hundreds are Dying Who Should Not Die', *The Age* (21 April 2003).
99. UNICEF. 'Iraq Briefing Note' (21 April 2003).
100. Baker. 'Hundreds are Dying Who Should Not Die'.
101. United Nations. 'UN Relief Agencies Report Slow Improvement in Iraq, But Situation Still "Precarious"' (22 April 2003).
102. Amnesty International. 'Iraq: Looting, Lawlessness and Humanitarian Consequences' (11 April 2003), AI Index: MDE14/085/2003.
103. 'US Soldiers Fire on Iraqi Protesters; Hospital Chief Says 13 Iraqis are Dead', Associated Press (29 April 2003).
104. Normand. 'Special Report'.
105. *Arab News* (8 April 2003).
106. Carol Giacomo. 'Aid Groups Oppose Pentagon Control of Aid Effort', Reuters (2 April 2003). See also Shanta Bryan Gyan. 'Statement on Military Control of Iraq Relief; Reconstruction', *InterAction* (3 April 2003).
107. UN Office for the Co-ordination of Humanitarian Affairs Integrated Regional Information Network. 'UN Relief Agencies Praised Iraqi Health Workers', United Nations (21 April 2003).
108. UN Office for the Co-ordination of Humanitarian Affairs Integrated Regional Information Network. 'Iraq: Conditions in Basra's Main Hospital Still Dire', United Nations (17 April 2003).
109. Robert Fisk. 'Final Proof that War is About the Human Spirit, *Independent* (10 April 2003).
110. David Wilmhurst. 'Iraq: Looting, Lawlessness and Humanitarian Consequences', UNHCI (9 April 2003).
111. For more details, see: www.iacenter.org/franks-infra.htm.
112. Ibid.
113. ICRC. 'Iraq: Daily Bulletin – 10 April 2003': www.icrc.org/web/eng/siteeng0.nsf/iwpList550/C4F4D01059E327CFC1256D04004E2E42.
114. For more details, see www.iacenter.org/franks-infra.htm.
115. *Observer*. 'Saddam's Land Mines and Coalition Clusters Litter the Map of Iraq' (1 June 2003): http://observer.guardian.co.uk/international/story/0,6903,968208,00.html.

116. Kamal Ahmad. 'Revealed: The Cluster Bombs Litter Iraq', *Observer* (1 June 2003).
117. AAP. 'Civilian Death Toll Terrific: Priest', About News.com (23 August 2003): www.news.com.au/common/story_page/0,4057,6255211% 255E1702,00.html.
118. Ibid.
119. Andrew Cawthorne. 'US, UK "Ignore" Iraq's 20,000 Wounded Civilians', *Middle East Times* (8 August 2003).
120. For more information see also: www.iraqbodycount.net.
121. Simon Jeffery. 'War May Have Killed 10,000 Civilians, Researchers Say', *Guardian* (13 June 2003): www.guardian.co.uk/international/story/ 0,3604,976295,00.html.
122. Ibid.

CHAPTER 6

1. In 1916–17 during the First World War, the Russian Army even occupied the northeastern part of present-day Iraq, which at that time had been a province of the Ottoman Empire. See Haim Shemesh. *Soviet–Iraqi Relations, 1968–1988: In the Shadow of the Iraq–Iran Conflict* (Boulder, CO and London: Lynne Rienner Publishers, 1992), p. 14, f. 2.
2. Oles M. Smolansky with Bettie M. Smolansky. *The USSR and Iraq: The Soviet Quest for Influence* (Durham and London: Duke University Press, 1981), p. 63.
3. Majid Khadduri. *Independent Iraq 1932–1958: A Study in Iraqi Relations* (London: Oxford University Press, 1960), p. 252.
4. Shemesh. *Soviet–Iraqi Relations*, pp. 2–3.
5. Smolansky. *The USSR and Iraq*, p. 14.
6. Ibid., p. 280.
7. Ibid., p. 281.
8. Shemesh. *Soviet–Iraqi Relations*, p. 6.
9. Ibid.
10. Ibid.
11. *Pravda* (Moscow, 18 and 19 July 1967).
12. Francis Fukuyama. *The Soviet Union and Iraq Since 1968* (Santa Monica: Rand Corporation, 1980), p. 46.
13. A. Agarkov. 'Rossiisko-Irackiie otnosheniia no novom etapie razvitiia sotrudnichestva: problemy i perpektivy', *Vostok i Rossiia no rubieze XXI veka* (Institute of Oriental Studies, Russian Academy of Sciences, Moskva, 1998), p. 214. According to the always well-informed Middle Eastern French expert Eric Ruleau, Saddam Hussein was the real architect of the treaty (*Le Monde*, 14 April 1972).
14. TASS (in English, 9 April 1972).
15. Ibid.
16. Smolansky. *The USSR and Iraq*, p. 31.
17. Ibid., p. 33.
18. Radio Baghdad (*FBIS*, 8 January 1980).
19. Shemesh. *Soviet–Iraqi Relations*, p. 163.

20. *Mezhdunarodnaia zhizn*, no. 3, 1987, p. 83.
21. *Pravda*, 1 October 1980.
22. A. Vassiliev. *Rossiia no Blizhnem i Srednem Vostoke ot Messianstva k pragmatizmu* (Moskva: Nauka, 1993), p. 335.
23. Ibid.
24. Ibid., p. 336.
25. Ibid.
26. BBC news (2 February 1980).
27. Agarkov. 'Rossiisko–Irackiie', p. 214.
28. Ibid., p. 215.
29. Ibid.
30. Ibid.
31. Ibid.
32. Ibid.
33. On 2 August 1990 there were exactly 7791 Soviet citizens there (A. Vassiliev. *Rossiia no Blizhnem*, p. 363).
34. V.Z. Sharipov. *Persiskii Zaliv: Neft – politika i voina* (Moskva: Institute of Oriental Studies, Russian Academy of Sciences, 2000), p. 107.
35. Ibid., p. 109.
36. Agarkov. 'Rossiisko–Irackiie', p. 215.
37. *Izvestia* (10 January 1996), p. 3.
38. *Pravda* (Moscow, 3 August 1990).
39. That was indicated soon afterwards by a prominent Russian scholar who noted that: 'We lost the confidence of the Arab countries when we trampled upon the Treaty of Friendship and Co-operation with Iraq.' In A. M. Khazanov (ed.) *Posledstvia voiny v Persiskom zaliv'e i situatsia v regione* (Moscow: Prometei, 1993), p. 9.
40. Agarkov. 'Rossiisko–Irackiie', p. 215.
41. Vassiliev. *Rossiia no Blizhnem*, p. 350.
42. *Izvestia* (Moscow, 4 August 1990).
43. Yelena S. Melkumyan: 'Soviet Policy and the Gulf Crisis', in Ibrahim Ibrahim (ed.) *The Gulf Crisis: Background and Consequences* (Washington, DC: Center for Contemporary Arab Studies, Georgetown University, 1992), p. 84.
44. Vassiliev. *Rossiia no Blizhnem*, p. 352.
45. Ibid.
46. Sarah Graham-Brown. *Sanctioning Saddam: The Politics of Intervention in Iraq* (London, New York: I.B. Tauris Publishers, 1999), p. 10.
47. A.M. Vassiliev. 'Budushtieie Rossiiskoj Politiki na Blizhnem Vostoke', *Vestnik Rossiyskoj Akademii Nauk*, 68, no. 6, (1998), p. 494.
48. Galia Golan, 'Gorbachev's Difficult Time in the Gulf', *Political Science Quarterly*, **107**, no. 2 (1992), pp. 216–17.
49. Vassiliev, *Rossiia no Blizhnem*, p. 358.
50. Golan. 'Gorbachev's Difficult Time', p. 218.
51. Vassiliev. *Rossiia no Blizhnem*, p. 360.
52. *International Herald Tribune* (28 January 1991).
53. TASS (4 February 1991).
54. Golan. 'Gorbachev's Difficult Time', p. 218.
55. Melkumyan. 'Soviet Policy', p. 87.

56. Vassiliev. *Rossiia no Blizhnem*, pp. 359–60.
57. Melkumyan. 'Soviet Policy', p. 87.
58. Ibid.
59. Vassiliev. *Rossiia no Blizhnem*, p. 359.
60. However, there is also the opinion that supporting Primakov's mission, Gorbachev only wanted to 'please his domestic opponents in the hope of ultimately resuming his own policies' (Golan. 'Gorbachev's Difficult Time', p. 219). Shevardnadze was definitely against Primakov's mission and any efforts towards Soviet mediation and a more independent stand in the conflict (Vassiliev. *Rossiia no Blizhnem*, p. 358). See also Primakov, *Gody v Bolshoi Politike* (Moskwa: Sovershenno Sekretno, 1999), pp. 309–10.
61. Golan. 'Gorbachev's Difficult Time', p. 219.
62. Agarkov. 'Rossiisko–Irackiie', p. 216.
63. *Izvestia* (Moscow, 15 November 1991).
64. For a detailed analysis of the unprecedented Soviet-Russian collapse, see V. Pogodin. 'Rossiya i SSZA na poroge XXI veka' (Russia and the USA at the Threshold of the XXI Century), *Svobodnaya Mysl* (April 1997), pp. 30–4.
65. Russell E. Travers, 'A New Millenium and a Strategic Breathing Space', *Washington Quarterly*, **20**, no. 2 (Spring 1997), pp. 103–4.
66. *Middle East International* (9 October 1992), p. 8.
67. *Rossiia – SNG – Asia. Problemy i Perspectivy sotrudnichestva* (Moscow: Institute of Oriental Studies, Russian Academy of Sciences, 1993), p. 6.
68. *Mezhdunarodnye otnosheniia na Blizhnem i Srednem Vostoke u Politika Rossii* (Moscow: Institute of Oriental Studies, Russian Academy of Sciences, 2000), p. 41.
69. Abdalla Abdalla Omar, *SSZA, Islamskij Vostok i Rossiia* (Moscow: Russian National Fund, 1995), p. 76.
70. Ibid., pp. 76–7.
71. Agarkov. 'Rossiisko–Irackiie', p. 216.
72. Abdalla Abdalla Omar, *SSZA*, p. 77.
73. *Izvestia* (10 January 1996), p. 3.
74. *Middle East International* (9 July 1993), p. 5.
75. Ibid.
76. Ibid.
77. Agarkov. 'Rossiisko–Irackiie', p. 216.
78. *Mezhdunarodnye otnosheniia na Blizhnem i Srednim Vostoke*, p. 29. Also personal interview with A. M. Vassiliev, a noted Russian Middle Eastern scholar in Moscow, on 4 January 2000.
79. Abdalla Abdalla Omar, *SSZA*, p. 78.
80. Ibid.
81. *Izvestia* (8 December 1994).
82. S. Lavrov, Pora li oslabliat' sanktsii protiv Iraka?' *Moskovkiye Novosti*, no. 30 (24–30 June 1994).
83. Agarkov. 'Rossiisko–Irackiie', p. 217.
84. Ibid., p. 218.
85. *Izvestia* (17 October 1995). For comments about Kozyrev's political fickleness, see also *Izvestia* (10 January 1996), p. 3.

86. Abdalla Abdalla Omar, *SSZA*, p. 78.
87. Ibid., p. 80.
88. *Diplomaticheskii Vestnik* (Moscow, September 1995), p. 21.
89. Gawdat Bahgat. 'The Iraqi Crisis in the New Millennium: The Prospects', *Asian Affairs*, **XXXI**, part 2 (June 2000), p. 15.
90. *Diplomaticheskii Vestnik* (Moscow, September 1995), p. 21.
91. *Mezhdunarodnye otnosheniia na Blizhnem i Srednim Vostoke*, p. 30 and personal interview with A.M. Vassiliev (4 January 2001).
92. Ibid.
93. Ibid.
94. According to some American sources, the Russian oil company Zarubezhneft has already started up as the first foreign company since the Second Gulf War to drill oil wells in the Kirkuk field in northern Iraq. See Leon Barkho. 'Russian Firm Drilling for Iraq Oil', Associated Press (2 December 1999). Online at: www.Washington post.com/wp-srv/openline.
95. Bahgat, 'The Iraqi Crisis', p. 150. See also *Current Digest of the Post-Soviet Press*, **XLVI**, no. 10 (1994), p. 28 and No. 28 (1994), p. 24.
96. Sharipov. *Persiskii Zaliv*, p. 113.
97. ITAR-TASS (21 October 1994), issue 165, s. 1–8 (in Russian).
98. Ibid.
99. *Current Digest of the Post-Soviet Press*, **XLVII**, no. 23, p. 26 (1995).
100. Vassiliev. 'Budushtieie Rossiiskoi Politiki na Blishnem Vostoke', p. 495.
101. Agarkov. 'Rossiisko–Irackiie', p. 218.
102. *Current Digest of the Post-Soviet Press*, **XLVIII**, No. 2 (7 February 1996), p. 14.
103. See for instance V. Kolossov. 'Geopolititsheskiie polozeniie Rossii', *Polis*, No. 3, 2000, pp. 55–60 and K. Brutens. 'Vneshnaia politika Rossii; Novyi etap', *Svobodnaya Mysl*, **XXI**, No. 11 (1501) 2000, p. 7.
104. Kolossov. 'Geopolitiitsheskiie', p. 59.
105. Olga Aleksandrova. 'The 'Third World' in Russian Foreign Policy', *Aussenpolitik*, **III** (1996), p. 249.
106. *Haaretz* (31 October, 1997), online /www3.haaretz./eng.
107. Agarkov. 'Rossiisko–Irackiie', p. 218.
108. Ibid.
109. Ibid.
110. *Sevodnya* (Moscow, 6 September 1996), p. 1.
111. Ibid.
112. Ibid.
113. Agarkov. 'Rossiisko–Irackiie', p. 219.
114. Ibid., pp. 218–19.
115. *Diplomaticheskii Vestnik* (November 1997), p. 55.
116. Ibid.
117. Ibid. See also Sarah Graham-Brown. *Sanctioning Saddam: The Politics of Intervention in Iraq* (London and New York: I.B. Taurus, 1999), p. 86.
118. *Diplomaticheskii Vestnik* (November 1997), p. 56.
119. Ibid.
120. *Nezavisimaya Gazeta* (21 November 1997).
121. Ibid.

122. *Rossiyskaya Gazeta* (21 November 1997), p. 4.
123. Ibid.
124. See for instance Youssef M. Ibrahim. 'Higher Hopes in Baghdad for Ending UN Embargo', *New York Times* (18 October 1998), p. A4; Tim Weiner. 'US Spied on Iraq Under UN Cover, Officials Now Say', *New York Times* (7 January 1999), p. A1. Also UN Secretary-General Kofi Annan confirmed that he had obtained convincing evidence that the UNSCOM inspectors helped collect eavesdropping intelligence for the US government (*Washington Post*, 6 January 1999, p. A1).
125. *New York Times* (18 October 1998), p. A4.
126. *Rzeczypospolita* (Warsaw, 13 February 1998), p. 4.
127. See for instance K. Eggert, *Izvestia* (4 February 1998). For the predominant opinion among the political class and public opinion at large, see *Nezavisimaya Gazeta* (5 February 1998).
128. *Pravda* (3 February 1998).
129. *Nezavisimaya Gazeta* (5 February 1998).
130. Ibid.
131. RFE/RL, *Newsline* (13 February 1998), p. I.
132. Ibid.
133. *Guardian International* (23 February 1998).
134. *Diplomaticheskii Vestnik* (April 1998), pp. 49–50.
135. Ibid., p. 52.
136. Ibid.
137. Ibid.
138. *Current Digest of the Post-Soviet Press*, 50, no. 51 (20 January 1999), p. 1.
139. *Diplomaticheskii Vestnik* (January 1999), p. 7.
140. *Kommersant* (18 December 1998), p. 1. See also *Nezavisimaya Gazeta* (18 December 1998).
141. *Kommersant* (18 December 1998), p. 2.
142. *Diplomaticheskii Vestnik* (January 1999), p. 24.
143. Ibid.
144. Ibid., p. 25.
145. Ibid., p. 27.
146. Ibid., p. 24.
147. *Nezavisimaya Gazeta* (18 December 1998).
148. RFE/RL, *Newsline*, 2, no. 243 (December 18, 1998), p. I.
149. *Sevodnya* (Moscow, 11 December 1996), p. 3.
150. Ibid.
151. For an example of the political support of the Russian oil companies, see *Nezavisimaya Gazeta* (18 October 1996), pp. 1–2.
152. Ibid. See also *Sevodnya* (Moscow, 11 December 1996), p. 3.
153. A private interview with a prominent Russian Middle Eastern expert, member of the Russian Academy of Sciences, Prof. A.M. Vassiliev in Moscow on 4 January 2001.
154. Ibid.
155. *Mezhdunaradniye Otnosheniia no Blizhnem i Srednem Vostake*, p. 41.
156. *Sevodnya* (11 December 1996), p. 3.
157. *Mezhdunaradniye Otnosheniia no Blizhnem i Srednem Vostake*, p. 41.

158. *Diplomaticheskii Vestnik* (January 1999), p. 30.
159. During Iraqi Deputy Prime Minister Tariq Aziz's visit to Moscow on 18 November 1997, the Russian spokesman Tarasov stated: 'Russia's position remains unchanged...that the Iraqi authorities must annul their illegal steps to impose conditions on UNSCOM. After that, and only after that, should other issues be discussed' (*Christian Science Monitor*, 21 November 1997, p. 18).
160. RFE/RL, *Newsline*, 2, no. 244 (21 December 1998), p. 1.
161. *Middle East International* (25 December 1998), p. 10.
162. *Nezevisimaya Gazeta* (18 December 1998).
163. *Diplomaticheskii Vestnik* (July 1999), p. 50.
164. Ibid.
165. Interview with A.M. Vassiliev on 4 January 2001.
166. *Diplomaticheskii Vestnik* (July 1999), p. 50.
167. Interview with A.M. Vassiliev on 4 January 2001.
168. Ibid. See also C. Lynch and John Lancaster. 'UN Votes to Renew Iraq Inspections' (*Washington Post*, 17 December 1999), p. A1; and R. Khalaf. 'UN Adopts New Resolution on Iraq' (*Financial Times*, London, 18 December 1999).
169. Ibid.
170. Ibid.
171. *Diplomaticheskii Vestnik* (October 1999), p. 57.
172. Ibid.
173. *Mezhdunarodnye otnoshenia no Blizhnem i Srednem Vostoke*, pp. 40–1.
174. *Nezavisimaya Gazeta* (18 March 2001).
175. A. Malygin. 'Novaia Situatsia no Blizhnem i Srednem Vostoke', *Mezhdunarodnaia zhizn*, no. 10, 2000, p. 85.
176. Ibid., p. 86.
177. *Nezavisimaya Gazeta* (24 November 2000), pp. 1–2.
178. Ibid.
179. *Nezavisimaya Gazeta* (8 December 2000), p. 6.
180. Ibid. Another outcome of that policy is a planned north–south corridor which will link Russia with India via Iran, cutting in half the time for land transportation between the two countries (RFE/RL *Newsline*, 5, no. 11, part I, 17 January 2001).
181. Vitali Naoumkine. 'Le Russie et le Proche Orient', *Revue Internationale et Strategique*, no. 38 (2000), p. 203.
182. Ibid., pp. 202–4.
183. As a Lebanese scholar indicates: 'There is absolutely no evidence of defiance in the articulation of Russia's disagreements with the US on the issue of Iraqi sanctions. Russia just disagrees with Washington on Iraq, and it wants the world to know that it does.' Hilal Khashan. 'Russia's Middle Eastern Policy', *International Studies* (New Delhi) 36, 1 (1999) p. 27.
184. Agence France-Press (26 July 2000).
185. *Diplomaticheskii Vestnik* (July 2000), p. 59.
186. Ibid.
187. Ibid.
188. *Nezavisimaya Gazeta* (30 November 2000), p. 6.

189. *New York Times* (13 January 2001), p. A8.
190. RFE/R,L *Newsline*, **5**, no. 34 (19 February 2001), p. I.
191. RFE/RL, *Newsline*, **5**, no. 36 (21 February 2001), p. 1.
192. RFE/RL, *Newsline*, **5**, no. 39 (26 February 2001), p. I.
193. RFE/RL, *Newsline*, **5**, no. 35 (20 February 2001), p. I.
194. RFE/RL, *Newsline*, **5**, no. 39 (26 February 2001), p. 1.
195. RFE/RL, *Newsline*, **5**, no. 35 (20 February 2001), p. 1.
196. RFE/RL, *Newsline*, **5**, no. 38 (23 February 2001), p. I.
197. RFE/RL, *Newsline*, **5**, no. 39 (26 February 2001), p. I.
198. For instance, on 29 January 2001 two Russian delegations, one led by the Minister of Energy, A. Gavrin, and the other by the President of Kolmykia, Kirsan Ilymzhinov, left for Baghdad (RFE/RL, *Newsline*, **5**, no. 20 (30 January 2001), p. I). Between 16 and 18 March, an official visit was scheduled to take place by the Chairman of the Duma, G. Seleznev: www.mid.ru.>) 13 March 2001.
199. RFE/RL, *Newsline*, **5**, no. 47 (8 March 2001), p. I.
200. An interview with A.M. Vassiliev (4 January 2001).
201. For example, the head of the Moscow-based Arabists Association, Vadim Sementsov, who argues that the 'sanctions must remain in place until Saddam Hussein caves in' and that 'Russia's betting on Iraq has been a mistake', ITAR-TASS News Agency (11 July 2000). Quite recently, even Sergei Karaganov, influential president of the Council on Foreign and Defense Policy in Moscow, has blamed Putin's administration for 'the stepped up dialogue with Iraq' (*Sevodnya*, 20 January 2001, p. 4).
202. Politiken online (Copenhagen, 18 July 2002).
203. 'Many Hurdles Will Delay US Attack on Iraq', Stratfor.com (10 July 2002).
204. Ibid.
205. Interfax (Moscow, 17 July 2002).
206. Ibid.
207. ITAR-TASS (Moscow, 17 July 2002).
208. Ibid.
209. Interview with Jasim al-Khurafi, Speaker of the Kuwait National Assembly, *Al Sharq al-Awsad,* 20 April 2001 in FBIS-NES-2001–0421.
210. Ibid.
211. A.P. Worldstream (26 November 2001), Database: Newspaper Source.
212. *Kommersant* (19 April 2001), p. 2.
213. A. Roff, 'Envoy: Russia to Earn Billions in Iraq' (*Moscow Times*, 17 August 2001).
214. Ibid.
215. Nadezhda Spiridonova. 'Sanctions Against Iraq Lose Russia Billions', *Moscow News* (13 June 2001).
216. *Economic News Digest*, ITAR-TASS (17 January 2002).
217. ITAR-TASS (26 November 2001), Database: Newspaper source.
218. A.P. Worldstream (3 July 2001), Database: Newspaper source.
219. *Ibid.*
220. Associated Press Online (3 July 2001), Database: Newspaper source.
221. RFE/RL, *Iraq Report*, **4**, no. 20 (8 June 2001).
222. Ibid.

223. Associated Press Online (3 July 2001), Database: Newspaper source.
224. RFE/RL, *Iraq Report*, **4**, no. 23 (27 July 2001).
225. A.P. Worldstream (3 July 2001), Database: Newspaper source.
226. RFE/RL, *Iraq Report*, **4**, no. 23 (27 July 2001).
227. Xinhua News Agency (13 November 2001), Database: Newspaper source.
228. Canadian Press (27 November 2001), Database: Newspaper source.
229. *The Australian* (28 November 2001), Database: Newspaper source.
230. Ibid.
231. A.P. Worldstream (1 December 2001), Database: Newspaper source.
232. RFE/RL, *Iraq Report*, **4**, no. 40 (7 December 2001).
233. A.P. Worldstream (1 December 2001), Database: Newspaper source.
234. Ibid.
235. Ibid.
236. RFE/RL, *Iraq Report*, **4**, no. 39 (30 November 2001).
237. A.P. Worldstream (2 December 2001), Database: Newspaper Source.
238. ITAR-TASS (9 February 2001), Database: Newspaper source.
239. RFE/RL, *Iraq Report*, **5**, no. 3 (25 January 2002).
240. ITAR-TASS (22 January 2002), Database: Newspaper Source.
241. Ibid.
242. ITAR-TASS (1 February 2002), Database: Newspaper source.
243. Ibid.
244. *Nezavisimaya Gazeta* (25 January 2002).
245. ITAR-TASS (24 January 2002), Database: Newspaper source.
246. 'Iraq Losing Allies in Face of US Threats', Stratfor Global Intelligence Company (11 February 2002): www.stratfor.com.
247. President Bush directly accused Iraq as a leading member of an 'axis of evil' and criticised unnamed others for being 'timid in the face of terror'. He said: 'I will not wait on events, while dangers gather. The US will not permit the world's most dangerous regimes to threaten us with the world's most destructive weapons', *Middle East International* (22 February 2002), p. 22.
248. Stratfor Global Intelligence Company. That 'the Russian position collapsed after Bush's 29 January 2002 state-of-the-union address' (see note 246) is apparently inaccurate.
249. ITAR-TASS (27 February 2002), Database: Newspaper source.
250. ITAR-TASS (28 February 2002), Database: Newspaper source.
251. Ibid.
252. ITAR-TASS (1 March 2002), Database: Newspaper source. Russian Foreign Minister I. Ivanov,has made it clear again in an interview with the Italian paper *Corriere della Sera* on 2 March 2002.
253. ITAR-TASS in English (20 May 2002) in FBIS-SOV-2002–0520.
254. 'News Analysis on UNSC. Extending "Oil-for-Food" Programme for Iraq', *Xinhus* (14 May 2002) as found in FBIS-SOV-2002–0514.
255. ITAR-TASS in English (20 May 2002) as found in FBIS-SOV-2002–0520.
256. ITAR-TASS (17 May 2002); see also FBIS-SOV-2002–0517.
257. Interfax (Moscow, 18 June 2002).
258. Xinhua News Agency online (18 June 2002).
259. Associated Press online (18 June 2002).
260. Interfax (17 July 2002).

261. Ibid.
262. ITAR-TASS 16 July 2002.
263. Interfax (17 July 2002).
264. *Al Sharq al-Awsad* internet version. FBIS-WEU (14 July 2002). One of
     the leading American specialists went so far as to write on 'Moscow's
     apparent decision to sell out Iran and quietly sell out Iraq'. See: 'One
     year later – where are we?' Stratfor.com (8 July 2002).
265. Scott Peterson. 'Russia Rethinks its Longtime Support for Iraq', *Christian
     Science Monitor* (13 March 2002), p. 1.
266. ITAR-TASS (10 July 2002).
267. Ibid.
268. RFE/RL *Newsline*, **6**, no. 132 (17 July 2002), p. I.
269. ITAR-TASS (18 July 2002).
270. *Washington Post* (15 September 2002).
271. *Observer* (3 November 2002).
272. Associated Press (8 November 2002).
273. Ibid.
274. *Ha'aretz* (9 November 2002).
275. ITAR-TASS, in English (3 December 2002).
276. Interfax (3 December 2002).
277. Ibid.
278. Ibid.
279. *Russian Journal Daily* online (24 November 2002).
280. Interfax (3 December 2002).
281. ITAR-TASS (29 November 2002).
282. Ibid.
283. *Russian Journal Daily* online (28 January 2003).
284. Ibid.
285. Interfax, online in English (28 January 2003).
286. ITAR-TASS, in English (28 January 2003).
287. Interfax, in English (28 January 2003).
288. Ibid.
289. Ibid.
290. Ibid.
291. *Nezavisimaya Gazeta* (29 January 2003).
292. RFE/RL, *Newsline*, **7**, no. 22 (4 February 2003), p. I.
293. *Moscow Times* (7 February 2003).
294. Ibid.
295. *RIA Novosti* (6 February 2003).
296. RFE/RL, *Newsline*, **7**, no. 25 (7 February 2003), p. I.
297. Ibid.
298. Ibid.
299. Ibid.
300. RFE/RL, *Newsline*, **7**, no. 23 (5 February 2003), p. III.
301. 'Russia, US Said to Seek Common Position to Stabilize Situation in Iraq',
     ITAR-TASS (in English) (7 April 2003).
302. *Hong Kong Te Kung Pao* (internet version) FBIS-SOV-2003–0407.
303. Ibid.
304. Agence France-Press (in French) (4 April 2003), in FBIS-SOV-2003–0404.

305. Interfax (in English) (4 April 2003), in FBIS-SOV-2003–0404.
306. *Teheran Iran News* in FBIS-NES-2003–0419. See also 'The Visible and Invisible Battlefields', *Benjing Renmin Wang*, Internet version (in Chinese) (9 April 2003), in FBIS-CHI-2003–0409.
307. Interfax (in English) (25 April 2003), in FBIS-SOV-2003–0425.
308. Alexey Frolov. 'Could Iraq Pose Threat to Russian Economy?' Rasbald News Agency (15 June 2003).
309. Interfax (in English) (23 April 2003), in FBIS-SOV-2003–0423.
310. ITAR-TASS (in English) (25 April 2003), in FBIS-SOV-2003–0425.
311. ITAR-TASS (in English) (16 April 2003), in FBIS-SOV-2003–0416.
312. Pavel Ivanov. 'The Evian Summit: Russia's Future and the G-8', *In the National Interest* (Internet version) (28 May 2003).
313. Interfax (in English) (28 April 2003), in FBIS-SOV-2003–0428.
314. ITAR-TASS (in English) (12 May 2003), in FBIS-SOV-2003–0512.
315. Ibid.
316. ITAR-TASS (in English) (22 May 2003), in FBIS-SOV-2003–0522.
317. ITAR-TASS (in English) (23 May 2003), in FBIS-SOV-2003–0523.
318. 'Antirackiye Sankcii otmenyat sevodnia? Suschestvennyh Ustupok Rossiya tak I ne polutshila', *Nezevisimaya Gazeta* (21 May 2003).
319. Alexei Arbatov. 'Lessons of Iraq', *Vremya MN* (4 June 2003) in FBIS-SOV-2003–0604.
320. Ibid.
321. Ibid.
322. *Rossiyskaya Gazeta* (4 June 2003), in FBIS-SOV-2003–0605.
323. Interfax (in English) (3 June 2003), in FBIS-SOV-2003–0603.
324. See, for instance, Giandomenico Picco. 'New Entente After September 11? The United States, Russia, China and India (Global Insights)', *Global Governance*, **9**, no. 1 (January–March 2003); and Alexander Rahr. 'EU Does Not Want Russia Walking on its European Lawn', *Rosbalt. Ru* (30 June 2003).
325. 'Russian Specialist Views Emergence of "Pax Americana"', Interfax (in English) (19 April 2003).
326. Ibid.
327. Ibid.
328. *Rossiyskaya Gazeta* (27 April 2003), in FBIS-SOV-2003–0427.
329. Yevgeny Verlin and Dimitrii Suslov. 'After the Summits: Russia's Role as a Player in the International Arena', *In the National Interest*, **27**, no. 23 (11 June 2003).
330. ITAR-TASS (in English) (15 April 2003), in FBIS-SOV-2003–0415.
331. Interfax (in English) (15 April 2003), in FBIS-SOV-2003–0415.
332. See, for instance, Frederic Encel and Olivier Guez. 'Le Couple Washington – Moscow et la crise Tirakienne', *Politique International*, no. 99 (Spring 2003), pp. 171–83. See also the book of the same authors, *La Grande Alliance. De la Tchétchenie à L'Iraq: le nouvel ordre mondial* (Paris: Flammarion, 2003).
333. Interfax (in English) (29 April 2003), in FBIS-SOV-2003–0429.
334. Ibid.
335. Interfax (in English) (3 June 2003), in FBIS-SOV-2003–0603.
336. *Rossiyskaya Gazeta* (19 May 2003), in FBIS-SOV-2003–0521.

337. *Rossiyskaya Gazeta* (17 May 2003), in FBIS-SOV-2003–0518.
338. Ibid.
339. Ibid.
340. Ibid.
341. Ibid.
342. The possible exception to that political line may be the keeping open of the Iraqi Embassy of the former regime in Moscow. This issue might be an object of a subtle diplomatic game between the interested parties (*Nezavisimaya Gazeta*).
343. ITAR-TASS (in English) (26 June 2003). Online: www.-itar-tass.com.
344. Vergenyi Verlin. 'Mesopotamia prevrastchatsia y Checheniu', *Nezavisimaya Gazeta* (26 June 2003).
345. Jonathan Steele. 'Putin Urges Decisive UN Role in Iraq', *Guardian* (27 June 2003).
346. Ibid.
347. RFE/RL, *Newsline*, 7, no. 121, part I (27 June 2003).
348. Ibid.
349. Ibid.
350. Adnan al-Panachi, a well-known Iraqi politician, previous Foreign Minister of Iraq, and previous representative of his country in the UN. ITAR-TASS (in English) (5 June 2003), in FBIS-SOV-2003–0605.
351. Ibid.
352. *Russia Journal Daily* (online, 7 July 2003).

Bibliography

AAP. 'Civilian Death Toll Terrific: Priest', *About News.com* (23 August 2003): www.news.com.au/common/story_page/0,4057,6255211%255E1702,00. html.

Abu Khalil, As'ad. *Bin Laden, Islam and America's New 'War on Terrorism'* (New York: Seven Stories Press, 2002).

Agarkov, A. 'Rossiisko-Irackiie otnosheniia no novom etapie razvitiia sotrudnichestva: problemy i perpektivy', *Vostok i Rossiia no rubieze XXI veka* (Institute of Oriental Studies, Russian Academy of Sciences, Moskva, 1998).

Agence France-Presse. 'Iraq at Risk of Cholera Epidemic' (7 April 2003).

Agence France-Presse. 'Yemen Downplays US "Experts" Role on Anti-Terror Mission' (2 March 2002): www.inq7.net/brk/2002/mar/02/brkafp_3-1.htm.

Ahmed, Kamal, Jason Burke and Peter Beaumont. 'Bush Wants 25,000 UK Iraq Force: Britain Considers Joint Invasion Plan', *Observer* (10 March 2002): www.observer.co.uk/international/story/0,6903,665083,00.html.

Ahmad, Kamal. 'Revealed: The Cluster Bombs Litter Iraq', *Observer* (1 June 2003).

Air University. 'Strategic Environment: USCENTCOM' (15 January 2002): www.au.af.mil/au/database/projects/ay1995/acsc/95-002/chap1/stratgic. htm.

Aleksandrova, Olga. 'The "Third World" in Russian Foreign Policy', *Aussenpolitik*, **III**, (1996).

Ali, M.M. and I.H. Shah. 'Sanctions and Childhood Mortality in Iraq', *Lancet*, **355** (27 May 2000).

al-Khalil, Samir. *Republic of Fear* (Berkeley: University of California Press, 1989).

al-Panachi, Adnan. 'ITAR-TASS', FBIS-SOV-2003–0605 (5 June 2003).

Amnesty International. 'Iraq: Looting, Lawlessness and Humanitarian Consequences', AI Index: MDE14/085/2003 (11 April 2003).

Amnesty International. 'Iraq: Civilians Under Fire – April 2003', AI Index: MDE14/071/2003, UNICEF. 'Iraq Briefing Note' (20 April 2003).

Arbatov, Alexei. 'Lessons of Iraq', *Vremya MN* (4 June 2003) in FBIS-SOV-2003–0604.

Aronson, Geoffrey. 'Palestine Near and Far: A Sideshow to the Conquest of Iraq', *Le Monde Diplomatique* (17 May 2002).

Asherio, A., R. Chase, T. Cote, G. Dehaes, E. Hoskins, J. Laaouej, M. Passey, S. Qaderi, S. Shugaidef, M.C. Smith, 'Effect of the Gulf War on Infant and Child Mortality in Iraq', *New England Journal of Medicine*, **327**, No. 13 (24 September 1992), 931–6.

Bahgat, Gawdat. 'The Iraqi Crisis in the New Millennium: The Prospects', *Asian Affairs*, **XXXI**, part 2 (June 2000).

Baker, Mark. 'Hundreds are Dying Who Should Not Die', *The Age* (21 April 2003).

Baker, Peter. 'For US Forces, a Secret and Futile Hunt: Local Guides Describe Furtive Trip Into Pakistan in Search of Fugitives', *Washington Post* (5 May

2002): www.washingtonpost.com/ac2/wp-dyn?pagename=article&node=
&contentId=A33591-2002May4&notFound=true.

Baker, Raymond. 'Imagining Egypt in the New Age: Civil Society and the
Leftist Critique', in Tareq Y. Ismael and Jacqueline S. Ismael (eds). *The Gulf
War and the New World Order* (Gainesville: University Press of Florida, 1994),
pp. 399–434.

Berman, Ari. 'Payments for Perle', *The Nation* (18 August 2003): www.
thenation.com/docprint.mhtml?i=20030818&s=berman.

Birchard, K. 'Does Iraq's Depleted Uranium Pose a Health Risk?', *Lancet*, **351**
(9103) (28 February 1998).

Borger, Julian. 'US Paves Way for War on Iraq: Attack Base to be Moved into
Qatar to Bypass Saudi Objections', *Guardian* (27 March 2002).

Borger, Julian. 'US Hawk "Tried to Sully Iraq Arms Inspector". Pentagon No
2 ordered CIA to Investigate Record of UN Agency Chief', *Guardian* (16
April 2002).

Blix, Dr Hans. 'Oral Introduction of the 12th Quarterly Report of UNMOVIC',
UN News service (7 March 2003).

Brisard, Jean-Charles and Guillaume Dasquie. *The Forbidden Truth* (trans. Lucy
Rounds) (New York: Thunder's Mouth Press/Nation Books, 2002).

Brutens, K. 'Vneshnaia politika Rossii; Novyi etap', *Svobodnaya Mysl*, **XXI**, No.
11 (1501) 2000.

Bryan Gyan, Shanta. 'Statement on Military Control of Iraq Relief;
Reconstruction', *InterAction* (3 April 2003).

Brzezinski, Zbigniew. *The Grand Chessboard: American Primacy And Its Geo-
strategic Imperatives* (New York: Basic Books, 1997).

Bush, George W. 'Address to a Joint Session of Congress and the American
People' (20 September 2001). Found at: www.whitehouse.gov/news/
releases/2001/09/20010920-8.html.

Bush, George W. 'President Bush Outlines Iraqi Threat', The White House (7
October 2002): www.whitehouse.gov/news/releases/2002/10/20021007-
8.html.

Butler, Amir. 'The Euro and the War with Iraq' (29 March 2003):
www.atrueword.com/index.php/article/articleview/49/1/2.

Campaign Against Sanctions on Iraq. 'Confidential UN Document Predicts
Humanitarian Emergency in Event of War on Iraq', Press Release (7 January
2003).

Cawthorne, Andrew. 'US, UK "Ignore" Iraq's 20,000 Wounded Civilians',
Middle East Times (8 August 2003).

Centre for Security Policy. 'What To Do Now About Iraq' (28 November 2001):
www.centerforsecuritypolicy.otg/index.jsp?section=papers&code=01-D_76.

Chaddock, Gail Russell. 'A Revival of Public Religion – on Capitol Hill', *Christian
Science Monitor* (7 January 2002): www.csmonitor.com/2002/0107/p1s4-
usgn.html.

Chomsky, Noam. *A New Generation Draws the Line: Kosovo, East Timor and the
Standards of the West* (New York: Verso Books, 2000), p. 25.

Chomsky, Noam. 'Iraq: Invasion that will Live in Infamy', *Z-magazine* (11
August 2003).

Chossudovsky, Michel. 'The Anglo-American Military Axis', *Global Research*
(10 March 2003): http://globalresearch.ca/articles/CHO303B.html.

Clark, William. 'The Real Reasons for the Upcoming War with Iraq': www.ecapc.org/eurodollariraq.asps.

Cockburn, Patrick. 'CIA Survey of Iraq Airfields Heralds Attack', *Independent* (18 March 2002): http://news.independent.co.uk/world/middle_east/story.jsp?story=275699.

Cohen, William S. 'DoD News Briefing' (19 December 1998): www.defenselink.mil/news/Dec1998/t12201998_t1219coh.html.

Cox, Robert and Michael G. Schechter. *The Political Economy of a Plural World: Critical Reflections on Power, Morals and Civilisation* (London: Routledge, 2002).

Deibel, Mary. 'Tax Shortfall Feeds Seas of Red Ink' (11 May 2003): www.gomemphis.com/mca/business/article/0,1426,MCA_440_1950272,00.htm.

Dinmore, Guy and James Harding. 'Iraqi Arms Find Not Likely, US Official', *Financial Times* (3 May 2003).

Dolny, Michael. 'Spectrum Narrows Further in 2002', *FAIR* (July/August 2003): www.fair.org/extra/0307/thinktanks2002.html.

Dreyfuss, Robert. 'The Misinformers', *Mother Jones*: www.motherjones.com/news.qa/2003/15/we_352_01.html.

Dreyfuss, Robert. 'Devising Bad Intelligence to Promote Bad Policy' (December 2002): www.truthout.org/docs_02/12.06E.pentagon.cia.htm.

Dreyfuss, Robert. 'The Thirty Year Itch', *Mother Jones* (March/April 2003): www.redrat.net/BUSH_WAR/dreyfuss.htm.

Durrani, Anayat. 'Trooping Across the World', *Al-Ahram Weekly Online* (7–13 March 2002, Issue No.576): www.ahram.org.eg/weekly/2002/576/re74.htm.

Eisenhower, President Dwight D. *Public Papers of the Presidents* (1960), pp. 1035–40: http://coursesa.matrix.msu.edu/~hst306/documents/indust.html.

El Baradei, Mohammed. 'The Status of Nuclear Inspections in Iraq', Statement to the United Nations Security Council (7 March 2003).

Encel, Frederic and Olivier Guez. 'Le Couple Washington – Moscow et la crise Tirakienne', *Politique International*, no. 99 (Spring 2003).

Encel, Frederic and Olivier Guez. *La Grande Alliance. De la Tchétchenie à L'Iraq: le nouvel ordre mondial* (Paris: Flammarion, 2003).

Everts, Steven. 'Why should Bush take Europe Seriously?', *Observer* (17 February 2002): www.observer.co.uk/Print/0,3858,4357611,00.html.

Fahey, D. 'DoD Analysis; The Good, the Bad and the Ugly' (June 1999): www.globaldialog.com/~kornkven/DOD_Analysis_II_Fahey.pdf.

FAIR. 'Media Advisory: Media March to War', *Fairness & Accuracy in Reporting* (17 September 2001): www.fair.org/press-releases/wtc-war-punditry.html.

FAO – Technical Co-operation Programme. 'Evaluation of Food and Nutrition Situation in Iraq: Terminal Statement', FAO Prepared for the Government of Iraq (1995).

FAO – Technical Co-operation Programme. 'Assessment of the Food and Nutrition Situation: Iraq', Technical Report prepared for the government of Iraq by the Food and Agriculture Organisation of the United Nations (2000): www.reliefweb.int/library/documents/iraqnutrition.pdf.

Federation of American Scientists (FAS) Military Toxics Project. 'Depleted Uranium; Agent Orange of the 90's: Another Pentagon Cover-up' (June 1999): www.miltoxproj.org/DU/DU_Faqs/Du_Faqs.htm.

Fenelon, K.G and V. Manjiakin, W. Rasaputram. *National Income in Iraq: Selected Studies* (Republic of Iraq: Ministry of Planning, Central Statistical Office, 1970).

Fetter, S. and F.N. von Hippel. 'The Hazard Posed by Depleted Uranium Munitions', *Science & Global Security*, 8(2), (1999).

Fierke, K.M. 'Logics of Force and Dialogue: The Iraq/UNSCOM Crisis as Social Interaction', *European Journal of International Relations*, 06, no. 03 (15 September 1998).

Finkelstein, Norman G. *Image and Reality of the Israel–Palestine Conflict* (New York: Verso, 1995).

Fisk, Robert. 'Final Proof that War is About the Failure of the Human Spirit', *Independent* (10 April 2003).

Fisk, Robert. 'Books, Priceless Documents Burn in Sacking of Baghdad', *Independent* (14 April 2003).

Fisk, Robert. 'For the People on the Streets, this is Not Liberation but a New Colonial Oppression', *Independent* (17 April 2003): http://argument.independent.co.uk/commentators/story.jsp?story=397925.

Fisk, Robert. 'Censorship of the Press', *Independent* (11 June 2003).

Fisk, Robert. 'Iraq Collapse', *Independent* (20 August 2003).

Freedland, Jonathan. 'Patten Lays Into Bush's America: Fury at President's "Axis of Evil" Speech', *Guardian* (9 February 2002): www.guardian.co.uk/bush/story/0,7369,647554,00.html.

Freeman, Alan. 'Blair's MPs Threaten Revolt', *Globe and Mail* (12 March 2003).

Friedman, Thomas. 'Foreign Affairs; Noblesse Oblige', *New York Times* (31 July 2001).

Friedman, Thomas. 'World War III', *New York Times* (13 September 2001).

Friedman, Thomas. 'Vote France off the Island', *New York Times* (9 February 2003).

Frolov, Alexey. 'Could Iraq Pose Threat to Russian Economy?', Rasbald News Agency (15 June 2003).

Fukuyama, Francis. *The Soviet Union and Iraq Since 1968* (Santa Monica: Rand Corporation, 1980).

Geisler, Jill. 'Minute by Minute with the Broadcast News', Poynter Institute: www.poynter.org (11 September 2001).

Giacomo, Carol. 'Aid Groups Oppose Pentagon Control of Aid Effort', Reuters (2 April 2003).

Golan, Galia. 'Gorbachev's Difficult Time in the Gulf', *Political Science Quarterly*, 107, no. 2 (1992).

Golub, Philip S. 'Background to Washington's War on Terror: American Caesar', *Le Monde Diplomatique* in English (16 January 2002).

Graham-Brown, Sarah. *Sanctioning Saddam: The Politics of Intervention in Iraq* (London and New York: I.B. Taurus, 1999).

Gray, Christine. 'From Unity to Polarization: International Law and the Use of Force against Iraq', *European Journal of International Law* 13, no. 1 (2002).

Hammad, Abdel Azim. 'Al-Muwagaha min Agl al-Ta'awun: Al-Rad al-Almani ala Istratejyyat al-Takhweef al-Amrikiyya', *Al-Ahram* (26 May 2003): www.ahram.org.eg/Index.asp?CurFN=REPO1.HTM&DID=7767.

Harley, H. N., E. C. Foulkes, L. H. Hilbourne, A. Hudson and C. R. Anthony. 'A review of the scientific literature as it pertains to Gulf War illness', *Depleted Uranium, Volume 7*. RAND: National Defense Research Institute (1999).

Harvard Study Team. 'The effect of the Gulf Crisis on the Children of Iraq', *New England Journal of Medicine*, **325** (1991), pp. 977–980.

Hedges, Stephen J. 'Ex-Inspector: Butler OK'd Spying Device: US purported to have sole control of eavesdropping equipment in Baghdad office', *Chicago Tribune* (10 January 1999).

Herman, Edward S. and Noam Chomsky. *Manufacturing Consent* (New York: Pantheon Books, 1988).

Hersh, Seymour. 'Lunch With the Chairman: Why was Richard Perle Meeting with Adnan Khashoggi?', *The New Yorker* (17 March 2003): www.newyorker.com/printable/?fact/030317fa_fact.

Hill, Enid. 'The New World Order and the Gulf War: Rhetoric, Policy, and Politics in the United States' pp. 184–223, in T. Ismael and J. Ismael, (eds) *The Gulf War and the New World Order* (Gainesville: University Press of Florida, 1994).

Hobsbawm, Eric. 'America's Imperial Delusion', *Guardian* (14 June 2003).

Hodges, Michael. 'Grandfather Economic Report Series': http://home.att.net/~mhodges/debt.htm.

Hoffman, David. 'About US and Iraq: Why Were We Lied To?', *Pravda* (17 June 2003).

Ibrahim, Youssef M. 'Higher Hopes in Baghdad for Ending UN Embargo', *New York Times* (18 October 1998).

Ignatius, David. 'Washington is Paying for its Lack of Arabists', *Daily Star* (14 July 2003): www.dailystar.com/ib/opinion/14_07_03_b.asp.

Institute of Oriental Studies. *Rossiia – SNG – Asia. Problemy i Perspectivy sotrudnichestva* (Moscow: Institute of Oriental Studies, Russian Academy of Sciences, 1993).

Institute of Oriental Studies. *Mezhdunarodnye otnosheniia na Blizhnem i Srednem Vostoke u Politika Rossii* (Moscow: Institute of Oriental Studies, Russian Academy of Sciences, 2000).

International Committee of the Red Cross. 'Red Crescent Maternity Hospital Damaged in Attack' (3 April 2003): www.icrc.org.

Ismael, Jacqueline S. 'Social Policy and Social Change: The Case of Iraq', *Arab Studies Quarterly*, **2** (3), (1980).

Ismael, Jacqueline S. and Shereen T. Ismael. 'Gender and State in Iraq', in S. Joseph (ed.) *Gender and Citizenship in the Middle East* (Syracuse: Syracuse University Press, 2000).

Ismael, T.Y. and William Haddad. *Iraq. The Human Cost of History* (London: Pluto Press, 2004).

Ismael, T.Y. and J.S. Ismael. 'Cowboy Warfare, Biological Diplomacy: Disarming Metaphors as Weapons of Mass Destruction', *Politics and the Life Sciences* (March 1999).

Ivanov, Pavel. 'The Evian Summit: Russia's Future and the G-8', *In the National Interest* (Internet version) (28 May 2003).

Jane's Foreign Report. 'The Israeli General's Plan' (10 July 2001): www.janes.com.

Jeffery, Simon. 'Baghdad Hospital Bombed', *Guardian* (2 April 2003).

Jeffery, Simon. 'War May Have Killed 10,000 Civilians, Researchers Say', *Guardian* (13 June 2003): www.guardian.co.uk/international/story/0,3604, 976295,00.html.

Khadduri, Majid. *Independent Iraq 1932–1958: A Study in Iraqi Relations* (London: Oxford University Press, 1960).

Khalaf, R. 'UN Adopts New Resolution on Iraq', *Financial Times* (London, 18 December 1999).

Khammas, E.A. 'A Closed Circle of Collaborators', *Occupation Watch Centre* (28 July 2003): www.occupationwatch.org/print_article.php?id=340& print=1.

Kissinger, Clark. 'The New Domestic Order' (25 July 2003): www.zmag.org/ content/print_article.cfm?itemID=3955&sectionID=43.

Klein, Naomi. 'Bush to NGO's: Watch Your Mouths' (24 June 2003): www.zmag.org/content/showarticle.cfm?SectionID=43&ItemID=3826.

Kolossov, V. 'Geopolititsheskiie polozeniie Rossii', *Polis*, No. 3 (2000).

Labaton, Stephen. 'Pentagon Advisor is also Advising Global Crossing', *New York Times* (21 March 2003).

Lacroix-Riz, Annie. 'When the US Wanted to Take Over France', *Le Monde Diplomatique* (May 2003): www.mondediplo.com/2003/05/05lacroix.

Lawton, Kim. *Religion and Ethics Newsweekly* (7 February 2003): www.pbs.org/wnet/religionandethics/week623/news.html.

Lemoine, Maurice. 'Uncle Sam's Manifest Destiny', *Le Monde Diplomatique* (May 2003): www.mondediplo.com/2003/05/03lemoine.

Lewis, Bernard. 'Did You Say "American Imperialism"?', *National Review* (17 December 2001).

Lind, Michael. 'Distorting the US Foreign Policy: The Israeli Lobby and American Power', *Third World Traveller* (May 2002): www.thirdworldtraveler. com/Israel/Israel_lobby_US.html.

Liu, Henry C.K. 'US Dollar Hegemony Must Go', *Asia Times* (11 April 2002).

Liu, Henry C.K. and Javad Yarjani. 'The Choice of Currency for the Denomination of the Oil Bill' (14 April 2002): www.opec.org/newsInfo/ Speeches/sp2002/spAraqueSpainAp14.htm.

Lobe, Jim. 'Pentagon Steps Closer to "GloboCop" Role', *Asia Times* (14 June 2003).

Lobe, Jim. 'US Fails Post-war Iraq Examination', *Asia Times* (27 June 2003).

Lynch, Colum. 'US Spying Goals in Iraq Called Difficult', *Boston Globe* (7 January 1999).

Lynch, Colum. 'Powell Accuses Iraq of Undermining Inspectors: At U.N., Secretary of State Says Iraqis Dispersing Rockets', *Washington Post* (5 February 2003).

Lynch, Colum and John Lancaster. 'UN Votes to Renew Iraq Inspections', *Washington Post* (17 December 1999).

Lustick, Ian S. 'The Absence of Middle Eastern Great Powers: Political Backwardness in Historical Perspective', *International Organisation* (51)4, (Autumn 1997).

Malygin, A. 'Novaia Situatsia no Blizhnem i Srednem Vostoke', *Mezhdunarodnaia zhizn* No. 10 (2000).

Martin, Patrick. 'How and Why the US Encouraged Looting in Iraq': www.wsws.org/articles//2003/apr2003/iraq-a15_prn.html.

Mattson, Ingrid. 'Saving Islam From the Terrorists: American Muslims Have a "Special Obligation"': www.beliefnet.com/frameset.asp?pageLoc=/story/89/story_8987_1.html&boardID=26483.

Melkumyan, Yelena S. 'Soviet Policy and the Gulf Crisis', in Ibrahim Ibrahim (ed.) *The Gulf Crisis: Background and Consequences* (Washington DC: Center for Contemporary Arab Studies, Georgetown University, 1992).

Milbank, Dana and Mike Allen. 'US Will Take Action Against Iraq, Bush Says: "All Options Are on the Table" Against States That Pose Threat', *Washington Post* (14 March 2002): www.washingtonpost.com/wp-dyn/articles/A22091-2002Mar13.html.

Moore, Michael. *Stupid White Men* (New York: Regan Books, 2001).

Morgan, Dan and David B. Ottaway. 'In Iraqi War Scenario, Oil is Key Issue: US Drillers Eye Huge Petroleum Pool', *Washington Post* (15 September 2002).

Naoumkine, Vitali. 'Le Russie et le Proche Orient', *Revue Internationale et Strategique*, no. 38 (2000).

Normand, Roger. 'Special Report: Water Under Siege In Iraq. US/UK Military Forces Risk Committing War Crimes by Depriving Civilians of Safe Water', *Centre for Economic and Social Rights* (April 2003).

Nye, Joseph S. Jr. *The Paradox of American Power* (Oxford: Oxford University Press, 2002).

Observer. 'Saddam's Land Mines and Coalition Clusters Litter the Map of Iraq', (1 June 2003): http://observer.guardian.co.uk/international/story/0,6903,968208,00.html.

O'Connor, H. *World Crisis in Oil* (New York: Monthly Review Press, 1962).

Office of the Iraq Programme. 'Oil-for-Food, Basic Figures', United Nations (18 May 2002): www.un.org/Depts/oip/background.

Office of the Iraq Programme. 'Oil-for-Food', United Nations (18 May 2002): www.un.org/Depts/oip/cpmd/roleofoip.

Omar, Abdalla Abdalla. *SSZA, Islamskij Vostok i Rossiia* (Moscow: Russian National Fund, 1995).

Omestad, Thomas. 'One War at a Time', *US News & World Report* (23 December 2002).

Orbinski, James. 'New Frontiers in Health in a Changing Global Context', in J.S. Ismael (ed.) *Social Welfare in a Changing World* (Calgary: Detselig Enterprises, 1996).

Pearson, Graham S. *The UNSCOM Saga: Chemical and Biological Weapons Non-Proliferation* (New York: St. Martin's Press, 1999).

Peterson, Scott. 'Russia Rethinks its Longtime Support for Iraq', *Christian Science Monitor* (13 March 2002).

Phythian, M. *Arming Iraq: How the US and Britain Built Saddam's War Machine* (Boston: Northeastern University Press).

Picco, Giandomenico. 'New Entente after September 11? The United States, Russia, China and India (Global Insights)', *Global Governance*, 9, no. 1 (January–March 2003).

Pilger, John. 'Who are the Extremists' (22 August 2003): www.zmag.org/content/print_article.cfm?itemID=4079&sectionID=40.

Pincus, Walter and Colum Lynch. 'Crisscrosses Hamper Arms Inspection in Iraq', *Washington Post* (15 April 2002).

Rahr, Alexander. 'EU Does Not Want Russia Walking on its European Lawn', Rosbalt. Ru (30 June 2003).

Rampton, Sheldon and John Stauber. 'How to Sell a War', *In These Times* (4 August 2003): http://inthesetimes.com/print.php?id=299_0_1_0.

Ratner, Steven R. 'Image and Reality in the UN's Peaceful Settlement of Disputes', *European Journal of International Law*, 6, no. 3 (1995).

Research Unit for Political Economy. *Behind the Invasion of Iraq* (New York: Monthly Review press, 2003).

Reuters. 'UN Inspectors Withdraw to Bahrain from Iraq' (11 November 1998).

Richardson, J.J. 'Clinton's Other War', *Mother Jones* (6 April 1999).

Richardson, J.J. 'Depleted Uranium: The Invisible Threat' *Mother Jones* Online (23 June 1999): www.motherjones.com/total_coverage/kosovo/reality_check/du.html.

Rodinson, Maxime. *Europe and the Mystique of Islam* (trans. Roger Veinus) (Seattle: University of Washington Press, 1987). Translation of *La Fascination de l'Islam.*

Roelofsma, Derk Kinnane. 'US, Islam, and Central Asia', United Press International/*Washington Times* (7 March 2002): www.washtimes.com/upi-breaking/07032002-110409-5870r.htm.

Roff, A. 'Envoy: Russia to Earn Billions in Iraq', *Moscow Times* (17 August 2001).

Rooney, Andy. 'Why Islam has a Hold on Muslims' (17 December 2001): www.cbsnews.com/stories/2001/12/14/60minutes/rooney/main321447.shtml.

Rowat, Colin. 'UN Agency Reports on the Humanitarian Situation in Iraq', *Campaign Against Sanctions on Iraq* (12 August 2000).

Russia Journal Daily. 'Kurdistan Leader: Russia to Support Democracy in Iraq' (10 July 2003).

Said, Edward. *Orientalism* (New York: Vintage Books, 1979).

Said, Edward. *Covering Islam: How the Media and the Experts Determine How We See the Rest of the World* (New York: Vintage Books, 1997).

Said, Edward. 'American Zionism: The Real Problem', *Media Monitors Network* (14 March 2001): www.mediamonitors.net/edward13.html.

Said, Edward. 'Israel, Iraq and the United States', *Al-Ahram Weekly*, Issue # 607 (10–16 October 2002).

Said, Edward. 'A Monument to hypocrisy', *Al-Ahram Weekly,* Issue # 625 (February 2003).

Said, Edward. 'The Other America', *Counter Punch* (21 March 2003).

Said, Edward. 'The Academy of Lagado', *London Review of Books*, 25, no. 8 (17 April 2003).

Said, Edward. 'Archeology of the Road Map', *Al-Ahram Weekly* (12–18 June 2003).

Said, Edward. 'Imperial Perspectives', *Al-Ahram Weekly* (24–30 July 2003).

Salmon, Christian. 'Palestine Near and Far: The Bulldozer War' *Le Monde Diplomatique* (17 May 2002).

Sands, David R. 'Petroleum Fuels Debate on Iraq War', *Washington Times* (7 October 2002).

Scherer, Michael. 'Daniel Pipes, Peacemaker?' (26 May 2003): www.motherjones.com/news/update/2003/22/we_420_01.html.

Schneider, Howard. 'Mideast Allies Warn US Not to Attack Iraq: Leaders of Jordan, Turkey Say Move Against Hussein Could Destabilize Region', *Washington Post* (11 March 2002): www.washingtonpost.com/wp-dyn/articles/A5422-2002Mar10.html.

Schwarz, Peter. 'European Foreign Ministers Attack Bush's Policy' *World Socialist Web Site News* (15 February 2002): www.wsws.org/articles/2002/feb2002/euro-f15.shtml.

Shafer, Jack. 'Richard Perle Libel Watch, Week 9: What Happened to Richard Perle's Big, Bad, Libel Stick?' *The Slate* (7 May 2003): http://slate.msn.com/toolbar.aspx?action=print&id=2082676.

Sharipov, V. Z. *Persiskii Zaliv: Neft – politika i voina* (Moskva: Institute of Oriental Studies, Russian Academy of Sciences, 2000).

Shemesh, Haim. *Soviet-Iraqi Relations, 1968–1988: In the Shadow of the Iraq–Iran Conflict* (Boulder and London: Lynne Rienner Publishers, 1992).

Sikora, K. 'Cancer Services are Suffering in Iraq', *British Medical Journal* (16 January 1999).

Silverstein, Ken. *Private Warriors* (New York: Verso Books, 2000).

Simons, Geoff. *Targeting Iraq* (London: Saqi Books 2002).

Simons, M. 'Gulf War Studies Link Cancer to Depleted Uranium', *New York Times* (29 January 2001).

Sipress, Alan. 'Jordan Advises US Against a Military Campaign in Iraq', *Washington Post* (13 March 2002): www.washingtonpost.com/wp-dyn/articles/A16757-2002Mar12.html.

Sipress, Alan. 'Cheney Plays Down Arab Criticism Over Iraq', *Washington Post* (18 March 2002): www.washingtonpost.com/wp-dyn/articles/A42203-2002Mar17.html.

Sivard R.L. *World Military and Social Expenditures*, 11th edition (plus the 12th, 14th and 15th editions) (Leesburg, VA: World Priorities 1980).

Smolansky, Oles M. with Bettie M. Smolansky. *The USSR and Iraq: The Soviet Quest for Influence* (Durham and London: Duke University Press, 1981).

Spiridonova, Nadezhda. 'Sanctions against Iraq Lose Russia Billions', *Moscow News* (13 June 2001).

Staunton, Denis. 'EU Refuses to Adopt French Middle East Plan', *Irish Times* (11 February 2002): www.ireland.com/newspaper/world/2002/0211/3780008927FR11EUDENIS.html.

Steele, Jonathan. 'Putin Urges Decisive UN Role in Iraq', *Guardian* (27 June 2003).

Stratfor Global Intelligence Company. 'Iraq Losing Allies in Face of US Threats' (11 February, 2002): www.stratfor.com.

Toenjes, Laurence. 'US Policy Towards Iraq: Unravelling the Web of People, Think Tanks, etc' (19 July 2003): www.opednews.com/toenjessummary.htm.

Travers, Russell E. 'A New Millenium and a Strategic Breathing Space', *Washington Quarterly*, **20**, no. 2 (Spring 1997).

Traynor, Ian. 'Georgia: US Opens New Front in War on Terror', *Guardian* (20 March 2002): www.guardian.co.uk/international/story/0,3604,670542,00.html.

Tyler, Patrick. 'After the War: The Political Scene; Iraqis Frustrated by Shift Favouring US-British Rule', *New York Times* (26 May 2003).

United Nations. 'Report to the Secretary-General Dated 15 July 1991 on Humanitarian Needs in Iraq Prepared by a Mission Led by the Executive Delegate of the Secretary-General for Humanitarian Assistance in Iraq'. S/22799, Geneva, (17 July 1991).

United Nations. 'Report on Humanitarian Needs in Iraq in the Immediate Post-Crisis Environment by a Mission to the Area Led by the Under-Secretary General for Administration and Management', 10–17 March 1991, S/22366 (20 March 1991).

United Nations. 'Report of the Second Panel Established Pursuant to the Note by the President of the Security Council of 30 January 1999 (S/1999/100), concerning the current humanitarian situation in Iraq' (30 March 1999): www.un.org/Depts/oip/panelrep.html.

United Nations. 'UN Relief Agencies Report Slow Improvement in Iraq, but Situation Still "Precarious"' (22 April 2003).

United Nations Development Programme (UNDP). '1999–2000 Report', Iraq Country Office: www.iq.undp.org.

United Nations Development Programme (UNDP/UNDESA). 'Analysis of Contracts On Hold (As of 31/10/10/2000) Electricity Sector (Centre/South)' (November 2000): http://mirror.undop.org/iraq/; United Nations Development Programme (UNDP), '1999–2000 Report: as of June 2000' Iraq Country Office (July 2000): http://mirror.undop/iraq/REPORT.pdf.

United Nations Development Programme (UNDP/UNDESA). 'Analysis of Contracts On Hold, (As of 31/10/10/2000) Electricity Sector (Centre/South)' (November 2000): http://mirror.undop.org/iraq/.

United Nations Development Programme (UNDP). 'S/2001/566. Report of the Team of Experts Established Pursuant to Paragraph 15 of Security Council Resolution 1330' (6 June 2001): www.un.org/Depts/oip/reports/2001.

UNICEF. 'Situation Analysis of Children and Women in Iraq – 1997', United Nations (April 1998).

UNICEF. 'Iraq Briefing Note' (21 April 2003).

UNICEF. 'Child and Maternal Mortality Survey 1999: Preliminary Report', United Nations (July–August 1999).

UNICEF. 'UNICEF: Questions and Answers for the Iraq Child Mortality Surveys', (Baghdad, 16 September 1999).

UNICEF. Press release located at: www.unicef.org/newsline/99pr29.htm and the report itself at http://www.unicef.org/reseval/iraqr.html.

UN News Service. 'Press Briefing on Humanitarian Preparations for Iraq' (13 February 2003): www.un.org/News/briefings/docs/2003/OshimaBriefing. doc.htm.

UN News Service. 'Transcript of the UN Humanitarian Briefing in Amman, Jordan' (20 March 2003): www.un.org/apps/news/printfocusnews.asp? nid=440.

UN News Service. 'Transcript of the UN Humanitarian Briefing in Amman, Jordan' (24 March 2003): www.un.org/apps/news/printfocusnews.asp? nid=449.

UN Office for the Co-ordination of Humanitarian Affairs Integrated Regional Information Network. 'UN Relief Agencies Praised Iraqi Health Workers', United Nations (21 April 2003).

UN Office for the Co-ordination of Humanitarian Affairs Integrated Regional Information Network. 'Iraq: Conditions in Basra's Main Hospital Still Dire', United Nations (17 April 2003).

United Press International. 'US May Grant $50mn to Iran Dissidents', *Middle East Times*: www.metimes.com/2k3/issue2003-15/reg/us_may_grant.html.

US Department of State. 'Patterns of Global Terrorism 2001' (May 2002): www.state.gov/documents/organization/10319.pdf.

Vassiliev, A. *Rossiia no Blizhnem i Srednem Vostoke ot Messianstva k pragmatizmu* (Moskva: Nauka, 1993).

Vassiliev, A.M. 'Budushtieie Rossiiskoj Politiki na Blizhnem Vostoke', *Vestnik Rossiyskoj Akademii Nauk*, **68**, no. 6 (1998).

Verlin, Yevgeny. 'Mesopotamia prevrastchatsia y Checheniu', *Nezavisimaya Gazeta* (26 June 2003).

Verlin, Yevgeny and Dimitrii Suslov. 'After the Summits: Russia's Role as a Player in the International Arena', *In the National Interest*, **27**, no. 23 (11 June 2003).

Verter, Yossi and Aluf Benn. 'Israel to US: Don't Wait for Calm Here Before Hitting Iraq', *Ha'aretz* (3 May 2002): www.haaretz.co.il/hasen/pages/ShArt.jhtml?itemNo=151228&contrassID=2&subContrassID=1&sbSubContrassID=0.

Vidal, Gore. 'The Enemy Within', *Observer* (27 October 2002).

von Sponek, Hans. Public address at 'A Day and Night for the People of Iraq', 6 May 2000, as quoted in Colin Rowat. 'UN Agency Reports on the Humanitarian Situation in Iraq' Campaign Against Sanctions on Iraq (12 August 2000).

Weiner, Tim. 'US Spied on Iraq Under UN Cover, Officials Now Say', *New York Times* (7 January 1999).

Whitaker, Brian. 'US Think Tanks Give Lessons in Foreign Policy', *Guardian* (19 August 2002): www.guardian.co.uk/elsewhere/journalist/story.

Williams, Ian. 'Of Pipes and Sources', *Middle East International* (8 August 2003).

Wilmhurst, David. Special Note, UNHCI (9 April 2003).

World Health Organisation. 'Depleted Uranium: Sources, Exposure and Health Effects' (2001).

Wright, George. 'Amnesty Accuses the US-Led Forces of Abuses', *Guardian* (23 July 2003). See also: www.guardian.co.uk/international/story/0,3604,1004537,00.html.

Yarjani, Javad. 'The Choice of Currency for the Denomination of the Oil Bill', A Speech to the EU on the International Role of the Euro (14 April 2002): www.opec.org/newsInfo/Speeches/sp2002/spAraqueSpainApr14.htm.

Zaidi, S. and M.C. Smith-Fawzi. 'Health of Baghdad's Children', *Lancet*, **346**, no. 1485 (December 1995).

Index

Compiled by Sue Carlton